The Nevada Advantage

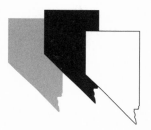

"*The law provides incredible financial incentives to seek out a victim with deep pockets, drag him into court, ruin his reputation, wear him down with endless discovery demands, pay a fortune to defend himself, and then extort a settlement from him. This is not justice in any sense of the word.*"

The Tort Informer

Terry L. Neal

The Nevada
Advantage

WHEN, WHY & HOW TO INCORPORATE;
REGARDLESS OF WHERE YOU LIVE AND WORK

MasterMedia Publishing Corp.

Contact:
MasterMedia Publishing Corp.
1005 Terminal Way, Suite 110
Reno, NV 89502
Phone: 800-334-8232 Fax: 503-668-0494

Library of Congress Cataloging-in-Publications Data:
Neal, Terry, 1946–
        The Nevada Advantage: When, Why & How to Incorporate;
Regardless of Where You Live and Work / Terry Neal

All photos in this book © 2002 www.arttoday.com

IBSN 1-57101-947-2

Manufactured in the United States of America

Dedication

This book is dedicated to the memory of three deceased friends, each of whom was associated with the evolution of that unique financial environment my colleagues and I have come to regard as the "Nevada advantage," which has inspired the title of this book.

Harley and Lewis Laughlin, father and son, the visionary and the leader. Together they developed an entire corporate formations industry in Nevada. Their vision and example was eventually duplicated by the state of Wyoming. Virtually on his own, the irascible Harley Laughlin assailed the Nevada legislature and prevailed upon the thinking of the majority, thereby securing a legal setting to support the dreams and aspirations of business owners and professionals from across America, and around the world.

The third friend and close associate was Chuck Carter, a family man of great depth, and one committed to doing the right thing, easy or not. In his professional life, Chuck was a CPA, an enlightened man who helped develop working strategies that have benefited people from all walks of life.

Table of Contents

SECTION II   BUSINESS STRUCTURES

Chapter 6 – Acts of the Corporation

Chapter 13 - Alternative Considerations

SECTION IV   Corporate Formalities & Forms

**Chapter 14 – Forms, Minutes, Resolutions, Notes
Agreements and Contracts**

SECTION V – Appendices

Acknowledgements

Many individuals have contributed to the writing of this book. The list is so long I have decided not to include their names for fear of inadvertently leaving someone out. I thank them all, and hope that my efforts measure up to the invaluable contributions they have so freely given.

Dr Sherry L Meinberg, my sister and an author of several books herself, is always an inspiration. I thank her particularly for her help. I owe a debt of deep gratitude to Laughlin Associates for providing draft materials included in the text, as well as for various sample documents.

Once again, I extend my thanks to Albert Yokum, editor and publishing consultant, who personally converted the manuscript into a book and who has provided invaluable expertise in this publication and three prior books entitled, *The Offshore Solution, The Offshore Advantage,* and *Barter & The Future of Money.*

My sweetheart, best friend, and the love of my life of forty years, deserves more credit than could ever be properly acknowledged. Maureen is truly my better half and without her continued and unselfish support, virtually nothing would ever get done.

Preface

The Genesis

Harley Laughlin founded Laughlin Associates in Nevada over thirty years ago. His firm grew to become the oldest, and certainly one of the most sophisticated company formation and management firms in the western United States. I have known the Laughlin family for at least twenty of those years and have used their services, and referred them to numerous others. But when Laughlin Associates, now Laughlin International, suggested I write a book on the advantages of doing business through a Nevada corporation, it struck me as unnecessary. After all, I had already included a chapter on Nevada in two of my previous books, which dealt with the offshore world, and there are other publications available touting Nevada as the premier jurisdiction in the United States.

It seemed to me that many sophisticated business owners and professionals already understood the values inherent in operating a private company based in Nevada in order to encumber assets in their home state, enact privacy strategies, reduce taxes, and protect business and personal assets. However, after conducting a somewhat informal survey, it became abundantly clear that not only did most business owners not have a clue as to how to adequately protect themselves, but most lawyers did not understand these basic concepts either.

Philosophical Content

The first four chapters of this book comprising Section I outline some of the reasons that enlightened entrepreneurs, professionals, and anyone who has anything of value are implementing Nevada strategies. To be abundantly clear, I am solely responsible for the compilation of these "rationales" which, admittedly, may offend some readers and irk the occasional bureaucrat. But I can say with a clear conscience that the problems set forth do, in fact, substantially represent the reasons more and more Americans are searching for strategic solutions.

Perhaps I have taken greater license in these first four chapters than is justified, particularly in view of the book's title and reason for production. But being "politically correct" is nothing more than de facto censorship. And the older I get, the more I resist the notation of being "PC." After Section I, the reader will discover the balance of the book to be an easily digestible text on the forms of doing business, how and why things work the way they do, what the reader needs to consider, and a fairly pragmatic approach as to how to proceed. In other words, my tendency to rant is limited to the first four chapters. So if you simply cannot abide my thinking in these regards, move on to the next section where the material is explanatory and not philosophical.

Analysis

Nevada is the jurisdiction of choice for many non-U.S. persons and it is also a great place to go "offshore" for the enlightened American. What? Offshore for an American? Yes! Actually, if you are a U.S. person and live and do business from any of the other 49 states, Nevada is considered a "foreign" jurisdiction by your home state. Perhaps that's not technically going offshore, but as far as your home state legislation is concerned, there is little difference between a corporation formed in Nevis, West Indies and one formed in Nevada, USA.

So why would someone go to Nevada, or anywhere else for that matter, to form a corporation? And why would you want or need a corporation anyway? Well, that is what this book is designed to expand upon. In the following pages you will learn what you need to know about corporations and other legal structures and how to use them effectively to protect yourself, your assets, your business affairs, and your family possessions. You will learn how to reduce your taxes, increase profits and income, and build a better and more secure future in these tumultuous times.

The majority of this publication constitutes a "how to" book prefaced with the day-to-day rationales as to why so many people have decided to form a corporation or similar legal entity in a jurisdiction other than the one in which they live. After the philosophical musing mentioned above I get down to the business of outlining a step-by-step approach to providing all the information you need to improve your position now!

I hope you enjoy reading this book as much as I have writing it.

Terry Neal

SECTION I

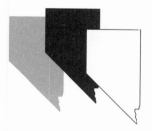

The Whys

THE PERSONAL SOVEREIGNTY PARADIGM
THE PRIVACY FACTOR
THE LITIGATION EXPLOSION
CONCERNS OVER GOVERNMENT

THE PERSONAL SOVEREIGNTY PARADIGM

"Freedom is the recognition that no single person, no single authority of government has a monopoly on the truth, but that every individual life is infinitely precious, that every one of us put on this world has been put there for a reason and has something to offer."

Ronald Reagan

The Purpose

In the following pages you will learn what you need to know about corporations and other legal structures and how to use them effectively to protect yourself, your assets, your business affairs, your family possessions. You will learn how to reduce taxes, increase profits and income, and build a better and more secure future in these tumultuous times.

This book was written to afford the reader an expanded reality map on a number of related subjects that may be thought of as political and philosophic, economic and structural. Much of the material in later chapters is corporate entity resource information and it is designed to serve as a reference tool for years to come. However, the ultimate objective of this production is to provide you with practical knowledge and working solutions for real-world application.

The concepts presented herein are centered on legal structuring for your personal and business dealings and are designed to achieve privacy, asset protection, tax reduction and to allow you to enjoy enhanced freedom and flexibility in your day-to-day affairs.

Preamble

As a general rule people feel threatened when faced with new information because if they integrate it as foundational to their thinking, they must revise their mental maps of reality, and this takes too much thought and reflection. As a result, more often than not, we tend to fight against new information rather than for its assimilation. It may help to recognize that this is a normal human reaction as you proceed through what follows.

Nation States

The democratic experiment fostered by renegade colonists in America spawned a whole new world of open thought, personal liberty and private property rights. These foundational principals in turn, formed the cornerstone of the United States Constitution which, notwithstanding its scandalous beginning, matured into a force so potent as to impact, and to a great extent change, the entire civilized world. The fundamental concepts of individual freedom and the right to own and control one's own property form the basis of free-market capitalism and its attendant political partner, democracy. America remains the champion of these ideals.

U.S. patriotism aside, countries, states, and nations may not survive much longer as we currently recognize and understand them. The United Nations generally defines a country by its borders and by a single secular authority in charge of the territory and representing it to the rest of the world. National governments have an authority that is superseded by no other body within a given country. In other words, national governments consider themselves the ultimate power and authority on questions related to the individual's rights within their territorial boundaries.

This conviction in a national government's ultimate sanctity is changing, openly in democracies, violently under other forms of government. But the heart and soul of what ultimately constitutes a sovereign nation, and to a great extent what identifies a state, province, principality, or other legal jurisdiction within a nation, is the power to tax. No matter what you call an area, if it does not have the right to demand money of its citizens and have the power to take it from them if they don't pay, you don't have a country.

Instantaneous communications and greater world awareness have put political leaders of almost every ilk under pressure to be more sensitive to the rights and needs of their citizens while projecting the image of good fiscal judgment. On the other hand, it is the nature of virtually every political leader to expand his or her influence and control. These objectives are frequently in conflict.

All political survivors are skilled in using whatever media is available to them to get their message across in such a way that it supports and defends their personal objectives. Although the direct use of force is very much alive in our newly connected world, media spin driven towards legislative enactments ultimately plays an even greater part in citizen control.

Notwithstanding the power of television and its ubiquitous talking heads, enlightened individuals who refuse to accept the current party line and think clearly for themselves are generally able to sort the information overload and intuit the underlying objectives of those pushing any particular political agenda. Whether one has articulated specific mental rules with which to measure proposed legislation, or not, most of us ultimately recognize the validity of these three political axioms:

1   Follow the money;
2   Identify those to gain in power and influence; and
3   Power corrupts, absolute power corrupts absolutely

There are other valid rules for assessing political objectives, but these three summarize the healthy skepticism the "personal sovereign" must have.

Of course, if skepticism is carried too far it can easily evolve into cynicism, which if not balanced by solid principals and a love and respect for others, is simply a fast track to misery.

Political Change is Inevitable

Even a cursory look at world history validates the old adage that the only thing constant in the universe is change. The evolution of politics is now being quickened by the abundance of information of every kind. Countries are in a state of flux and some portion of these changes will play a crucial role as you chart your individual course towards enhanced freedom, personal sovereignty, and the protection and expansion of your resources. Facing new realities is critically important when deciding where and how to conduct business, place money, and control assets. There are several safe harbor jurisdictions from whence to handle various components of your business and personal affairs.

In one of those odd congruities of history, the friction between the world's largest political ideologies – communism and capitalism – largely disappeared at the same time the means to unite them appeared. These two contending ideologies that divided the world into hostile camps ceased being an issue by the 1990s. At that very moment in history, the Internet emerged as a fast, economic way to communicate and do business across borders.

Respect and tolerance, or perhaps more correctly the lack of same, particularly as it relates to religious interpretation and ethnic preference, now tends to shape and define countries as much as their historical precedents. For example, consider that of the fifty-four[1] predominantly Muslim countries, repressive governments rule all but two. In other words, kings, dictators, warlords, or militant clerics, administer virtually all of these. Tolerance for competing political ideologies or religious views, other than those perpetuated by the state, are almost always condemned in these countries.[2]

---

[1] My research indicates Islam claims control of 66 countries and unincorporated territories, the latter being such places as the unincorporated area of the Western Sahara, Gaza Strip, Palestine, the West Bank, etc. However, 9 of these locations are not recognized as nation states by the U.N. A somewhat deeper analysis reveals that 3 of the countries loosely controlled by those claiming ties to Islam are ones where Muslims as a group make up less than 50% of the actual population, ergo I calculate the figure 54 predominantly Muslim countries.

[2] The 2001 annual Human Rights Watch reporting on Muslim States says: "Women continued to suffer from severe forms of institutional and societal discrimination in nearly every aspect of their lives." It further cites Egypt, Tunisia and Bahrain — all commonly thought of as moderate Arab states — for using the courts to harass and intimidate critics of regimes there. Saudi Arabia was hit with some of the report's most harsh criticism. "Freedom of expression and association were nonexistent rights, political parties and independent local media were not permitted, and even peaceful anti-government activities

Just as Christianity was hijacked by feudal warlords in the Middle Ages to enhance their power and justify their actions, so has Islam become the tool of political leaders to gain and maintain control in under-developed Middle Eastern and African countries.[3] **These acts are not about religion they are about power**. Karl Marx, the author of the Communist Manifesto, maintained that religion was the "opiate of the masses." Although it pains me to give him credit for any kind of truth, there is merit in the statement.

Despots of every kind have played on ignorance and mixed it with the passion of religion to gain power over the masses. Unfortunately they have done so all too often without the average person discovering their deceit, at least until after the tyrant had solidified his control. Curiously, the atheism that Karl Marx preached bore all the hallmarks of the state-sponsored, radical, religious fundamentalism that we see in a number of Muslim countries today.

Radical fundamentalists of every political or religious persuasion tend to have in common a lack of tolerance for the thoughts, ideas, and opinions of anyone who does not think and act the way they do. This is the diametric opposite of the libertarian view of America's Founding Fathers.

Note that the term used above was "radical" fundamentalists, those that represent the unyielding extremists of any particular social-political-religious group, as opposed to mainstream "fundamentalists" which generally represent the semi-opened minded moderates that form the essential core of most stable society. It seems that no matter how valid or vital one's belief system might be, one undermines that system and ultimately negates it when one gets rigid and dogmatic in its adherence.

The Freedom Ideology

Surely all of us have been deeply touched in many ways by the horrific events of September 11, 2001. There are people in diverse places that do not think as we do; that do not share our values, principals and morality. There are those who do not respect the sanctity of human life or value

---

were virtually unthinkable."2 The 2001 annual Human Rights Watch reporting on Muslim States says: "Women continued to suffer from severe forms of institutional and societal discrimination in nearly every aspect of their lives." It further cites Egypt, Tunisia and Bahrain — all commonly thought of as moderate Arab states — for using the courts to harass and intimidate critics of regimes there. Saudi Arabia was hit with some of the report's most harsh criticism. "Freedom of expression and association were nonexistent rights, political parties and independent local media were not permitted, and even peaceful anti-government activities were virtually unthinkable."

[3] Islam exploded on the world scene in the 6th century AD, however it did not spread by the sword, as is commonly thought in western society. While the Arabs (most of which are Muslim) conquered huge territories, they did not force conversions. The Islam of the Middle East was uniformly more tolerant of minority religions than was medieval Christianity in Europe.

one's rights to personal property. Sadly, dreadful people really do exist, both inside and outside America. It is up to us, both individually and collectively, to prepare for our own protection and that of our families.

On a personal level I am proud to be an American and believe strongly in its foreordained mission to protect personal liberty and freedom and the basic inalienable rights of its citizens.[4] However, that is not to say that as the pendulum of power swings, we as Americans should be willing to sacrifice our individual rights and our personal liberty in exchange for what appears to be physical safety. In the words of Benjamin Franklin "Those who give up essential liberty to obtain a little temporary safety deserve neither liberty nor safety."

This is a crucial time, a time where each of us should carefully explore our thoughts and feelings and consider with great gravity how our reaction to current events could change the look and feel of freedom forevermore. We must secure America against tyranny, and work to ensure our personal safety, but we must also secure and preserve our liberty and the freedom that makes America the greatest nation on earth. To sacrifice one for the other is to smother the child to protect her from the cold.

Freedom as a political ideology is the right to think and act according to your own conscience within the constraints of civil law. Therefore, who authors, implements, and controls legislation should be of great concern to us, and contrary to contemporary liberal thought we should be very concerned with our elected legislator's conduct and they way they live their personal lives. Why? Because it presents a window on their underlying thought patterns and provides insight to their true objectives.

Enlightened individuals must guard with fervor every other person's right to liberty, regardless of their religious or political persuasion, and it is vital that we protect every individual's right to hold, own and control their own possessions. A simple review of the last century should convince us that anytime a country enacts laws that legislate prejudice it backfires on the general populace at large and erodes the freedoms the people may

---

[4] In the old State House in Philadelphia, on July 4, 1776, a group of men were gathered for the momentous task of severing the tie between the old country and the new. It was a grave moment, and not a few of those present feared that their lives would be forfeit for their audacity. In the midst of the debate a fierce voice rang out. The debaters stopped and turned to look upon the stranger. Who was this man who had suddenly appeared in their midst and transfixed them with oratory? They had never seen him before, none knew when he had entered; but his tall form and pale face filled them with awe. His voice ringing with a holy zeal, the stranger stirred them to their very souls. His closing words rang through the building, "God has given America to be free". As the stranger sank into a chair exhausted: the Declaration of Independence was signed. But where was the man who had precipitated the accomplishment of this immortal task—who lifted for a moment the veil from the eyes of the assemblage and revealed to them a part at least of the great purpose for which the new nation was conceived? He had disappeared, nor was he ever seen or his identity established." (Complete text included in the Appendices)

once have had. Nazi Germany, Soviet Russia, Iran, Iraq, Ethiopia, Yugoslavia, Rwanda, and Afghanistan, are just a few of numerous examples in the past half-century.

Martin Luther King, Jr., surely had it right when he said: "Injustice anywhere is a threat to justice everywhere."

Government's Challenge

Many things of great importance have a way of ignoring borders these days. Family and business relationships are no longer the mark of a local area but are increasingly stretched around the world. They are connected by more than just blood and mutual objectives, but because they have the capacity for almost instant communication.

Consider international terrorism. Even though Osama bin Laden and his terrorist connections were focused on America, the first strikes were in Africa, Yemen, and Lebanon. Eventually it spread into the U.S. itself and engulfed it with such fury that it literally changed the views, and to some extent the conduct, of millions of Americans virtually overnight.

Consider the Laplanders in northern Scandinavia, who could not eat their reindeer meat because even a decade after Russia's Chernobyl nuclear power plant meltdowns, it was still contaminated with radiation. There was literally nothing Sweden and Norway could do to prevent the winds from carrying contaminates across their borders.

Reflect for a moment on the parents of children hooked on cocaine-based drugs imported into the U.S. through any number of holes in the borders. Or ask the residents of California, Texas and Florida, (three nations masquerading as states), along with other U.S. border states where illegal aliens have come to roost in such quantity that the balance of power in their social institutions have tipped towards the new comers. (An interesting footnote on history may be the observation that the Mexican American War of the mid 1840's was ultimately won post 2000 by Mexico, as the Hispanic residents of the southern Border States are out-populating all other ethnic derivations.)

The Internet poses a threat to intolerant national governments because it facilitates trans-national loyalties and affiliations in a way that governments cannot control. Notwithstanding the above, the main threat to national bureaucracies is the loss of their control over money. It is now possible to conduct major transactions across borders using the Internet coupled with smart cards, offshore banking and credit cards, or various forms of barter currencies and private money. This is not just a possibility; it is a huge phenomenon very much on the increase.

Governments are in a weakened position to get a piece of the action with a tax. Taxing is the kind of thing governments are able to do well when goods or people or cash are passing through checkpoints at borders or ports or train stations or airports. But when deals are made for information or for goods already within the jurisdiction, how does government track and tax?

The established bureaucracy knows the handwriting is on the wall. That's why there is so much talk about controlling the exchange of information over the Internet, cell phones and faxes. This is true in America and it is true in Pakistan, and regardless of whether it is Canada or Libya, governments want more control over their citizen's capacity to communicate. Of course, when this highly explosive political issue is spun for the public's consumption, it is all about protecting our children, getting the terrorists, and the war on drugs, while the larger issue of how to tax and control is rarely mentioned.

Expanded anti-money laundering legislation coupled to the greatly enlarged federal investigative powers passed under the political umbrella of tracking Osama bin Laden and company, provided the perfect cover for regulatory agencies to gain greater control over you and your assets. The passion for anti-terrorist control has allowed for increased power to be granted government agencies, such that in some political corners the September 11th tragedy is considered more like Christmas than the national disaster that is permanently registered in the hearts and minds of most Americans. This is particularly worrisome in view of claims by many reputable authorities, including the published statements by the government agencies of Germany, England, Russia and Israel, that the CIA, FBI, and NSA, were all aware of the intent and the timing of the tragic events of September 11th, and for reasons we may never really know decided to ignore that knowledge.

Freedom Verses Chaos

Americans are increasingly being asked —or simply told — that they must give up their freedoms in the name of freedom. Surely this is a paradoxical enigma. How many of our personal liberties must we sacrifice to be safe? This dilemma is the kind of balancing act that freedom itself seems to thrust upon us. This demand upon our freedoms does not necessarily come from outside, but in fact may be a natural and logical consequence of freedom itself. Those that seek the high road of personal sovereignty must decide how far to push the marker on the slide between freedom from danger and the personal freedoms we demand as a result of our civil liberties. We seem to be moving constantly between one and the other as we endeavor to balance order against chaos.

The Queen of England, in her coronation broadcast in 1953, considered the value of ceremony and its effect upon order as contrasted to disorder and chaos when she said: "The ceremonies you have seen today are ancient, and some of their origins are veiled in the mists of the past. But their spirit and their meaning shine through the age...the need for formalized conduct lies deep in the human subconscious, whether it is expressed in the bosom of the family, in a gathering of friends, or in the expression of national emotions."

Following this line of thinking, it appears that many of our family, cultural and national traditions are guards against the chaos that would surely overtake us if we abandon past formalities in favor of complete unrestricted liberty. And, yet the belief in personal liberty is the gift America brought to the world. Our individual positions become even more complicated when one realizes that every point on the sliding scale of personal liberty carries with it a potentially separate definition that can change lives qualitatively. There does not appear to be a simple answer or a clever phrase to sum up the essence of what it means to pursue personal sovereignty, but at its heart it demands personal accountability.

Curiously the very government that was once formed by the people and for the people is now in some quarters a threat to these basic liberating notions. The world is indeed changing and those who are insensitive to these changes will surely be in harm's way. In this vein we might dare to consider a frightening statement by the infamous Reichsmarschall Hermann Goering of Nazi Germany:

> "It is the leaders of the country who determine the policy and it is always a simple matter to drag the people along, whether it is a democracy, or a fascist dictatorship, or a parliament, or a communist dictatorship. Voice or no voice, the people can always be brought to the bidding of the leaders. That is easy. All you have to do is tell them they are being attacked, and denounce the peacemakers for lack of patriotism and exposing the country to danger. It works the same in any country."

Frightening words. Let us hope beyond hope, that America will conduct herself with greater honor than that contemplated by the infamous Goering and that America's leaders will hold themselves to a higher ethical standard than that to which many have become accustomed.

The Underlying Force

Forces found within the nautical world seem to provide apt metaphors that can give us insights into scenarios unfolding on the world stage. For me they provide powerful handles by which we may grasp and understand these events.

Contrasting offshore sailing as a method to interpret personal decision-making in light of current events boils down to this: A sailing yacht is almost always able to make good it's destination regardless of the way the winds blow. If the wind is blowing against you it may take longer to get where you're going but that same force may be used to tack upwind.

Whether you are a weekend sailor or a wealthy yachtsman you will understand these principals and make the connection quickly. If you are not, simply consider that there are forces in motion in the world that are so great that if you resist them you can be washed away. But if you understand how to set your course and trim your theoretical sails, you will reach your goal regardless of the direction the current political and social winds are blowing.

Another force from which we can learn is that of the tidal wave. If you've ever seen the aftermath of one of these giants of nature, you can't help but be moved by its devastating power. Boats smashed to pieces and scattered on the shore, buildings collapsed — a vast scene of destruction and disarray. And yet, if you have boating experience and are out to sea, you know that a tidal wave can move right beneath your hull and you might never even sense its presence. That's the way it is with the truly massive changes in the world. They seem to happen with sudden fury, but in reality the big transformations move beneath us so silently we rarely know they are taking place.

Look Around

A tidal wave is sweeping under us today. Money and instantaneous communications have burst through the floodwalls of national borders and now flow freely. No longer is any single legal jurisdiction the champion of freedom or a safe haven for wealth. The old scenario of risk verses return has never been more pertinent than it is right now. Yes, there are places from where you may control assets, conduct business, and sleep the better for it because risks are reduced and opportunities for expansion are enhanced.

There is a sea change going on. It is part of the process that may end up causing the death of many national governments or at least force upon them dramatic change — a change that is inevitable if governments can't control the exodus of money and assets. Feeling the threat, bureaucracy reacts with ever harsher means of exacting wealth from the people whom government was created to protect. In many jurisdictions, nation states are being superseded by a host of overlapping quasi-governmental bodies, while at the same time national borders are uncontrollable — opening to a flow of drugs, illegal immigrants, terrorists, and cash. In some countries, nationality has more meaning now as an ethnic preference than a political persuasion.

In the United States, some federal agencies seem to increasingly ignore the separation of powers deemed critical by the Founding Fathers, and implement their own rules — which have the effect of law — behaving thereby as if they were a legislative body. They establish their own regulatory enforcement programs. Forty-five federal agencies are now authorized to carry guns. They administer their own programs and all too

frequently answer to themselves as the highest authority. This is a dangerous scenario that must be curtailed, as the axiom "power corrupts and
absolute power corrupts absolutely" is universally valid and America cannot escape this fundamental truth.

Claiming Autonomy

The alert individual is claiming personal sovereignty as nations lose
their authority over knowledge, communication, and thinking. Slowly,
quietly, as if waking from a dream, we take control of our lives and make
the decisions that are best for us. Government is not capable of delivering
what they promise — protection and security. It is the task of the autono-
mous individual to assume more of these responsibilities.

It's been said that there are three kinds of people in the world: those
who make things happen; those who watch things happen, and those who
wonder what happened. Continuing with the nautical theme we might
suppose that those who steer their ships safely to harbor are the ones who
make things happen; those who never get off the dock are the ones who
watch things happen; and those whose ships get dashed on the rocks for
lack of understanding and direction are the ones who simply wonder what
happened.

By understanding the processes that are in play, the self-directed individual who makes things happen has the opportunity to conduct business from more secure locations and place assets where they may grow
more rapidly beyond the grasping hands of predators. These pages tell how
to chart that course and make good your destination.

Legal Documents and Video

In chapter 7, entitled *A Classic U.S. Strategy*, a process is outlined that
could render considerable savings in state income tax, close the curtains
on those peering in your financial windows, and provide you with rock
solid asset protection. You need not expect to understand it all the first
time; further details and a more complete explanation are included in
other chapters. In addition, there is a twenty minute video review of this
sample strategy included in the Compact Disk which is enclosed on the
inside front cover of this book.

Why Nevada

The title of this book is "The Nevada Advantage", so let's move on
to the question of why Nevada. As a point of clarification, almost anywhere you read the word Nevada you could probably substitute it with
Wyoming and the statement would likely be correct. Wyoming has made
a huge effort to level the playing field and compete directly with Nevada
as the U.S. jurisdiction of choice for corporate domicile. For simplicities'
sake, Nevada will generally be referenced throughout this book because its

acceptance worldwide is well known. But, Wyoming is probably just as good a jurisdiction in terms of developing a corporate strategy to achieve privacy, asset protection, tax reduction, and allow you to enjoy enhanced freedom and flexibility in your day-to-day affairs.

Nevada and Wyoming, along with eight other U.S. states, have no state income tax. Nevada, like Texas and Alaska, simply does not need a state income tax because the revenues from other sources are sufficient to support the state budget. In Nevada the gaming industry carries about half the tax load. In Texas and Alaska oil revenues provide significant additional income thus eliminating the need for a state income tax. If you live almost anywhere else in the U.S., even if you are in a non-state income tax jurisdiction like Florida, New Hampshire, New Mexico, South Dakota, Tennessee, or Washington, you are paying extra fees to live there.

Many taxes you find common in the U.S. simply do not exist in Nevada. There is also the somewhat old fashioned mentality that conveys the sense that "what a person earns a person ought to be able to keep." It's a mindset that I share and I suspect you do as well.

If you've visited Nevada, you quickly sense something in the air. It isn't necessarily the sound of coins jingling into the pan of a slot machine. It isn't the sound of buccaneers fighting it out on pirate ships in front of a casino. It isn't the sound of people on street corners handing out advertising for cabarets. What's in the air is the freedom that makes all these things possible.

Nevada and Wyoming are perhaps unique in the United States, where the frontier spirit of independence and personal freedom still holds full sway. That spirit of freedom carries through to personal economics as well. And, you can enjoy the economic freedom either of these States has to offer — and never even go there.

Both Nevada and Wyoming, and a host of other safe harbor jurisdictions around the world, exhibit particular respect for privacy, a critical component in your quest for "personal sovereignty" and the topic of the next chapter.

THE PRIVACY FACTOR

"We are not afraid to entrust the American people with unpleasant facts, foreign ideas, alien philosophies, and competitive values. For a nation that is afraid to let its people judge the truth and falsehood in an open market is a nation that is afraid of its people."

John F. Kennedy

Freedom Requires Privacy

There is a great debate raging over your personal privacy. It has been gathering steam for years and has brought together such unlikely bedfellows as Ralph Nader, Rush Limbaugh and the American Civil Liberties Union. In the wake of the terrorist activities of September 11, 2001, the debate has become much more than philosophical.

Americans feel an urgent need for government to protect them and their property. In order to succeed, government has required greater access to our personal communications and private financial records. Federal law enforcement has garnered broad authority to screen telephone calls, review e-mail transmission, and examine all manner of financial records, including bank, credit card and brokerage activities. Unfortunately, many Americans forget, if they ever really knew, that the war on drugs made the honest citizen its most common casualty. It is a lesson of recent history that when personal affairs are made more easily identifiable, personal property often becomes the target of unwarranted government intervention and predatory lawsuits.

This is the heart of government's dilemma: on the one hand, free governments are instituted to protect citizens and their rights — including the right to privacy. On the other hand, government believes they must violate that privacy in order to protect us and to gather the revenue they need to exist. Given the choice between protecting your rights and funding government's expansion, which do you think bureaucrats will choose?

Surely military and law enforcement require temporarily expanded power during times of national emergency, but at what cost and for how long? Consider the value of your rights to privacy and personal property. And consider that it is in the defense of those very rights, in spite of personal peril, that has made ordinary individuals into national heroes.

Americans are now increasingly being told that they must forgo personal freedoms in the name of freedom. In Chapter 1, with tongue held firmly in cheek, I observed that this might be called "a paradoxical enigma."

But perhaps the issue was better summarized by Lord Acton, several hundred years ago, when he observed: "Power corrupts; absolute power corrupts absolutely."

Nothing to Hide

Some argue that if they have nothing to hide, privacy simply does not matter. Nothing to hide or not, privacy *does* matter, and it matters a great deal! My guess is that you close your drapes at night, not because you have anything wrong going on, but simply because people looking through your windows may not have honorable intentions. Aside from your need to protect yourself from the socially corrupt and the criminal, one should not expect that a private investigator or a law enforcement agent is somehow more honest than others. To do so is to ignore their humanity. In other words, to grant others the right to leaf through your personal life without restriction is to set yourself up for terrible harm.

Newsweek, Business Week, Forbes, and a host of other magazines, along with many of the major U.S. newspapers, have carried articles in the recent past dealing with the loss of privacy in America and the negative impact it is having on us all. *Newsweek* seemed to sum it up best when they wrote: "The legitimacy of laws in a democracy grows out of the democratic process. Unless the people are free to discuss the issues — and privacy is an essential component of many of those discussions — that process cannot take place."

Privacy is an essential ingredient to freedom, and when government invades your rights to personal privacy, the liberty of the people are directly at risk.

Privacy is Paramount

Privacy and freedom are irrevocably linked, remove one and the other is soon lost. For those who believe in individual free agency and suppose that each of us should have the right to think and act for ourselves, there follows a moral imperative that we protect our rights to individual privacy. A world in which seclusion is curtailed undermines our individual dignity and our freedom, while threatening our security and well being.

To be an enlightened citizen, from whatever country or nationality you hail, is to be a person who understands that it is his or her responsibility to protect the rights of the individual. The right to privacy is core because it most closely evokes the concept of individual sanctity. All other rights will simply not exist for any length of time, if and when those in power are permitted to abuse this fundamental of all civil liberties.

Robert S. Peck provides this insight as to our basic need for privacy: "The chilling effect of the loss of privacy is an undesirable incentive to conform to societal norms rather than assert one's individuality. Ultimately, what is lost is not only the private emotional releases we all need but, most importantly, the creativity that leads to human achievement. Privacy makes possible individuality, and thus freedom. It allows us to cope with the larger world, knowing there is a place where we can be by ourselves, doing as we please without recrimination."

Phone Records Are Not Sacred

Larry Ponemon, CEO of the Privacy Council, as quoted in a *Forbes* magazine article in 2001, said, "Telephone information is actually pretty sacred to people like me. Your telephone behavior is one of your most personal behavior patterns. It probably defines more about you then any other behavior pattern —— and most people don't realize just how easy it is to gather that information and to buy it."

Offers abound all over the Internet to provide personal information about others. "Give us a name, address and telephone number, we'll give you the toll calls, dates and numbers, for one monthly billing cycle by their long distance carrier," claims one. Residential Toll Records $100.00 per month. Business Tolls $130.00 per month. These aren't false promises, says Rob Douglas of American Privacy Consultants, Inc. "It's widespread. You could easily say more than 1,000 times a day across the country this occurs," says Douglas.

It may be easy and it may be widespread, but it's legal. The Telecommunications Act of 1996 declared such data to be "customer proprietary network information." Still, private investigators routinely get around this restriction. All it takes is for someone to call the phone company and say "I've just got to have my last phone bill. Please fax it to the hotel at which I'm staying." Al Schweitzer, has spent the last twenty years hunting down electronic information like phone records for clients, and testified before Congress regarding the matter. In short, he claims the practice is so widespread it can't be stopped.

Technology's Expanding Effect

Facial recognition software can match your facial features against a database of people the government is watching. Iris-scanning cameras make sure you're the real, living thing, by checking the pulse inside your eyeball. Tiny high-resolution digital cameras have already become ubiquitous as prices fall below $100.

For decades the job of surveillance was hindered by practical, economic and legal limitations. Technology dealt with the first two obstacles and concern over terrorism has removed the last. We ought rightly worry that, as we embrace intrusive monitoring tools to hound the few plotting terrorist attacks, that millions of Americans will lose another layer of the right to be left alone.

The controversy over privacy is an unwelcome outgrowth of the

Space Race and the microchip and computer that were its offspring. With them came a Pandora's box of electronic devices that have made information about you readily available. The War on Terrorism has put rank and file citizens in the line of fire and within ready earshot of constant electronic snooping. There are those in government and many in the media that suggest everyone should be provided with a unique national identity smart card that tracks where you have been and everything you do.

Surveillance technology, once it is installed for public safety purposes, quickly infiltrates other parts of our lives. Iris scanning was first developed for identification but is used to scan eyes to detect recent drug use, legal or illegal. It claims 95% accuracy. Recently, Panasonic unveiled a PC camera that uses iris-ID. "Once you create these tools, it's very tempting to use them," says Jonathan Zittrain, a Harvard Law professor. "Once the information exists, it's very hard to say you can't access it because that wasn't its intended use."

In May 2001, US Airways supplemented the use of ID tags at the Charlotte, N.C. airport and installed iris scanners that can, from 1 foot away and in a fraction of a second, confirm a pilot's identity. In one test, an iris scanner made by Iridian, matched 2.7 million records to photographs without an error. It even distinguished between identical twins. Evidently their genes are the same, but their irises aren't.

Businesses everywhere are now using cameras, motion sensors and smart ID cards. Biometric ID methods are being built into digital cameras, and as costs fall they will proliferate into every nook and cranny of America. In 2001, cameras in Tampa made national news as it scanned crowds in a business district with facial recognition equipment. Software from Visionics of Jersey City, N.J. picks out human faces, locates key features and calculates the dimensions of a person's skull. The software matches "face prints" against a database of millions in less than a second. Evidently gaining weight or getting a nose job won't fool the system because skull dimensions don't change. New software recognizes faces in a crowd even if they are in profile or tilted up at a 45-degree angle.

Advances in electronics have made it possible to tap telephone lines — to listen in to private conversations from a central control position without ever actually having to physically tap into anything. Other devices make it possible to eavesdrop on things going on inside your home. Radio transmitters are now small enough to be hidden inside cardboard or behind wallpaper.

In many countries the judicial systems have made such evidence inadmissible in court. For example, in 1967, in Katz v. United States, the Supreme Court broadened this prohibition to make wiretapping and other electronic surveillance illegal without a valid warrant. However, the next year saw the Crime Control Act, which set up a system through which courts can approve wiretapping.

Although the Supreme Court ruled that even in cases involving national security, there must be a court order for wiretapping, new legislation in late 2001 was passed granting expanded powers to law enforcement, which simply wiped away restraints on the invasion of personal privacy, at least by government.   However, most governmental agencies, less scrupulous competitors, and those that deal in the gray zones of propriety, have no intention of telling anyone how they got their information. They gather data to seek advantage. Government and private organizations both are in the business of gathering information about you.

Government agencies such as law enforcement, regulators and taxing authorities, as well as private groups like banks, credit card companies, insurance underwriters, employers, and medical merchandisers, all have reams of information about you. And they share it, and they use it, in ways over which you have neither knowledge nor control.

Many scholars and observers, who report on the loss of privacy and its corollary, the consequent loss of freedom, indicate that people generally feel as though their financial life has become part of the public record, a result of the computer age. Frequently we feel powerless to deal with the technology that has stripped away our privacy.

Internet Detectives

Ubiquitous spam email advertisements seem to arrive daily. A recent one states: "Cyber-Spy 2002 just released! Be your own Internet spy and investigate with the best cyber tools! Investigate anyone and everyone! Access information sources just like those used by professional private investigators. Locate, skip trace or access specialty investigative databases instantly at any time, its all just a few clicks away!"

"Secrets never intended to reach your eyes, get the facts on anyone! Find out secrets about your relatives, friends, enemies, and everyone else, even your spouse. Get anyone's name and address with just a license plate number, find that girl you met in traffic. Get anyone's driving record, get unlisted phone numbers, discover dirty secrets your in-laws don't want you to know, learn about your mysterious neighbors. Find out what they have to hide."

Promotions say things like: "The Internet is a powerful mega-source of information, if you only know where to look. I tell you how to find out nearly anything about anybody, and tell you exactly where to find it." For example, you can "find out a juicy tidbit about a co-worker," or "check out your daughter's new boyfriend."

One promotion advised you to "Research yourself first! You'll be horrified, at how much data has been accumulated about you." And now, for twenty bucks, any yahoo with a computer can find it out as well. (Pun intended.) That's not even the worst of it. A company called International Intelligence Network conducts "Public Information and Asset Tracking" seminars, through which anyone can learn how to get more than 50 pieces of financial information on anyone through Internet public records search. By 2002 the price of this program had increased to $29.50, but included access to additional databases and a software system designed for private detectives to help one in organizing search information and reports.

People are buying and selling information about you, combining it with information from other sources and creating profiles on you. Most of this is for commercial purposes — someone wants to sell you something. But this information is available to anyone who might spend the money to buy it — a former spouse or business partner, or anyone else seeking leverage over you for any reason. You may find yourself the target of someone who sues others for a living, or a down and dirty competitor, stalkers, kidnappers, or simply those that deal in the kind of gossip that ruin people's lives.

Other information seekers may be legitimate, although still invaders of privacy. Some very well known hotels put the names of their guests together with records of the vehicles they drive, and the property they own, to find out who is most likely to respond to their mailings. The news media has carried multiple articles about major U.S. banks collating and selling information about their customer's private financial activities. Even as you read this, somebody may be ransacking databases gathering information about you — finding out what you have and where you have it.

Legislative Protection

There are rules that give you some rights — "fair informational practices" laws. These were enacted in various countries beginning in the 1980s, when it became clear the safeguards to protect privacy were not sufficient for the computer age. These rules cover credit, insurance, banking and law enforcement.

In November 2001, the Federal Aviation Administration advised all American pilots, both private and commercial that: "Congress and the President have enacted the Aviation Investment and Reform Act for the 21st century, which requires the FAA to make airmen's addresses available to the public." The logic for this requirement is all bound up in the word "investment" meaning that banks, credit cards companies, lenders, insurance companies, etc., (organizations with tremendous legislative clout), will all now be able to track pilots down in order to sell them something. But what about those of us interested in privacy? Well, it seems that the government has decided, for reasons only it understands, that those of us holding a pilot's license are now open game and not allowed to maintain a quiet, low profile lifestyle.

In America, the purported champion of individual freedom, one does not have the same privacy protection as those who live in Sweden, France, Germany and several other countries. These countries have national data protection or privacy protection commissions that license computer data banks, receive complaints from citizens and enforce the rules. But if you live in the U.S., you're pretty much on your own.

Legislation Ripe for Abuse

The Federal Communications Commission, at the behest of regulations precipitated by the Federal Bureau of Investigation, ordered cellular and digital phone companies to install tracking technology. In January of 2000, Internet privacy organizations unsuccessfully sought a reversal of this mandate through the federal appeals court. As it now stands, law enforcement agencies are supposed to be able to triangulate the exact whereabouts of any cellular or digital phone user without oversight, which means without a warrant or court order.

This may mean that any law enforcement person having access to this technology can track their neighbor, their wife, husband's, or paramour's whereabouts at any time of the day or night, or anyone else they have a grudge against or want something from, and no one will know they've done it.

What may be even worse is that cellular service providers must give authorities the packets of information that constitute the calls themselves and provide lists of the phone numbers being called and the numbers from whence inbound calls are coming. In some places, law enforcement already has access to tracking your every whereabouts, whenever you're carrying a cellular or digital phone. According to FCC rules, the technology must pinpoint within 125 meters any cellular or digital phone that is turned on, whether a call is in progress or not. George Orwell's famous book *1984* seems to have been incredibly prophetic. Big brother is indeed watching and listening in on its citizens.

Whereas governments seem to be in the business of violating personal privacy rights they are at the same time careful to retain privacy over the information they generate. Once again, this situation is in diametric reverse of the concepts outlined by the Founding Fathers of America. Government was to be transparent to the people, not the other way around. From the Great Bathroom Book III comes this quote: "The estimated annual cost to U.S. taxpayers for keeping government documents secret is $20 billion per year. That's $6 billon more than the entire NASA budget!"

Echelon

The vast international global eavesdropping network Echelon is said to be able to monitor ALL, as in EVERY one, of the world's telephone and fax transmissions and sift out messages it finds interesting. According to published reports it is alleged that computers are now automatically analyzing every phone, fax, and data signal, and can also identify calls to say, a target telephone number in London, no matter from which country the call originates. Originally designed to snoop on the Russians, the system has been expanded to eavesdrop on domestic citizens of all nationalities, and it is now believed that much of the work appears to be focused on commercial and private civilian targets.

So where was Echelon prior to September 11th? According to a story in Germany's daily *Frankfurter Allgemeine Zeitung*, both U.S. and Israeli intelligence agencies received warning signals at least three months prior to the assault on the World Trade Center and the Pentagon. They were clear that Middle Eastern terrorists were planning to hijack commercial aircraft to use as weapons to attack important symbols of American and Israeli culture. The article went on to say that U.K. intelligence services also had advance warning and that American intelligence took the warnings seriously, and intensified surveillance, but could not agree on how to prevent the looming attacks. Subsequently, Russia's president Putin made public statements that his country's intelligence apparatus had several times warned the U.S., in the most direct and serious terms, of the pending attack on U.S. soil.

Initially it was the British Broadcasting Corporation that reported that an Australian government official had finally confirmed what both the Americans and British had consistently denied — that the super-secret spy network code-named Echelon, did in fact exist. As it turns out, Britain, Australia, Germany, Japan, and surprisingly, the People's Republic of China are jointly operating Echelon, a global spying network whose existence was first revealed by Duncan Campbell at a symposium held in Luxembourg.

Campbell presented an in-depth report, which included as an example of the potential for abuse of power, specific evidence that the National Security Agency in Fort Mead, Maryland, intercepted a phone call from a French firm bidding on a Brazilian contract and then allegedly passed the information along to an American competitor, which subsequently won the contract. So much for government integrity. But does it really surprise us that anyone who has access to this kind of unbridled power and the right to snoop without balanced civilian oversight would find a way to use it to advance their own agenda?

Carnivore

In 2000, it was discovered that the U.S. Department of Justice had secretly developed and implemented a surveillance system code-named "Carnivore" being used and tested without the courts permission and without seeking or receiving warrants to intercept and examine private communications. Carnivore is a combination hardware/software system, with far-reaching electronic snooping capabilities that can access, read and collate e-mails.

Legislative hearings were convened in Washington when the story broke. The circumstances of its development and the political intrigue surrounding its evolution was widely reported and became the basis of multiple news articles over a several month period. The FBI backed away from installing Carnivore at the major Internet Service Providers (ISPs), which constitute the backbone of the Internet system. On September 12, 2001, I received surreptitious calls from techs with two of the largest ISPs; the FBI had arrived and were installing Carnivore.

A Washington AP release, dated October 26, 2001, stated that Stewart Baker, an attorney at the Washington D.C.-based Steptoe & Johnson and a former general consul to National Security Agency, said the FBI now has plans to change the architecture of the entire Internet and route traffic through central servers so that it would be able to monitor e-mail more easily. He claims that their plans go well beyond the Carnivore e-mail-sniffing system that generated so much controversy among privacy advocates and civil libertarians before the September 11th terrorist attacks.

The country now appears to be seeking more, not less, law enforcement on the Internet, and even those who once complained are afraid to speak up. The FBI is clearly using people's current state of mind to their advantage. "The new FBI plans would give the agency a technical backdoor to the networks of Internet service provider's like AOL and Earthlink and Web hosting companies," Baker said. It would concentrate Internet traffic in several central locations where e-mail and other web activity can be more easily wiretapped. So…where was the national debate on this action? Where is the civilian oversight? Is the fox guarding the hen house? And, if not, how would we know?

Sue Ashdown, executive director of the Washington-based American ISP Association, an Internet company trade group, said most Internet companies aren't healthy enough financially to take on the government in court to protect their subscribers' privacy rights. And no one, she says, wants to appear hostile to law enforcement right now. "In the current patriotic climate, enterprises of all types will likely play along with the FBI in order to avoid a public relations disaster," said Gene Riccoboni, an Internet attorney with the Stamford, Connecticut-based Grimes & Battersby.

The good news for those who value privacy in their personal communications is that recent reports on Carnivore indicate that the use of any one of several e-mail encryption systems will defeat Carnivore and give you back the privacy you seek.

Computer Scanning

In Newark, New Jersey the FBI rigged a suspects computer in late 2000, in such a way that they were able to monitor their target's every keystroke. Not just email messaging or where and what sites he choice to visit on the web, but actually every keystroke of information related to his home financial accounting, personal journal entries, and private correspondence.

Normally, communications between a lawyer and his client are considered sacrosanct under the concept of solicitor-client privilege. However, in this case, the suspect's correspondence with his personal lawyer was retrieved right along with everything else.

In December 2001, it was reported that the FBI had developed a Trojan horse style computer virus, code named "Magic Lantern," similar to the Badtrans worm that have infected many computers around the globe. This virus installs a keystroke logger that monitors everything you type on your home or business computer, and then whenever you access the Internet, it sends these records out to the FBI in the background so that you are unaware that it is happening. If you are using an ISDN line, cable or broadband service, it happens whenever your computer is turned on and works without your knowledge.

An Associated Press article reported that McAfee Corp. (one of the largest anti-viral software providers) contacted the FBI to ensure its software wouldn't inadvertently detect the bureau's snooping program and alert a suspect.

Columnist Brett Glass, probably representing the majority of computer geeks, system operators and IT personnel, lashed out with immediate condemnation of any anti-viral company who would stoop to selling faulty anti-viral software. He went on to say; "Network Associates has shown that it is willing to compromise its integrity by selling intentionally faulty products. For this reason, it is no longer appropriate or wise for those concerned about the security of their networks, systems, or confidential data, to use them."

Whereas most of us do not want to limit law enforcement from having the sophisticated tools necessary to catch the bad guys, the question looms as to whom is providing balanced civilian oversight on the Department of Justice's expansion of powers. At least for the FBI, it now appears that the requirement to secure a warrant in order to spy on the general populace is out the window. Does anyone hear the heavy breathing of Darth Vader in the wings?

The Clipper Chip

The Clipper Chip is a cryptographic device that was designed to permit government agents to obtain "backdoor keys" held by government "escrow" agents that would enable them to defeat encrypted communications and provide them with access to scrambled voice transmissions.

Although the clipper chip was designed to defeat only voice encryption, its sister chip, code named "Capstone" was developed to decrypt private data transmissions. Eventually, both became what is referred to as the "Clipper Chip." In 2001, *Newsweek* stated in their cover article entitled "Beating Big Brother: "What if you had to leave a copy of your front-door key at the police station? Even Joe Six-pack, who didn't know encryption from a forward pass would be an anti–Clipper convert."

The ACLU found itself agreeing with Rush Limbaugh, who attacked Clipper on his radio show. Digital hippies savored the William Safire column "Sink the Clipper Chip," where he noted that the solution's name was well chosen "as it clips the wings of individual liberty."

Privacy and Government Needs

The U.S. Constitution guarantees many things — such as the right to free speech, freedom of religion, and assembly, as well as the right to keep and bear arms. But the "right to privacy" is not guaranteed in the Constitution. What you have in the States is a tradition of Supreme Court rulings and interpretations of various Amendments to the Constitution — primarily the Fourth and Fourteenth.

The Fourth Amendment shields one from "unreasonable search and seizure" and other law enforcement arrest and pre-arrest techniques. The Fourth Amendment is part of the Bill of Rights — a sacrosanct element of the protection citizens demanded for themselves during the formation of the Republic. Unreasonable search and seizure was abhorrent to the framers of the Constitution because at one time, the British used to enter colonial homes, ransack their dwellings and take things without probable cause that a crime had been committed. The British had meaningless, easy-to-get writs and pieces of paper to justify their intrusions. Often enough, these unacceptable violations of privacy came because the Crown wanted to extract more taxes and expand upon their own resources.

The Fourth Amendment is the one that prevents officials from searching a person, automobile or home without "probable cause" or a valid search warrant. But this is a Constitutional Amendment protecting one from the government — not from other private citizens. If you are an American, someone may be executing an electronic search of your possessions right now, with complete immunity.

The gap in protection of the "right to privacy" in the Constitution has been noted and — short of adding an Amendment — the judicial system has gone a long way toward guaranteeing privacy rights. Other Amendments to the Constitution have been broadly interpreted so as to protect the individual. Technology is moving ahead at such a pace that secret governmental projects not open to public scrutiny may have already made these guarantees all but useless except in the direct prosecution of an event.

The Fourteenth Amendment has been used by the U.S. Supreme Court in (Mapp v. Ohio) to, in effect, prevent police from using evidence against a defendant gathered through an illegal search. The Court said that one could not be forced to testify against one's self with such evidence —

a violation of the Fifth Amendment protection against self-incrimination.

The Fourth Amendment is not enough to protect privacy today, because it was written in the Eighteenth Century long before either the Electronic or Information Revolutions. After all, who could have imagined in the days when information traveled at the speed of a horse or a ship, or when it took days or even weeks to find out important news, that information about private citizens would someday be bought and sold in an instant?

In the United States, the question might be well posed as to whether or not you have the right to keep your affairs to yourself: Do you have a right to privacy?" The answer is "yes and no." As noted above, there is no Constitutional protection of your rights to privacy, but the legal system has rallied to interpret many Amendments in a favorable way.

The First Amendment, for example, guarantees the right for people to associate with whomever they wish. The Third and Fourth Amendments protect us from unlawful search and seizures. Although, these have been significantly weakened as of late. The Fifth defends against self-incrimination. And the Ninth says that the rights enumerated in the Constitution "shall not be construed to deny or disparage others retained by the people." These Amendments have been woven together into a broad tapestry that includes privacy. But what does the term privacy really mean?

There is no single definition of privacy that everyone accepts. According to Justice William O. Douglas, the "right to privacy is older than the Bill of Rights." He made that decision in the case of Griswold v. Connecticut. Douglas said that privacy was protected under the "penumbra" or shadow of other constitutional guarantees.

Earlier, in 1928, Justice Louis Brandeis when referring to privacy, said it is the "right to be let alone." A political scientist, Alan Westin, in his book *Privacy and Freedom*, said we ought to define privacy as the right of persons to control the distribution of information about themselves. His definition does not have the force of law, but it is a valuable thought. If we use his concept, privacy is invaded when someone gathers information about you, and perhaps makes public what only you should have the right to disclose.

The Crux of the Privacy Problem

The reason "privacy" is such a problematic "right" is that it runs counter to governments interests. An absolute protection of your right to privacy means assassins, criminals, drug dealers; revolutionaries, saboteurs, spies, terrorists and other troublemakers could hatch their plots behind the cover of their right to privacy.

On the other hand, citizen control laws tend to precede significant shifts in dictatorial power, i.e.: Nazi Germany, Soviet Russia, Fundamentalist Iran, etc. The historical list is incredibly long, and, without exception, the people are always worse off after the transition period. The tendency of people to ignore history, believing that somehow "this time things will be different" brings to mind the famous quotation of Will Durant, author *The History of World Civilization,* when he said, "Those who ignore history are bound to repeat it." Sobering words we should consider with great gravity.

The problem seems to have begun in 1913, when the U.S. instituted an income tax. Prior to that, excise taxes and other taxes carried the burden. World War I, and the huge cash drain it brought to America meant that government needed a greater flow of revenue. One problem with an income tax is, how does the government know how much you have earned? It relies for the most part on the honesty of its citizens. But let's face it, people lie – especially when it comes to paying out money they would prefer not to. Knowing that fact about human nature, the government took action by prying into the personal financial affairs of its citizens.

The U.S. government admits to having about 25 files on every American, with some having as many as 200. Several recent authors claim the government has approximately 70 files on every adult in America. Whatever the number, these files are stored predominantly on computer, and they know a lot about you. It sort of reminds me of the cold war, and the huge efforts the free world put forth, so that we would never be subject to the type of information gathering the KGB performed on its citizens.

The Privacy Act of 1974 was intended to protect citizens from federal invasions of privacy. It prohibits agencies from exchanging personal information they have on file. But the Paperwork Reduction Act (1980) had the effect of allowing any agency to have access to personal data that any other agency had gathered about you. This makes it possible for their computers to cross check your activities — the IRS checking with banking, or the passport office, for example. Although the Computer Safeguards Bill of 1988 set new limits on government's use of computer records, agencies quickly found new ways to subvert the intentions of this bill.

Violence and Privacy

The world's remaining super power seems to be wasting much of its youth. The U.S. sadly sees too many of its young people destroyed by violence. American children are twelve times more likely to die of violence than children in the rest of the industrialized world. And it is getting worse. From 1950 to 1993, murder rates have tripled and suicide has quadrupled in children younger than 15.

During a three-day anti-money laundering conference I attended in Miami, Florida in 1997, a banking panel from Switzerland was responding to questions from the floor. One of the questions dealt directly with street violence in Europe, a concept virtually unknown to the Swiss. About half of the 400 people in attendance were from U.S. three-letter enforcement agencies. The balance of the attendees comprised legal and financial professionals from forty countries. U.S. enforcement spokespersons were disturbed that the Swiss were not enthusiastic about allowing them routine access to the banking records of American's who maintained bank accounts in Switzerland – an act which at that time would cause the Swiss to violate their country's privacy laws. From the Swiss perspective it would seem that whenever the U.S. government wanted confidential financial information from Swiss bankers, they immediately alleged that drug money was involved whether or not there was any demonstrable evidence to support such allegations.

A U.S. law enforcement person speaking from the floor was embarrassingly outspoken in his opinion that citizen rights to privacy were the underpinnings of violent crime. He went on to say that any one who wanted personal privacy had something to hide and it should be assumed that they were conducting some kind of criminal activity. (A sentiment shared by U.S. anti-money laundering trainers sent to all the Caribbean island jurisdictions in late 2000 to teach bank employees about the evils of Americans using offshore banks.) It was quite dramatic when a spokesperson for the Swiss delegation quietly pointed out that there were only five violent crimes that ended in the death of someone in his home city of Geneva, Switzerland during all of 1996. He readily admitted that he did not understand the profusion of violent crime in the U.S. where possibly as many people were killed in the greater Miami area in the past twenty-four hours as for an entire year in Geneva.

You could have heard a pin-drop when he softly made the point that rights to privacy had not spawned violent crime in Switzerland notwithstanding they had supported privacy for the individual for almost 700 years!

Progress

Privacy advocates tend to love cash and fear such things as smart cards. Dollar bills are dumb. They don't know where you dine out, whom you call or where you spent your last weekend. Cash and possible some smart card technology allows a certain level of anonymity. But there is a massive movement by governments to eradicate the use of cash in all but the most incidental of purchases. Once again this puts the individual squarely in jeopardy from bureaucrats and powerful authorities. The bottom line is that when someone is able to access your transaction records they have incredible details about your life. Whereas commercial institutions gather information on us for benign reasons, a government's underlying motives may be another matter entirely.

The privacy issue has now become a big deal with larger companies. Chief Privacy Officers are joining the executive ranks at major technology companies and many financial institutions. No one had ever heard of a "chief privacy officer" just two years ago. Now they are popping up everywhere. Companies are finally realizing that privacy will not arise by accident.

In Summary

Governments argue that they have the right to keep tabs on your activities for the sake of domestic security and to prevent tax evasion. But do they, or should they really have this right? Assuming they do, primarily because they say they do, then what about commercial snoops? Are they too entitled to ransack your personal information at will?

There are private firms known as "asset locators" whose job it is to find out where your keep your stuff and how much stuff you have. Disgruntled employees or others often employ them with a lawsuit in mind. Crooks, swindlers, competitors, long-lost relatives and others who want what you have can access important confidential information by retaining these investigators.

The erosion of personal privacy coupled with the alarming increase in citizen control laws, have been achieved under the cover of fighting the war on drugs and more recently on the war against terrorism. The assault on personal rights, including privacy, is justified with convincing arguments about the common good and how the state is improving the quality of the protection it provides its citizens. On closer examination, one may observe that the "common good" always happens to benefit the political concepts of those in power and that the individual's loss of personal power is quickly transferred to the bureaucracy.

With the war on terrorism in full swing, the loss of privacy in America has been accelerated. Lord Acton's epic warning that "power corrupts, and absolute power corrupts absolutely" is a standard by which we ought gauge all governmental demands for broader authority to act without careful external oversight.

There is a direct link between privacy and freedom and those who violate our private space by acquiring confidential information without permission may use it to exercise control over our activities. We must defend the individual's right to privacy, whether on the battlefield, in the courtroom, or in financial institutions. Justice Louis Brandeis, formerly with the U.S. Supreme Court sums it up:

"The right to be left alone is the most comprehensive of rights, and the right most valued by civilized men."

Part of the personal defense of freedom-loving people, personal sovereigns if you will, may be to guard their personal financial affairs through the use of legal strategy and structures. Make sure you have something safe, beyond prying eyes and grasping hands. Ultimately, it is the only way to ensure you are able to gain, or retain, a measure of personal privacy and the attendant personal freedom it can provide.

THE LITIGATION EXPLOSION

"The law provides incredible financial incentives to seek out a victim with deep pockets, drag him into court, ruin his reputation, wear him down with endless discovery demands, pay a fortune to defend himself, and then extort a settlement from him. This is not justice in any sense of the word."

The Tort Informer

The Problem

According to Walter K. Olson, senior fellow at the Manhattan institute:

"America has deregulated the business of litigation. In a series of lamentable legislative and judicial changes over the past few decades, we have encouraged Americans to sue each other. The changes amount to a unique experiment in freeing both the legal profession and the litigious impulse from their age-old constraints.

The experiment has been a disaster—an unmitigated failure. The unleashing of litigation in its full fury has done cruel, grave harm. It clogs and jams the gears of commerce, sowing friction and distrust between the productive enterprises on which material progress depends and all who buy their products or work at their plants and offices. It seizes on former love and intimacy as raw materials to be transmuted into hatred and estrangement. It sets parent against parent, doctor against patient. It exploits the bereavement that some day awaits the survivors of us all and turns it to an unending source of poisonous recrimination. It torments the provably innocent and rewards the palpably irresponsible. It devours hard-won savings and worsens every animosity of a diverse society. It is the special American burden, the one feature hardly anyone admires of a society that is otherwise envied the world around."

The Threat To Business

Everyone who has anything is vulnerable, but professionals and business owners, large and small, are the prime targets for lawsuits. New York officials have estimated that payouts in suits against doctors and hospitals in their state alone have risen 300 times in a single generation; that's not 300%, but rather a whopping 300 times increase!

As an example of this pernicious quandary, a study performed by Harvard researchers regarding medical malpractice litigation demonstrates that of four out of five lawsuits filed, the care given was not in fact negligent. Their findings indicate that most malpractice lawsuits have nothing to do with actual negligence but are rather an opportunity for a joint-venture speculation between legal counsel and the claimant to stake a claim and hope to strike it rich. Information provided from this exhaustive study points out that as medical litigation increases patients, taken as a group, are far worse off. The quality of medicine is being curtailed rather than expanded upon due to the risk to which medical professionals are exposed to litigation.

A recent National Institute of Medicine study found that "defensive medicine" had seriously compromised the quality of care, leading, for example, to thousands of unnecessary surgeries, unnecessarily prescribed medications, and the sometimes very serious side effects of these self-protection mechanisms.

Joint and Several Liability, or the "deep pockets" approach, is an open door for assaults on both business and personal assets. Through the Joint and Several Liability approach, if a firm so much as does business with another company that is the target of a lawsuit, it can be dragged in as a defendant to pay damages. It's sometimes called the "tort tax," and every year it costs business owners hundreds of billions of dollars.

Contingency-fee litigation, (lawsuits on a commission basis), or perhaps more correctly, "predatory litigation," has made more overnight millionaires than just about any business next to Microsoft and Intel. Forbes magazine reported on the richest lawyers in America and found that the big fortunes were overwhelmingly made in contingency-fee work. Among the top scorers on its list were a Detroit lawyer whose practice hauls in an estimated $100 million a year in settlements; another who specializes in suing doctors and carts home an estimated $12 million a year; a Wichita attorney who sues vaccine makers and has made more than $ 5 million in each of the last 10 years.

Richard Grand of Tucson, Arizona didn't make the list, but Laurence Bodine of the trial lawyers' newsletter "Lawyers' Alert" reports that Grand has collected $200 million in verdicts and settlements over his career, with 60 cases exceeding $1 million.

Predatory litigation is quite simply the most profitable work in law. Contingency legislation has spawned an entire industry that is boldly and openly run for profit. In a trend that is full of implications for the future, contingency litigation is spreading into employment matters, child support issues, will contests, copyright infringement, tax issues, divorce, and most ominously, into bureaucratic arenas where agencies search for new ways to expand on their discretionary budgetary funds.

Funding Government Through Litigation

In an article authored by Amy Moritz Ridenour, president of The

National Center for Public Policy Research, entitled "Government Use of Contingency Fee Lawyers Works Against Public Interest" comes this:

"Question: If on election day you were asked to choose between a political candidate who promised to work for a reasonable salary, and another candidate who wanted to be paid 25% of the government's receipts, an amount which could reach billions of dollars, which candidate would you vote for? Many voters thought they were voting for the former, but are getting the latter.

That's because several dozen states have chosen to farm out legal work to lawyers who will be paid not for the number of hours they work but a percentage of the proceeds from lawsuits.

In Florida, for instance, a recent settlement means a $2.8 billion payment for lawyers, an amount the Florida Attorney General's office likens to $100,000 per hour. Six other states have offered lawyers 25% of the take from tobacco deals

Advocates for trial lawyers give several reasons why lawyers should be paid large contingency fees instead of for work performed, like other state employees.

First, they say that contingency fees are the only way states can afford to hire top-notch lawyers. Nonsense. Tobacco litigation pits forty states with extensive revenues (the Texas state government alone collected $40.4 billion in 1996, which is about $4 billion more than the domestic and international tobacco revenues of the largest tobacco company for the same year) against tobacco companies who pay their lawyers by salary or by the hour. If tobacco companies can do it, so can the states.

Private lawyers will likely reap tens of billions from tobacco settlements. After they do, won't they try to keep this cash cow going? If lawyers can make billions saying that states are due dollars for the adverse health effects of tobacco, won't they want to say the same about junk food? Or liquor? Or fast cars?

The answer is: Yes. And that's why private profit-making has no place in government decision-making. Government policies should be based on their merits, not on opportunities to give private lawyers billion-dollar profits. "

There have been Congressional efforts to limit punitive damage awards to $250,000 or three times the compensatory damage, whichever is greater. But there are powerful forces at work against such limitations. One obvious reason is that class action lawsuits for product liability amounts to billions per year in income for plaintiff's attorneys, plus the legal fees defendants must pay their lawyers. And, now with government agencies leaping on the bandwagon to garner funding from business owners of all sizes the attempts by some to control this awful mess is unlikely to happen any time soon.

America The Litigators

No other country's legal system operates like that in America. A study in the 1987 Duke Law Journal concluded that America had almost three times as many lawyers per capita as Great Britain, with American tort claims running at least 10 times higher, malpractice claims 30 to 40 times higher, and product claims nearly 100 times higher as calculated on a per capita basis.

Another survey found that America spends five times as much as its major industrial competitors on personal-injury wrangling as a share of its economy, and that the gap is widening. The survey concluded that over the last two generations the cost of injury litigation has risen 14-fold after inflation, while the size of the real U.S. economy rose only three-fold.

Mushrooming litigation is also taking an economic toll on individuals. It used to be that mostly doctors among professionals had to worry about buying liability insurance. Now it's a crushing expense for accountants, nurses, amateur sports umpires, and local charity volunteers. Most hairdressers and veterinarians reportedly buy it. It is the coming thing among social workers, school counselors, and the clergy, who have been sued in much-publicized cases for giving wrongful advice. Lawyers pay dearly for their own coverage, and judges have been added to the list in the wake of rulings that they may now be sued in some circumstances for handing down wrongful decisions.

Some parts of the country are worse than others. Alabama is known to be the best place in the country for plaintiffs seeking damages in product liability cases. Juries there have made some of the highest awards anywhere in the country. The situation is so bad the U.S. Supreme Court in 1996 actually struck down several Alabama laws that required high damage awards and declared them unconstitutional.

Few reasonable people would suggest that companies should not be held liable for defective or dangerous products. But it is also true that product liability lawsuits have stifled entire industries, from breast implants to water slides. For example after paying out billions of dollars in breast implant settlements and judgments for difficult to define side-effects ranging from mental instability to constantly being tired, medical researchers finally concluded that breast augmentation had no real medical side effects whatsoever. That hasn't kept lawsuits from being filed or specialized law firms from continuing to gain huge settlements or jury judgments based on the claimant's charge that their lifestyle has been plagued with a whole host of aches and pains.

A Legal Joint Venture

In virtually everywhere but America, it's assumed that lawyers face serious temptations to behave badly in order to improve their clients' chances of winning a lawsuit. It is also commonly understood that because there are no effective means of policing such misconduct that the first line of ethical defense for lawyers is to NOT allow them a direct stake in the outcome of the lawsuits they create. In other words, predatory litigation, which allows plaintiff's legal counsel to share the spoils of legal warfare, is simply against the law.

Is anyone surprised that it's the upward middle class and the wealthy that get sued? People who do not have readily available resources to seize, or are considered "judgment proof" rarely find themselves a target of predatory litigation, unless they have major insurance coverage. It's simple economics. If lawyers don't believe you've got access to a large pool of assets, their primary negotiating leverage is gone.

In addition to allowing joint-venture style litigation, America is the only major country that denies to the winner of a lawsuit the right to force the loser to pay the legal expenses for pursuing or defending the case. In other countries, the promise of a fee paid by the opponent gives lawyers good reason to take on a meritorious case for even a poor client. The obvious result of not providing for legal fees to be paid by the loser is that clients must find some other way to compensate their lawyers. Unless the client has independent sources of cash, the only place for the fee to come from is out of the recovery itself, hence the rationale behind the despicable practice of predatory litigation.

Virtually every nation's legal system understands that to allow lawyers and clients to work jointly as pack predators is effectively an assault on the general public. But, in the good ole USA the lawyers control the game and the game keeps expanding. For example, it has been widely reported that the America has about 70% of the world's total legal professionals, and a whopping 94% of the world's litigation! And, if that's not enough, there are apparently more students in law school than are now practicing law within the country. So.... how do you think the new crop of lawyers will proceed to build their financial futures once they are practicing and are established litigators?

European lawyers are often astonished to learn that in America expert witnesses are recruited, sent into courtrooms and paid by the contending litigants themselves. Credentials are impressive to jurors, and jurors taken as a group do not seem able to separate expert's partisan positioning.

"I would go into a lawsuit with an objective, uncommitted, independent expert about as willingly as I would occupy a foxhole with a couple of noncombatant soldiers," former American Bar Association President John Shepherd has said. Frequently lawyers write the testimony for the expert to deliver on the stand.

"An expert can be found to testify to the truth of almost any factual theory, no matter how frivolous," noted federal Judge Jack Weinstein.

Countersuits

Leona Serafin was supposed to have a routine kidney-stone removal. Instead, hemorrhaging set in on the operating table and she died a few days later. An autopsy found the cause of death to be thrombotic-thrombocytopenic purpura, a rare and nearly always fatal blood disorder whose origin is unknown.

Two years later lawyers representing the Serafin family filed malpractice suits against the hospital and three doctors. Three years after that the case went to trial. The lawyers could not offer any testimony to indicate that the doctors or hospital had fallen short of any accepted standards in recommending or conducting the surgery. Upon hearing their case the judge promptly ordered a verdict for the defense.

After being drug through such a life-alternating event, defendants are somehow supposed to go back to pursuing their profession and forget what happened to them. In this particular case, one of them, Dr. Seymour Friedman, couldn't forget. He filed a lawsuit against the two attorneys who filed the original nuisance lawsuit saying they had good reason to know their action was groundless. And, that because of their endeavor to extort the equivalent of legal blackmail, he was put to huge direct expense: He would now have to pay higher insurance rates for as long as he practiced medicine; he lost two medical associates who could not afford to pay the higher liability premiums being charged to his office; his professional reputation had been seriously defamed; and he had been put through intense personal embarrassment and severe anguish.

The Supreme Court of Michigan in response essentially said that the doors of the courts were closed against him. Dr. Friedman could not prevail even if he could prove the lawyers knew the claim was spurious. The court held that a lawyer can't be sued for malicious prosecution even if he "has no probable cause and is convinced that his client's claim is unfounded."

Even though these lawyers were seeking a pre-court settlement, and not actually seeking adjudication, it did not matter. The court's opinion boiled down to one far-reaching declaration: A predatory lawyer has no "duty of care" to avoid hurting those he pursues, even where the circumstances are clear that the only objective was to garner a settlement from legal extortion.

America is the litigious society it is because our lawyers wield unparalleled powers of imposition. No other country gives a private lawyer such a free hand to select a victim, tie him up in court on undefined charges, force him to hire lawyers of his town at dire expense, trash his privacy through discovery, wear him down on the perpetual-motions treadmill, libel him grossly in documents that become permanent public records, and keep him scrambling to respond to self-anointed experts. Other countries let lawyers or litigants do some of these things, but never with such utter impunity.

City Governments Join the Fray

In a paper prepared by Michael I. Krauss, a senior fellow in constitutional studies at the Cato Institute in Washington, D.C. comes this:

"Hot on the heels of the carnage in Littleton, Colorado, President Clinton proposed a grab bag of new gun-control measures— never mind that they wouldn't have stopped the Littleton murders, whose perpetrators broke a dozen laws already on the books. An unspeakable event rocks the public, and our politicians seize on the ensuing anti-gun sentiment to advance their otherwise frustrated gun-control agenda."

Doubtless the same opportunism will spark a new round of litigation by mayors against the firearms industry. Already at least eight cities have filed suit — Atlanta, Bridgeport (Conn.), Chicago, Cincinnati, Cleveland, Detroit, Miami, and New Orleans — to recoup public outlays stemming from gun-related violence. Their suits are the leading edge of a novel and dangerous approach to public policy that ultimately threatens the rule of law.

When governments use the judiciary to recover "damages," the courts intrude on the regulatory and revenue responsibilities of legislatures. And when lawsuits based on tenuous legal theories impose high costs on defendants, due process gives way to a form of extortion, with public officials serving as bagmen for private contingency fee lawyers. The predictable result is growing public contempt for our legal institutions.

All eight cities' gun suits share an important characteristic of the tobacco settlements: They claim damages for indirect harm. The plaintiff cities do not argue that their property was hit by gunfire, only that they lost revenue when gunfire harmed others. Tort law, however, is classically based on direct harm. Suing for indirect damage flies in the face of 150 years of tort law. On this threshold issue alone, the cities' suits against gun makers are losers. But there's more.

To hold gun makers liable for selling an unsafe product, tort law requires that the product be truly defective, not merely dangerous. American case law has consistently rejected claims that firearms are inherently defective. Indeed, empirical data gathered by Gary Kleck, professor of criminology at Florida State University, and by John R. Lott Jr., law professor at the University of Chicago, reveal that handguns, far from being defective, in fact deter and substantially reduce violent crime when they are carried by non-felons. The lead plaintiff's counsel in the New Orleans case, Wendell Gauthier, himself carries a gun — presumably because he assigns to it greater utility than risk.

Then there is the public-nuisance argument. The American Law Institute defines a public nuisance as "an unreasonable interference with a right common to the general public." David Kairys of Temple University Law School, co-counsel in the Chicago case, has urged the adoption of that doctrine in gun cases. But Kairys has it backwards. It is Chicago's lawsuit that constitutes a public nuisance. The sale of guns does not violate any right common to the general public."

On the contrary, individuals have a right to protect themselves against criminal conduct. Gun ownership, by facilitating self-defense, helps secure that right. Wrongful behavior, not an inanimate object, is the cause of gunshot injuries. Legitimate ownership of firearms, which are present in almost 50 percent of American homes, cannot be a predictor of violent behavior. The manufacture, sale, and ownership of hand-guns are highly regulated. Statutes ban certain guns. It is a federal crime for felons or drug users to purchase or possess any firearm. It's illegal for retailers to sell hand-guns to minors. Sales of more than one firearm must be reported to authorities. Background checks of purchasers are federally mandated. Handguns are the only consumer products for which manufacturers, wholesalers, and retailers are all required to have federal licenses. Handguns are also the only products that may not be purchased outside one's state of residence. The design of every new model must be inspected and approved by the Bureau of Alcohol, Tobacco and Firearms.

If the cases against gun manufacturers are so insubstantial, why is the litigation so threatening to the industry and to the rule of law? A number of factors conspire to transform weak legal cases into effective means of accomplishing a shakedown: the use of juries in civil cases, procedural rules that make it difficult to have even lame cases dismissed prior to extensive litigation, huge potential damages, and the perverse incentives that drive lawsuits when public officials hire private attorneys on a contingency fee basis.

Because juries more than judges are willing to overlook legal niceties when an injured plaintiff seeks damages from an unpopular corporate defendant, jury verdicts tend to favor plaintiffs. Not only are plaintiffs more likely to prevail if a jury hears the case, but they are likely to recover a larger sum as well. Indeed, jurors can reduce their own taxes by holding defendants liable for public outlays. The effect is to make defendants more amenable to settlement.

Procedural rules also push defendants toward settlement, even when their case is strong on the merits. In many jurisdictions, courts are reluctant to dismiss a case prior to far-reaching discovery. Thus, plaintiffs can engage in fishing expeditions for documents that might support their case or embarrass the defendants.

Gun makers and other industries have reason to be concerned about the unholy alliance between government and the private bar. Although the gun suits are based on different legal theories than the tobacco suits, they enjoy a common lineage. Both series of suits were concocted by a handful of private attorneys who entered into contingency fee contracts with public officials. In effect, members of the private bar were hired as government subcontractors, but with a huge financial interest in the outcome. Imagine a state attorney general corralling criminals on a contingency-fee basis, or state troopers paid per traffic stop. The potential for corruption is enormous.

Contingency fee contracts between governments and private attorneys should be illegal. Free societies should not condone private lawyers' enforcing public law when those lawyers have a personal stake in securing severe penalties. Legislatures or the courts should shut down this plunder by the plaintiffs' bar.

Where will it end? More kids are killed by bicycles than by guns. What we have here is a legal system run amok — social engineering without restraint and without concern for personal responsibility. Yesterday tobacco, today guns, tomorrow bicycles, and who knows what will follow.

Can This Be True?

A highly educated, former CIA operative shared with the author the results of a U.S. study where those surveyed ranked their opportunities for achieving wealth. The following reveals the unfortunate results:

1. Win the lottery
2. Win funds from a lawsuit
3. Receive an inheritance

What does this tell you about the orientation of a growing number of people? What does this say about modern morality, self-reliance, and personal self-discipline?

It takes hard work to develop a business or invest wisely. It takes hard work to build assets and diligently accumulate them into an estate for your own security, your retirement, or as an inheritance for your heirs. Unfortunately a whole lot of Americans now believe it's a easier to put a buck into a slot, pull the lever and hope to get a cascade of free money. But what's worse is that a majority of people evidently also considers it perfectly acceptable to find a reason to sue someone in order to make their fortune.

Is it really okay to exploit a real or imagined harm, find a lawyer who'll take a suit on commission, and take a shot at getting into the pockets of a successful person who has spent the time to accumulate assets? Unfortunately it is easier and quicker to sue someone than it is to commit oneself to worthwhile goals, hard work, long hours, and ethical conduct.

The Future

What's the future of lawsuits in America? There will be a lot more of them if the lawyers have their way. Take California for example, this state prides itself on being the leader in so many things — and now in lawsuits as well. Attorneys and their clients have become increasingly creative in their reasons for suing. As a matter of fact, the trial lawyers there were the largest financial backers of a ballot measure that can be seen as a model of what may be in store for the entire country some day.

California lawyers sponsored Prop 211, which did not pass but represents a legal "wish list" for the lawyers who specialize litigation on commission. The ballot measure would have made it even easier for stockholders to sue if they lost money on a stock. "Strike suits" are those that target a company when its stock prices drop. There are people whose sole business directive is to buy stock they think will lose value. Then they sue. And there are law firms who specialize in just this type of lawsuit. One based in San Diego reports that they have secured $22 billion in settlements!

The idea was to protect the savings of retirees by giving them greater power against securities fraud. But the biggest winner would have been the state government and the lawyers. The measure would have allowed "punitive damages" against a defendant found guilty of "willful, outrageous or despicable conduct" in stock manipulation. But the people who lost money in such stock frauds would not benefit — such awards would have gone to the state! Punitive damages have not been previously allowed as blunder for state or the federal government security suits. If the measure had passed, there is no telling what heights governments may have, or may yet reach with the "punitive damages" concept.

At the federal level the U.S. Securities & Exchange Commission, certainly one of the world's great predators, already has so many ways to seize the assets of anyone unfortunate enough to show up on their radar screen that to give them greater resources to blunder and pillage would be to effectively turn the keys to the economic kingdom over to them. This is an agency, which has become essentially unaccountable to the American people and already has such poor external oversight that even the U.S. Congress has virtually no say in how it directs its activities.

Numerous government agencies have assumed authority not granted or even available to them under the Constitution, and with this power to "catch the guilty" they seize the assets of many innocents, frequently destroying their lives in the process. After all, chasing criminals can be hard and dangerous work, but plundering the naïve is easy pickings.

California also toyed with the idea of allowing plaintiffs to collect 100% of damages from deep-pocket defendants. This means that all expenses of a lawsuit could wind up the liability of someone only marginally involved in any given legal scenario. Even companies headquartered outside California could be dragged into their lawsuits. Several large accounting firms sponsored a study to learn the consequences of such laws. Among their findings was that an estimated 300,000 people would lose their employment over the next decade as businesses fled the oppressive atmosphere predicted were such legislation to be passed. Eventually state tax revenues would drop by almost $5 billion over a ten-year period.

The rest of us would be dragged into this lawyer's feast whether we wanted to be or not. The Economic Strategy Institute of Washington, D.C. estimated that such a law in California would cause a drop in U.S. GNP of between $48 billion and $102 billion, and that eventually almost two million Americans could lose their jobs. Thankfully the proposed legislation failed to make it into law, but the underlying point is that creative trial lawyers are seeking ever-broadening avenues toward more lawsuits. Whether they achieve their goal today or tomorrow, they are going to continue in that direction until they reach the Promised Land of your assets.

Facing The Legal Reality

We have a judicial system where a lady spilling coffee on herself after leaving a drive-through restaurant sues because the coffee was hotter than industry standards, and is awarded $2.8 million in damages. Has the American judicial system lost touch with reality?

Typically, a law firm working on contingency collects its expenses directly off the top of settlement or judgment receipts. It then usually takes half of any balance that is left. Contingency resolutions frequently end up paying the lawyers from 75% to 100% of actual receipts, thence comes the conventional wisdom: "In litigation, only the lawyers win."

According to U.S. News & World Report, in an article entitled "It's a tort world after all," coverage was given to some interesting contingency litigation.

- In a suit over faulty plastic plumbing installed in Sun Belt homes, lawyer George Fleming won a settlement of $170 million in cash, plus costs for reinstalling pipe. From the total award he demanded $108 million in cash, nearly two-thirds of the cash portion of the settlement. (I wonder how that computes on an hourly basis.)

- A Minnesota bank teller, pressed by her employer to take a lie detector test when she was questioned about missing funds, sued for emotional damages and won $60,000.

- A Hindu plaintiff mistakenly bit into a beef burrito and sued claiming he had clearly ordered a bean burrito and suffered emotional damage because beef is forbidden in his religion.

(Unearned income from lawsuits evidently is not.)

- A 56 year old Texan got $1.8 million when a dog scared him by darting in front of his bicycle, his wife got another $50,000 for loss of household help, companionship, and sexual affection.

- One couple sued for $10 million for injuries received when they were hit by a train while having sex on the tracks of the New York subway.

- In another case, one homeless man on heroin and another who had a bottle of wine for breakfast loitered on the tracks and got $13 million for having been burned by the third rail. (They got another $9,000 for loss of income as squeegee men washing car windshields at corner stop lights.)

- A New York drunk lost an arm when he fell in front of an oncoming train and got $3.6 million.

- An Illinois woman whose late husband, an immigrant from Korea, climbed down onto the New York subway tracks and urinated directly on the third rail, thus electrocuting himself. She was awarded $1.5 million because there were no signs in Korean warning against such behavior.

- A fleeing mugger was shot after trying to rob a 71-year-old man and was awarded $4.3 million.

- Recently a woman sued charging that her dog was killed by a neighbor's secondhand smoke.

What do you think, is the American judicial system on the right track? Given an out-of-control tort system where judges bend over backwards to help plaintiff's lawyers reach deep pockets, and where the plaintiffs' bar is able to frustrate tort reform by purchasing decisive political influence through campaign contributions, what is your recourse?

If you have anything or have accomplished anything or have served anywhere — from a school board to Little League — you may be the object of a lawsuit and your assets may be seized.

Conclusion

Most lawsuits, certainly in the high 90 percentile, get settled out of court, but you still have to pay an attorney and often large sums in "legal extortion." It's common knowledge among professional litigants that most people and companies will pay what equates to a "ransom" just to make the suit go away. Why? Because its much cheaper in the long run and besides once a case comes before court, especially if before a jury, you have no idea what the outcome will be. Your assets and your future are literally dangling in the wind.

One of life's most unpleasant experiences is receiving legal service. This is especially true if you pride yourself on personal honesty and integrity. You must now live with the stress and uneasiness of having litigation pending against you. It works on you; it disrupts your life, it interrupts your social relationships, it puts a cloud over your activities for the foreseeable future. And, you must deal with this, all the time knowing that the outcome is uncertain. Even if the litigation is frivolous, it will be vexatious, and there is always the chance that the presiding judge or jury might not agree with your view of matters.

U.S. juries tend to give awards to those they consider financially less fortunate, particularly if they are attractive or present themselves well. This appears to have more to do with whom jurors identify as opposed to any form of reasonableness. If a Plaintiff's lawyer were to paint you as one who has "deep pockets" that may be all it takes for you to find yourself with a legal judgment to pay.

Unfortunately the U.S. legal system is no longer about discovering truth, it's very much more about who presents the best case and, all too frequently, whom the jury feels can afford to pay. As a result of this reality, and other pressures that may be unique to your situation, such as your status in the community, the risk of a "finding" of negligence, how that might effect your professional career or business, the anticipated trial tactics that may expose your personal history, business secrets, or confidential family matters, you will surely find yourself under huge pressure to settle. Lawsuits — perhaps the fear of them as much as the reality — are the fundamental reason to invoke a well thought out asset protection strategy.

Before we move into the practical information section let's explore the threat of an increasingly powerful government and consider how that may impact you. All of us depend upon bureaucracy to implement and administer fair policy to ensure that our personal freedom and the rights to control our own property are not violated. But are we safe from the government itself?

CONCERNS OVER GOVERNMENT

*"My reading of history convinces me that most bad
government results from too much government."*

Thomas Jefferson

Government Expansion

The Nelson A. Rockefeller Institute of Government at State University of New York in Albany recently reported that government employment at all levels is substantially on the increase, regardless of political banter to the contrary. The most recent numbers readily available report that in 1998* government employment rose by 324,000 persons in that year alone, which represented the largest percentage increase in the preceding eight years.

Contrast this information with the quotation by Thomas Jefferson directly above.

Equal Rights

The Constitution and the Declaration of Independence endeavored to secure the equal right for any person to become as unequal as they want to become. Becoming unequal in knowledge, substance, and skill, is all about personal self-discipline, free competition, goal setting, and innovation. The concept of equal rights means that each of us ultimately has the right to choose for ourselves what we wish to make of ourselves and that there is no higher authority on earth making these choices for us.

The decision to pursue your own personal goals and objectives is exclusively yours, and that is just as it should be. Mature, independent, solid-thinking individuals should revel in this aspect of their personal sovereignty. You see people are simply superior to governments. People form governments, not the other way around.

Frederic Bastiat, the French political economist, said: "Life, liberty, and property do not exist because men have made laws. On the contrary, it was the fact that life, liberty, and property existed beforehand that caused men to make laws in the first place."

The proper role of government should be restricted to those activities within which any individual citizen has the right to act. Proper gov-

---

*Why is it that citizens have four months to reconcile and submit their prior year's activities to the government, whereas the government cannot seem to fully report on their internal activities for several years and oft times not at all?

ernment derives its power from the governed. Its responsibility is to protect its citizens from the loss of freedom, physical violence, theft, and other such matters.

Ezra Taft Benson, a fervent constitutionalist and former Secretary of Agriculture to President Eisenhower, was right on target when he said: "No individual possesses the power to take another's wealth or to force others to do good, so no government has the right to do such things either. The creature cannot exceed the creator."

The German sociologist, Franz Oppenheimer, dramatically stated the basic coercive and parasitic nature of government. He set forth the premise that there were only two means by which man could obtain wealth, and that these two methods were mutually exclusive. The first method was simply production and voluntary exchange. The second method was robbery by the use of violence. He refers to the latter as "political means." Political means are clearly parasitic, for it requires previous production for the exploiters to confiscate, and it subtracts from, rather than adding to, the total production in society. Oppenheimer goes on to define the State as "the systematization of the predatory process over a given territorial area." Strong words but insightful, none the less.

Certainly we need government. Good government is the basis for the quality of life one may hope to ultimately enjoy. But all entrenched bureaucracies eventually move to consolidate their power, and if not checked with well thought out, balanced, civilian oversight, will abuse that power to enrich themselves. In the words of Joseph Smith Jr., "We have learned by sad experience that it is the nature and disposition of almost all men, as soon as they get a little authority, as they suppose, they will immediately begin to exercise unrighteous dominion." And, so it is.

Justice for All

The number of adults in the U.S. prison system, either in jail, parole or probation, has jumped by 300% in the past twenty years according to information released in late 2001 by the Justice Department. Six and a half million people are clogging the U.S. correctional system stated Allen J Beck, chief researcher with the Justice Department's Bureau of Justice Statistics. This equates to from five to seven times more people in the prison system, on a per-capita basis, than other G-7 countries.

What is surely worse is that recent reports claim that more than half the people now in U.S. jails are there for victimless crimes, or in other words, crimes against the state. If this is true, then the huge increase in the correctional system's population says a lot about how U.S. authorities are criminalizing activities that were formerly considered relatively benign.

The number of people detained in the U.S. correctional system increased 49 percent in the 1990's. By the end of 2000 there were 2.1 million more adults in the correctional system that there were in 1990.

Unfortunately, the resources dedicated to prevention are slight compared to the billions being fed to an expanding prison system. Massive amounts of money have been dedicated to building huge new prison facilities — but for whom?

Why should the U.S. have so many more people in jail, on a relative percentage basis, than those of our global trading partners? Are U.S. streets safer than in England, France, Germany, Japan, Canada, Australia, Taiwan and South Korea? Certainly not. And, even though violent crime seems to have reached a relatively stable percentage in America, the number of people in the prison system is clearly on the increase. So what gives?

There is a fascinating story once told by Charles F Kettering, the founder of General Motors, where a friend of his bet he could not hang a bird cage in the entry way of his home for any length of time without putting a bird in it. Kettering accepted the bet but within the year bought a bird to fill the birdcage and thus lost the bet. He later said that he learned a good deal about human nature with this experiment, which if overlaid to our prison discussion would mean something like, "If you build it, they will come."

Yes, America is in danger, perhaps greater danger from within than without. We need be ever vigilant against all forms of tyranny, and we must make certain our voices are heard.

Non-Violent Crime

According to the 2001 FBI Uniform Crime Report, police arrested more people for non-violent marijuana offenses in 1999 and 2000 than for murder, rape, robbery, and aggravated assault — all combined. In 1999, 704,812 Americans were arrested on marijuana-related charges, while only 635,990 people were arrested for the crimes of murder, rape, robbery, and aggravated assault. Of those arrested for marijuana offenses, 88% were charged with mere possession, and 60,000 Americans are languishing in prison today on marijuana charges, according to the Marijuana Policy Project.

Federal figures show that a total of 4,175,357 people were arrested on marijuana charges during the Clinton-Gore administration alone, even though President Clinton openly admitted he smoked marijuana "but didn't inhale" and Vice President Gore admits he smoked marijuana in his twenties. The question might be asked if these two particular politicians might have been better off if they had been thrown in jail for their youthful indiscretions? As we have learned by repeated experience, and study after study, when you throw someone in jail for minor infractions, the chances are better than 90% you will produce a hardened criminal in short order.

The U.S. is fighting a loosing war against illicit drugs. But, because it is such a hot topic that can easily be sensationalized, politicians and law enforcement authorities are able to secure huge budgets to focus on this legitimate problem. The outcome of the focus on the war on drugs is that American citizens have lost many of their basic rights to privacy. Expanded search and seizure laws, passed explicitly to "catch the drug-dealers" were eventually refocused to include other activities that have more recently been dubbed "criminal."

Forfeiture and Seizures

The "war on drugs" has been subtlety changed to become the "war on crime," ergo, the application of rules and laws passed specifically to go after drug dealers are now being used against the rank-and-file. Unfortunately, these expanded powers granted to law enforcement agencies do not require legal conviction before asset seizure. Asset seizures have become an important part of many agencies budget funding activities. There are now over 200 forfeiture and seizure laws on the books in America that only require a suspicion of guilt before grabbing the goods. No lawsuit, no hearing, nothing. Government agencies can simply take your stuff, sell it, and add a portion of the funds to their budget, all based on their suspicion of your guilt. This incredibly unjust and incorrect principal is horribly un-American and it is just the kind of thing the war of Independence was all about.

During a CNN talk radio show where I was the guest, the host announcer Mr. Bert Lee, shared an impromptu story with his listeners about a young man in Arizona that was sentenced to 25 years in prison for transporting his own marijuana plants to Chicago. He posed the question on the air: "What's going wrong in a country where those that commit murder get out of prison in 7 years and a guy with a lame duck dope habit that grows his own stuff gets thrown in prison for 25 years?"

On a personal level I deplore recreational drugs and all that goes with them, but I also believe in personal liberty and our inalienable right to be just as wrong as we want to be right up until that right impinges upon another. This was the philosophy of the Founding Fathers of the Constitution. Now we criminalize things like the failure to wear a helmet or the use of seat belts, and we throw tens of thousands of young people in jail for minor indiscretions and expect to reduce crime. Of course, it is easier to incarcerate a rebellious youth than to love and teach them. And it is easier to believe that mandated jail sentences will fix a growing crime problem — you see, we all want simple, easily digestible answers to complex problems. Simple answers may make us feel more secure and keep our world grounded, even in a faulty belief system, but eventually we will reap what we sow. Society gets no special breaks for honest intentions where ignorance is involved.

Furthering the jail glut is the aggressive attitudes of federal agencies that have criminalized actions, which in European countries might be ignored or at most generate a fine, but certainly not jail time. For example, the Internal Revenue Service is the only tax collecting authority in the free world that threatens its citizens with prison terms for failure to "voluntarily" report and pay taxes correctly.

In addition to America's obsession with the drug war and taxes, sentences are now meted out for all kinds of infractions that only a few years ago were considered legal conduct. The prison system is big business, and the product is hardened criminals. If we want a more gentile society we must find ways to help our young before they've been polluted by the false doctrines of the day and been enamored away into diverse paths in pursuit of the fun and things hip.

Regulation Through Litigation

The Washington Post published an editorial in June of 2001 written by Robert J. Samuelson entitled, "Lawyers Unchained." The author provides a keen examination of the current climate of "regulation through litigation," citing numerous cases of national interest including the Justice Department's antitrust case against Microsoft; and the assaults against the tobacco, gun, and healthcare industries. "What is happening is that lawyers, acting on their own and deploying various legal devices, are increasingly trying to set government policies by themselves. Litigation substitutes for political debate and legislative struggle. It's not a healthy development... We are quietly delegating our democracy in unwise ways.

Democracy and politics are messy because it engages competing interests and attitudes. The conversion of difficult political choices into legal issues (disputes that can be litigated) usually involves a narrowing process that excludes important social considerations. Complex disagreements become simple questions of right and wrong. Compromise gives way to winner-take-all outcomes. We should be wary. Government policies need to achieve a certain level of fairness, popular acceptance and balance among legitimate, if inconsistent, public desires."

Government by litigation subverts democracy; litigation as politics subverts the law.

National ID verses National Security

News media pundits are fond of pointing out that the desire for personal privacy and the need for national security are exclusive of one another. Whereas it is clear that everyone has been called upon to sacrifice privacy to some degree as a consequence of the war on terrorism, it is not at all clear that the majority of incursions on our personal privacy are necessarily related to preventing terrorists from pursuing their trade.

The clamor for a national identity card in order to move around within America, comes uncomfortably close to a former time when the well-known phrase, "Your papers, please!" breathed out in heavily accented German, frightened virtually everyone.[1]

In a nationally syndicated editorial by William Safire, distributed on Boxing Day, December 26, 2001 comes this:

"The fear of terror attack is being exploited by law enforcement sweeping for suspects as well as by commercial marketers seeking prospects. It has emboldened the zealots of intrusion to press for the holy grail of snoopery — a mandatory national ID.

Police unconcerned with the sanctity of an individual's home have already developed heat sensors to let them look inside people's houses. But in the dreams of Big Brother and his cousin, Big Marketing, nothing can compare to forcing every person in the United States — under penalty of law — to carry what the totalitarians used to call "papers."

The plastic card would not merely show a photograph, signature and address, as driver's licenses do. That's only the beginning. In time, and with exquisite refinements, the card would contain not only a fingerprint, description of DNA and the details of your eye's iris, but a host of other information on you.

Hospital will say: How about a chip providing a complete medical history in case of emergencies? Merchants would add a chip for credit rating, bank accounts, and product preferences, while divorced spouses would lobby for a rundown of net assets and yearly expenditures. Politicians would like to know voting records and political affiliation.

Cops, of course, would insist on a record of arrests, speeding tickets, E-Z Pass automatic payment vehicle movements, and links to suspicious Web sites and associates. All this information and more is being collected already. With a national ID system however, it can all be centered in a single dossier, even pressed on a single card — with a copy of that card in a national databank, supposedly confidential but available to any imaginative hacker.

Soon enough, police as well as employers will consider those who resist full disclosure of their financial, academic, medical, religious, social and political affiliations to be suspect.

The universal use and likely abuse of the national ID — a discredit card —- will trigger questions like: When did you begin subscribing to these publications and why were you visiting that spicy or seditious Web

---

[1] An acquaintance of mine, the former head of a U.S. joint government agency "black operations" extraction force, similar to the now famous Delta Force, will only meet with me having traveled by train. According to him, air travel records are on-line and available at a moment's notice to numerous Washington operatives and this very credible person now insists that elements of certain agencies of the U.S. government have "turned." He adamantly refuses to provide "them" with a constant flow of information on his activities. This particular person, who previously worked at the pinnacle of power and can boast multiple post-graduate degrees, claims that Americans are already required to have the equivalent of an internal passport in that they must show photo identification to travel. As things now stand, this may be necessary, but again at what cost?

site? Why are you afraid to show us your papers on demand? Why are you paying cash? What do you have to hide?"

The 2000 congress and the president enacted new legislation that allows banks and other institutions to sell and share your social security number and other private information. This new law may well be the precursor to a national ID card program. As more and more institutions began using a social security number, Americans have had a creepy sense that this supposedly confidential number had already become one's national ID.

Privacy concerns were raised about the Social Security number when the retirement program was first implemented in the 1930s. The government was quick to guarantee that the government assigned SS# would only be used for that system — and none other. Of course, it was not long before the government itself began to use the SS# to track and identify everyone. Prior to the 1970s the FAA had already begun assigning pilots their social security number as their pilot's license number. Federally funded universities across America began using a student's SS# as their student number. And by the 1980's both private and public entities used this supposedly private number for customer tracking.

After the Genie was well out of the bottle, privacy concerns were finally addressed by federal prohibitions that made the sharing of personal social security numbers illegal. Well, that is until Congress reversed itself and passed the legislation in 2000 allowing banks and finance companies to share and sell this information. Robert Feinberg, a Washington attorney who specializes in banking and privacy issues, says the measure actually goes beyond that. "Not only your social security number but any data they happen to have, even if customers 'opt out' to share with third parties."

"There have also been cases in which banks have told customers they would not share data with third parties, but have gone ahead and done it anyway," says Feinberg. In this regard the U.S National Bank scandal quickly comes to mind, although dozens of major banks have been caught selling your data. In addition there have been dozens of articles written on identify theft that have been so easily facilitated by the free exchange of your social security number and other confidential details about you to third parties.

A typical illustration of this problem is contained in an article that appeared in the Oregonian in December 2001 reporting that two detectives went to a hotel room searching for a woman they suspected of identity theft and found Compact Discs filled with personal information including the entire database for the Oregon Driver and Motor Vehicle Services which contained every driver's license and automobile record active that year. Incidentally, the Federal Trade Commission is now offering advice on how to avoid becoming a victim of identity theft at (www.consumer.gov/idtheft).

Richard C. Shelby, U.S. Senator (R - Ala.) introduced a bill aimed at putting Genie back in the bottle, an impossible task but heroic in any event. The "Social Security Privacy Act of 2001" was designed to prohibit the sale and purchase of an individual's Social Security number by a financial institution. Social Security numbers would be designated "non-public personal information," subject to the privacy protections of the collective, Gramm-Leach-Bliley Act, passed in 2000. Robert Feinberg, who tracked this bill through Capitol Hill, quotes Shelby as saying during Senate debate that the privacy protections in that legislation were simply "a sham."

Senator Shelby commented: "I believe Congress has a duty to stop Social Security numbers from being bought and sold like some common commodity. Social Security numbers are key to just about all personal information concerning an individual. While Congress waits to act, the easy access and extreme availability of our personal information has lead to fraud, abuse, identity theft, and in more extreme cases, to stalking and death."

Feinberg, in a NewsMax interview, (www.newsmax.com), said that "from a strictly business standpoint, it's something that affects everyone. If your insurance company knows you have a given condition, your bank could know it when they consider you for a loan. On the other hand, if you've just gotten a check from the bank, the securities affiliate might call you and ask you to invest."

This, possibly illegal, but casual sharing of your personal information attached to a SS# seems to have been going on for some time. Senator Shelby adds he "knows of no one in this country who thinks financial institutions should be making money by trafficking in social security numbers." He went on to say that if the Congress did not act to protect privacy in these regards "the American people who overwhelmingly support this issue, will lose confidence in the U.S. Congress and our ability to lead."

Speaking of Social Security

President Bush's social security reform commission released a report in late July 2001 that outlines a desperate situation where the largest social welfare system in the world is plunging into deep crisis. This terrifying report outlines the financial and social catastrophe that will coalesce as longer life expectancies, falling birth rates, and fewer workers per retiree, explode an already staggering demand.

A major complaint in the report is that contrary to the belief that each worker's payroll taxes go into an investment account called a "trust fund" social security is not based on any real financial assets at all. "Today's beneficiaries are not living off financial assets accumulated in the past.

Today's workers are not accumulating financial assets for the future. Workers invest their payroll taxes not in financial assets but in the willingness of future politicians to tax future workers to pay future benefits," the report said.   It went on to say, " workers and retirees have no legal ownership over their social security benefits. Instead, what they have is a political promise that can be changed at any time, by any amount, for any reason."

On December 11, 2001 the social security panel met again and reported that the terrorist attacks of September 11th had sidelined congressional will to take on the restructuring of social security. Their recommendations however, include a needed requirement to cut benefits and implement tax increases to make up a predicted shortfall. If cutbacks are not politically feasible the government will somehow need to raise up to an additional $71 billion to fund 100% participation.

The clock is ticking; the disaster is predicted to strike when millions of baby boomers retire and begin to claim their social security checks. According to the report the system's finances are due to unravel in 15 years and be bankrupt by 2038.

On the other hand, the legislative elite has no reason to fear, neither Senators nor members of the House of Representatives, pay into the social security trust fund, nor do they collect from it.

Social security benefits are not adequate for the congressional aristocracy. Long ago legislators came to the conclusion that they should be entitled to a special deal and enacted a retirement program for themselves that is considerably more beneficial than the one to which the rank-and-file are entitled. When a Congressman retires, no matter how long he or she has been in office, they continue to draw their same pay until they die. Not bad, heh? This stable source of unearned income may also be increased from time to time by cost-of-living adjustments. So, for example, the former Senator, Bill Bradley (D-New Jersey) and his wife, may be expected to draw some $7,900,000.00 over the balance of their life span. Their contribution to this incredible retirement program was absolutely zero. Guess who pays the bill?

You and I are required to pay social security deposits into a so-called trust fund for our own retirement. Our employers must match these payments, or if you are self-employed you must pay double the amount that would normally be deducted from your payroll check. These "trust funds" have been open to constant use by legislators to fund government spending programs that are all too frequently designed to benefit private special interests. But why should we complain? After all, we might get lucky and receive $1,000 per month when we're sixty-five.

Tax Shelter America
Americans are frequently shocked to learn that the U.S. has had a two-tier tax policy that for many decades has allowed non-U.S. persons to

invest in the U.S. and not be subject to U.S. tax (if structured correctly.) At the same time America provides what is essentially a banking secrecy regime for non-U.S. persons that exceeds that available in many nations!

America is surely the largest tax haven nation in the world and within its borders are numerous international financial centers. Whereas Americans are blessed to enjoy an excellent standard of living under some of the best of all circumstances, they are not allowed to utilize the tax haven characteristics provided by America to non-Americans. Oh darn!

It is true that the U.S. government is deeply concerned about obtaining tax information on American's who are investing, banking, and trading abroad. It is also true that some agencies of the U.S. government have demonstrated that they are willing to violate other countries' sovereignty in order to get the information they want. On the other hand, the U.S. government is not accommodating in providing such information to other governments. Believe it or not, it is against the law in America to provide information on any foreign person's business activities in the U.S. unless a foreign government has previously entered into a treaty that provides for the exchange of information. This approach to foreign affairs actually screens non-U.S. persons that are investing in America from scrutiny from the tax authorities of their home country.

It is one thing to offer non U.S. persons an inducement to invest in America, which is a good idea for the economy. It is another matter altogether to learn that the U.S. was the prime motivator in causing the Organization for Economic Cooperation and Development (OECD), a UN organization of immense influence, to aggressively attack smaller countries with little to no income tax. And, that this was done on the basis that these countries had an unfair tax advantage over the U.S.!

The OECD produced a report in April 1998 entitled *Harmful Tax Competition: An Emerging Global Issue*, which crystallized the attack on small sovereign nations that supported offshore financial services. Previously denounced more or less unofficially by high-tax nations as conduits for money laundering and tax evasion, the report signaled the beginning of a formal attack on offshore centers.

The father of the OECD's harmful tax competition initiative, Mario Monte, was also instrumental in developing the Draft Code of Conduct on Business Taxation, which sought to include tax avoidance within tax evasion. In fact, high-tax governments looking for scapegoats have mounted a carefully orchestrated media campaign against offshore centers that link tax avoidance, which is legal, with tax evasion, which is not, thus intentionally blurring the differences in order to garner public and media support for their mission.

The OECD report made it clear that high-tax nations were attempting to change the rules of international commerce. Their goals were to attack smaller nations that offered low tax rates and banking confidentiality as ways of attracting investment into their respective jurisdictions. The campaign against small tax haven countries was combined with vast efforts exerted by the U.S., and other G7 countries along with their UN puppet, the OECD, to reduce "money laundering" around the world. The OECD report broke offshore financial centers into three groups based on the their legal infrastructures, levels of financial supervision and cooperation (cooperation with the powers that control the OECD that is) in order to combat the so called money laundering threat.

Money Laundering

The initial concept surrounding the term "money laundering" was simply that it represented the proceeds of major criminal activities, traditionally referred to as the proceeds of drug, kidnapping, and arms dealing. These criminal proceeds were then "cleaned" as it were, and re-introduced into the marketplace through normal investment channels. However, the misuse, and overuse, of the term money laundering has somehow morphed into meaning virtually anything the media or a prosecutor wants it to mean in order to solicit a strong reaction, intimidate and frighten. The OECD, for example seems to equate money laundering with income tax and estate planning, giving these normal and reasonable activities a sinister cast. The term is so frequently used in so many contexts today, including in the courts, that it is virtually impossible to any longer truly define it.

The OECD harmful tax competition initiative has surely violated international law in that the UN Economic, Social and Cultural Rights Covenant states: "All peoples have the right to self-determination. By virtue of that right they freely determine their political status and freely pursue their economic, social and cultural development."

States cannot unilaterally impose their tax policies on third states. In order to skirt this issue the authors of the OECD tax initiative have simply substituted the word "competitive" for the word "harmful." Competition in international business is deemed to be necessary and healthy. In the recent anti-trust case against Microsoft in the U.S., the court ruled that the company could no longer engage in tactics designed to eliminate the competition.

Is not the OECD harmful tax initiative simply attempting to accomplish exactly what the U.S. Justice Department condemned Microsoft for doing? Does anyone in government recall that the underlying principal regarding open competition remains the basis of the free world's economies? The attack on tax haven nations is in diametric opposition to the principals of freedom, it is anti-capitalistic, and ultimately, at its very core, it is completely un-American.

The Real Issue

Whereas the enhanced money laundering legislation was passed in what could accurately be described as an outpouring of blind-patriotism directly after the 11 September tragedy, legislators from both parties made impassioned speeches claiming that the sole reason for its almost unanimous passage was to put in place legislation to facilitate and track the financial dealings of Osama bin Laden and his terrorist organization commonly known as Al-Qaida.

The actions of the government tell a different story. The London Financial Times on December 3, 2001 carried an article of the first important accomplishment of the newly passed legislation. "The Cayman Islands and the U.S. have signed a tax information exchange agreement to give U.S. agencies access to records on U.S. federal income tax. The Cayman Islands is one of the world's biggest offshore centres. The Cayman government said that the agreement with the U.S. provides for confidential treatment of the information that is exchanged and that any such information may not be disclosed to any third party. It applies to criminal tax evasion for taxable periods commencing January 2004, and to all other tax matters for taxable periods commencing 1 January 2006. The agreement conforms to a commitment made by the Cayman Island to the OECD. The OECD has accused several offshore jurisdictions of indulging in harmful tax competition." So, what was the anti-money laundering bill really about? Taxes, not terrorism.

Tax Competition

A clear indication of the speed at which the use of offshore jurisdictions have grown and the reason for the overbearing actions of the U.S. government, is the amount of funds now residing offshore. In 1989 it was estimated that less than $500 billion was deposited in offshore funds compared with $5.2 trillion ten years later. As was noted in OECD report, a five-fold increase was sited between 1985 and 1994 to more than $200 billion flowing to tax havens in the Caribbean and South Pacific alone.

Of the estimated $5.3 trillion offshore today, more than $2 trillion is retained in trusts, of which the fastest growing segment are asset protection trusts as high-net worth individuals rush to counter the threat of litigation-happy lawyers and their jack-pot hopeful clients.

In the final analysis onshore high-tax nations have basically two choices in the competition for investment with offshore centers. They can reduce spending and the size of government, thereby reducing taxes to keep investment dollars at home or they can resist this movement and instead adopt draconian legislation and attack the competition. In America it is fairly obvious which tack the government has taken.

Predictions

Emerging evidence suggests that a carefully orchestrated campaign linking money laundering and tax issues together will ultimately backfire on the OECD and its American sponsors. Bloated unresponsive bureaucracies slowed by labor protectionist policies prevalent in many "onshore" nations are an anachronism to the emergence of the new e-commerce model. In our brave new world businesses and governments alike will be compelled to adapt quickly and efficiently if they are to survive.

As top-heavy pyramid corporate styles are besieged by new efficient computer savvy management team paradigms, inefficient, expensive and ponderous governments will find it increasingly more difficult to find acceptance with tax-weary voters who themselves are being forced to change with the times.

Information technology not only encourages money to flow more quickly and easily to jurisdictions with the least resistance, it is an absolute necessity. In this new economic spirit Robert Mundell, who was elected the Nobel laureate in economics in 1999, was rewarded for his time-proven theory that high taxes and big governments only contribute to economic malaise. Duh!

Governments responding positively to this challenge will emerge the winners in the new economy while those who insist on draconian tactics to intimidate and threaten will ultimately be left behind. Nations with oppressive regulatory and tax regimes continue to experience an exodus of capital to more friendly domiciles, even in light of September 11th. The harmful tax competition initiative of the OECD will not magically reverse this tendency.

Another surprising turn of events has been the entry of five American states (Montana, Colorado, Delaware, Alaska and South Dakota) into the offshore arena offering services such as tax-free trusts and tax-free offshore banking to foreign investors. This allows an offshore investor the potential for both federal and state tax concessions when investing in American enterprise. No Americans need apply.

An examination of projected world growth for the next decade reveals much about the potential future of offshore jurisdictions. While there are challenges facing all nations and issues to be settled between high and low tax governments, no one can deny the benefits that all will enjoy as goods and materials move across continents and oceans with greater ease and speed. The Internet is allowing such transactions to occur more simply and inexpensively.

It is expected that the funds residing offshore will surpass the $6 trillion mark towards 2010. This assessment underestimates the growth of international investment and stock trading made possible electronically from anywhere in the world. It is challenging indeed to estimate the effect in dollar value that this will have on capital flows, even in the face of efforts by various governments to stifle this activity. Short of erecting physical and electronic walls to curtail this movement, it will continue to expand.

Offshore Tax Havens

Something over a decade ago, *Offshore Investment Magazine* described 21 places an international investor should know about. In their latest update of *Tax Havens,* Walter and Dorothy Diamond outline more than 70 offshore financial centers in some detail. While the list of tax havens has tripled in the past eleven years, so have the products and services available. Vehicles such as the asset protection trust, purpose trust, charitable trust, spendthrift, debenture, and protective and unit trust, protected cell company, the offshore mutual fund, international business company and personal foundations are much more prevalent as are free trade, export and processing zones in a number of offshore jurisdictions around the world. There has also been a raft of new products such as limited liability companies, banking units, captive and re-insurance company charters and hybrid companies as well as permutations of existing structures to perform new, more complex duties.

A partial list of some tax shelters include: The Channel Islands — Jersey, Guernsey and Sark along with the Isle of Man, all of these are near Great Britain. Some of the largest financial institutions in the world are located in these smallish, out-of-the-way islands.

Within Europe are the long-time havens of Austria, Switzerland, Liechtenstein, and Luxembourg. And in more recent years Europe has gained Bulgaria, Ireland, and Hungary as new safe havens for wealth. In the Mediterranean are Gibraltar, (also part of Europe), and Malta. Not to be outdone, the Middle East now has a collection of tax haven jurisdictions of their own. The island nation of Mauritius in the Indian Ocean, along with the Seychelles, and the United Arab Emirates, serve as havens for Africa and the Indian subcontinent.

In the Far East, Hong Kong built itself into a financial center with its liberal corporate and banking laws. In 1999, over 15,000 new IBC's were formed in Hong Kong alone and pundits to the contrary this business continued to grow right into 2002 notwithstanding this jurisdiction is now under the control of Mainland China. The Philippines and Singapore have passed new laws to attract offshore money. These centers tend to serve the citizens of such countries as Japan and Korea.

Australia and New Zealand tend to use the Cook Islands, Marshall Islands, Vanuatu, Nauru, Western Samoa, and the Marianas, as their havens of choice although Australians are increasingly accessing services from the Caribbean. And, of course, the Caribbean and its numerous island nations, has long been considered the source of many of the world's best safe haven jurisdictions.

Both England and the United States draw vast sums of money from foreigners because they offer special tax advantages to them that are not available to their own citizens. Does it seem strange that the very countries whose citizens place their wealth offshore are themselves tax havens for citizens of other countries?

Corporate Structuring

The use of legal structures, both domestic and foreign, may allow one to more easily conduct business, ensure privacy, protect assets, grow retirement funds in a safer environment, and defer taxes where possible. The problem with government expansion for the honest and law-abiding citizen is greater exposure to risk, more complex compliance requirements, a severe loss of personal privacy, and increased taxes.

As a result, part of the personal defense of freedom-loving people is to place assets in corporate structures in jurisdictions like Nevada or Wyoming. Neither of these onshore jurisdictions lists shareholders in the public record.

Make sure you have something safe, beyond prying eyes and grasping hands. Ultimately, it is the only way to ensure you are able to gain and retain, a measure of personal privacy and the attendant personal freedom it can provide.

SECTION II

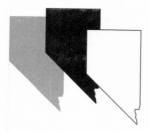

Business Structures

FORMS OF DOING BUSINESS
ACTS OF THE CORPORATION
A CLASSIC U.S. STRATEGY
ASSET TRANSFER COMPLICATIONS

FORMS OF DOING BUSINESS

"Man's mind, once stretched by a new idea, never regains its original dimensions."

Oliver Wendell Holmes, Jr.

Preamble

In the context of business entities, it becomes quickly evident that the corporation is by far the most versatile, powerful, and beneficial business entity of them all. However, this section begins by discussing the sole proprietorship, then both general and limited partnerships, followed by the limited liability company, and finally, the corporation. Each entity is described herein, what it is, how it is formed, and its advantages and disadvantages.

Sole Proprietorship

A sole proprietorship is the simplest form of doing business, and as a consequence the most common. The easiest way to understand the sole proprietorship is simply to understand that it is you. All you need to do is to begin doing business. In most areas you will need to obtain a business license, and if you've given your business a name other than your own, you usually need to file a fictitious name statement. That's all there is to it. You and your business are one and the same. As a sole proprietor you have no protection from liability, and as a result, your personal assets are always at risk.

A business operated as a sole proprietorship is simple. Its money is your money. If you wish to take money from the till to buy groceries on the way home from your business day, you are able to do so anytime you wish. If you want to use business inventory for your own personal needs, you are free to do so. There is no need to hire an attorney to set the company up, because there is no formation process other than obtaining the necessary licenses and permits. From a tax perspective, there is only one level of taxation, because the income or loss from the business is reported on your personal tax return by attaching a Schedule C form.

The advantage of a sole proprietorship is simplicity. It is also the downfall of this form of doing business. Since the assets of the business are your assets, in the event someone files a claim against your business, both your business assets and everything else you or your family owns is at risk.

Your house, your car, your child's college fund, everything is directly at risk, all of the time. In the tax arena, because the profits of the business are reported on your 1040, you are limited to personal deductions and are bound by personal tax rates. You are also liable for self-employment tax for Social Security and Medicare, which together will add another 15% or more to your personal tax burden. Taken as a whole, a sole proprietorship, while simple, is also dangerous, and in the end, almost always more costly than operating through some other form of legal entity.

General Partnership

Partnerships take two forms, general partnerships and limited partnerships, first the general partnership. The general partnership is the second most common method of doing business. Like the sole proprietorship, it is simple to form and has only one level of taxation.

A general partnership consists of two or more people who agree to enter into business together. They should see an attorney to draw up what is usually a simple partnership agreement, although very often they do not. They agree on how much money each will contribute to the business and who is going to do what in its operation. They then proceed to seek their fortune. Naturally, a partnership must obtain the necessary licenses and permits. From a liability point of view, a general partnership is in a worse position that a sole proprietor, for not only are all the partners' personal assets at risk for business liability, they are also at risk from each other.

Suppose one partner gets into an auto accident while driving on a pleasure trip wholly unrelated to business. A lawsuit results. The assets that the other party will seek to collect from include all of that person's individual assets, including their share of your company. If that party wins the lawsuit, you may well find yourself with a new partner. This new partner may decide that he or she wants nothing to do with the successful operation of the business, and may force its liquidation. Assuming your new partner has just as much decision-making ability as you do, they can make your life an utter nightmare.

A scenario such as this is bad enough if that were the only problem with general partnerships, but it's not the end of the story. Most business people who have been involved in partnerships of this type in the past will tell you that they would never do it again because of the management difficulties they experience. Who makes decision? If two partners share 50% each of the business, they must both agree on everything, and this is not a realistic scenario. In fact, most partners who enter business as friends leave business unfriendly to one another.

Tax wise, the partnership is quite similar to proprietorships in that the partner's share of the profit or loss is reported on their individual tax return by attaching form K-1. Again, the deductions and tax rates are personal, and of course there is self-employment taxes to be dealt with.

Limited Partnership

The limited partnership corrects some of the problems that are inherent in the general partnership. This legal entity has two different types of partners, general partners and limited partners. As in the general partnership, the general partner has unlimited personal liability for the actions of the partnership. To compensate for this, the general partner also has full management and decision-making power. The limited partner, on the other hand, has no liability for the actions of the partnership, and has no management or decision-making capacity.

From the point of view of formation, a limited partnership is much more complicated and expensive than the previous two entities discussed. An attorney normally prepares the Partnership Agreement, which sets forth the structure of the entity as well as its governing rules. In addition a filing with the Secretary of State must be made, listing the general partner(s). While limited partnerships are not usually used for operating businesses, if they are, they will also need the usual licenses and permits.

Limited partnerships are taxed in the same way as a general partnership, with the same disadvantages. However, they do have a great advantage over general partnerships in the liability arena. If there are more than one partner, (general partners can also be limited partners) and if a partner is sued individually, a judgment creditor cannot normally take away the interest of the other partners in the partnership.

In this case a judgment creditor is limited to a charging order, which entitles the judgment creditor to receive any partnership distributions that would have gone to the partner in question. Since a limited partnership generally has no obligation to make distributions of profits, the judgment creditor may have a long wait to be paid. During this waiting period they will be receiving the K-1 for of the debtor partner, and if the partnership is making money, the judgment creditor must pay the tax of the debtor, while not receiving the money. In many cases, this feature can motivate the judgment creditor to either settle with the debtor, or simply to leave the partnership interest alone.

A sample of a Limited Partnership agreement is contained within the Appendices.

The Limited Liability Company

The Limited Liability Company (LLC) is a hybrid between a limited partnership and a corporation. It is also one of the newest forms of doing business. The LLC combines the limited liability aspects of corporations with the partnership taxation aspects of a limited partnership into a flexible and workable way that has caught the eye of many businesspeople. The LLC is becoming more popular every day.

Rather than having partners or stockholders, the LLC has Members, who own an interest in the company, and who maintain management control in some circumstances. Called "Member Managed LLC's" these LLC's require votes of the members to make decisions. Like a corporation, they can also have officers. Another LLC option is to create "Manager Managed LLC's" wherein the members elect a manager, who exercises all management authority, thus acting as the general partner in a limited partnership, leaving the members acting as limited partners. Unlike the limited partnership, however, all parties within an LLC have limited liability for personal protection from business liability.

Taxation flexibility gives the LLC a great advantage when you are considering a form under which to do business. Partnership taxation can be a great thing if the company looses money, or if it makes certain types of investments where personal capital gains treatment would be preferable to corporate treatment, such as in real estate investment. In addition, because any U.S. person or entity may be a member in an LLC, an LLC offers advantages for income splitting which an S-corporation is unable to offer. (More about this under S-Corporations.)

Even with these advantages, however, LLC's have their share of problems. The biggest problem that they currently face is the fact that they are so new. The first LLC statue in the U.S. was passed in the state of Wyoming in 1976. Nevada passed one in 1991, California in 1995, and the last state joined the fold in 1997. Because the LLC is so new, there is simply a lack of case law to determine how LLC's will be treated in certain instances. In addition, tax treatment is not entirely carved in stone, and the IRS has from time to time made changes that could be adverse to people in particular situations. Questions as basic as whether or not an LLC needs to have corporate style formalities are still waiting for answers. Some expert's claim that LLC's do not need to worry about formalities, others claim that they do. Sooner or later a court will decide the issue, but for the near future no one knows for certain.

Consequently, LLC's remain something of a question mark in terms of solutions to business problems, and unless you've always dreamed of being a test case, you may wish to avoid them!

A chart of comparative analysis regarding LLC's is contained within the Appendices. Charts depicting LLC legislation in the various U.S. states and their tax rates are also contained within the Appendices.

Corporations

For over one hundred years, corporations have been the kings of business entities. Like an LLC, they offer limited liability for all involved, be they stockholders, directors or officers. They offer not only protection from lawsuits, but they offer two levels of taxation, with many more opportunities for deductions, perks with pre-tax dollars, as well as natural income splitting.

To understand a corporation, it is essential to recognize that it is very much like a separate person from you. You are not the corporation, and the corporation is not you. Legally, a corporation is called an "artificial person" while a human being is called a "natural person". You may want to think of a corporation as a paper person, after all it is made of documents, and yet it has the same rights under law that you have, and the same responsibilities as well. In operating a corporation, you must remember that you cannot do anything to a corporation that you couldn't legally and properly do to another person. You can't simply take money from the till to buy groceries like you might with a sole proprietorship because it is not your money, it's the corporation's money. While this may seem to be rather inconvenient to those who aren't used to it, it is also your salvation if the business gets sued, because when business liability occurs, the corporation is the "person" on the line, and not you.

Unlike LLC's, corporations have literally truckloads of case law. Your attorney can reasonably predict how courts will treat them in almost any situation, so you will know how to operate to achieve asset protection and tax savings. No wonder most business experts will not enter into a business relationship with any other form of doing business than a corporation. As you read on, you will learn the reasons that people incorporate, how corporations work, what things you need to do to keep your corporation healthy, what you can achieve by using multiple corporations, how to invoke asset protection strategies, tax strategies and much more!

A graphical chart depicting Nevada corporations verses other sample U.S. states is contained within the Appendices.

Corporate Structure

Corporations are not difficult to operate on a day-to-day basis, as many people seem to think. There are a few basic principles that, once learned, will provide the guidance you need to operate with a minimum of problems and few aggravations. The first and primary principal in corporate operations is also the main theory behind the corporate entity itself, and that is: **The corporation is not you, and you are not the corporation.**

A corporation, as a separate artificial person, must maintain its own separate identity, entirely distinct from that of its principals. This single factor is the basis of most of the material we will discuss in this section. It is also the cause of much of what has come to be called corporate formalities. Corporate formalities, which will be covered in depth later on, are simply the way that a corporation's activities are documented, so that they may be shown to be separate from your own actions and activities.

A corporation's identity is established by its Articles and Bylaws. Both of these documents have their own purpose and function, and should be read and understood by the principals of the corporation to ensure that they do not inadvertently violate the corporation's rules and thus confuse the corporation's distinct identity. Imagine that the corporation is a person, a very good friend. How would you treat it then? Wouldn't you be careful not to create offense by overlooking the individuality of the person? Hopefully, you would answer yes to that question. For if you would, and if you can get into the habit of thinking about your corporation in that way, then you can avoid many of the problems that business people create by "offending " their corporations' identities.

Articles of Incorporation

The Articles of Incorporation is the document that brings the corporation to life, literally. By filing the articles with the appropriate authority the corporation comes into existence. Generally, the articles set forth the structure of the corporation, include its name, period of life, and list of players. The articles also set forth the type, or types, of stock, its limitations, if any, and the total number of shares that are allowed to be issued. They even cite the actual purpose for which the corporation is being formed. This can be done in a very general way, or may be restricted to a narrow definition. Because of the fundamental importance of the articles and their function, you would be well advised to peruse your articles carefully. While you are looking them over, there are several issues you should be considering, which are listed and discussed briefly below. Incidentally, copies of generic articles of incorporation are included on the Compact Disc found on the inside cover of this book.

Corporate Name

Your articles should clearly state the exact name of your corporation. This is its legal name, just as your legal name is recorded on your birth certificate. If you are going to expect other people to recognize that they are transacting business with your corporation, and not with you personally, then they will need to know the corporation's legal name. While this may sound overly basic, or even silly, there are numerous court cases where business people lost everything because they failed in this one, obvious area. It is vitally important to your future!

Period of Existence

Most of the time, corporate articles will indicate that the period of existence of the corporation in question will be perpetual. As this would imply, that means that the corporation is immortal, and will never die on its own, or at least not of natural causes. This is one of the major factors in the doctrine of separateness alluded to above. Perpetual existence is not the only possibility. If need be, the corporate life span may be limited to a certain number of years. This is often referred to as a collapsible corporation. It is designed to die, or collapse, on a pre-specified date in the future – often thirty years.

Imagine how thrilled you would be after buying an existing corporation from someone, anticipating that its lifetime is perpetual, only to discover that it has already ceased to exist. Looking over the articles will eliminate this disaster from happening. It is important to note that a collapsible corporation can be amended, under most circumstances, before the termination date arrives.

The Corporate Purpose

Another important matter covered in the articles is the purpose for which the corporation is being formed. Most of the time, the purpose will be to conduct any lawful business activity. This allows the greatest flexibility, and is sometimes referred to as the "elastic clause." It is elastic because you are permitted to do anything you want to with the corporation, as long as it's legal. While this may be the most common feature, it is not the only way that purpose can be handled.

In some cases, an incorporator may wish to limit the potential activities of the corporation, and may so indicate in the original articles of incorporation. In other cases, a franchise or other business relationship with another entity may result in a limitation of activity to that approved by the franchiser, or other party. In any event, you need to be sure that your corporate operation does not violate any limitation contained in your articles, as this could result in a loss of your protection by the corporate veil.

More and more, as America careens into the litigation explosion, attorneys and others will add more descriptive material, along with the time honored language to the elastic clause, spelling out all of the possible activities they can imagine, to augment the declaration that the corporation is being formed to engage in any lawful activity. This is designed to circumvent those who would attempt to claim that any lawful activity doesn't necessarily include such and such. While it may seem silly, this long form of describing the business purpose of the corporation seems to be the wave of the future and is, after all, a reflection of our times.

Authorized Shares

Another important characteristic of the articles of incorporation is a listing of the number and types of authorized shares. The number of shares authorized means the number of shares of a particular class of stock, which may be issued by the corporation. Any shares, which are issued in excess of this number, are in violation of law and are, at best, invalid, and at worst are fraudulent. This number offers protection to the potential shareholder, who is trying to determine what his or her percentage of ownership will be. The number of authorized shares in many states is also the basis of calculating fees and taxes. A few states, such as Wyoming, have no provision at all for authorized stock and will allow a corporation to authorize any amount of stock, or an unlimited number of authorized shares. This provision can be quite convenient for its flexibility, but can be a little scary for investors.

Once a certain number of shares are authorized, a corporation is able to actually issue shares. The corporation may issue as few shares or as many shares as desired, as long as you don't exceed the total authorized share limit set forth in the articles.

Classes of stock

Usually, a corporation will have common stock. This is what most of us are thinking about when we talk about stock. Common shares are voting shares; they are usually considered no par value and are purchased from the company in exchange for contributions of cash, property or services. There can be many other types and classes of stock. Other types of stock, and their restrictions, are typically stated in the articles of incorporation, allowing for public record access to the entire picture, for the protection of potential investors, as well as for the edification of the corporate directors and officers. More discussion of stock types and their various features will be provided in the section on stock.

General Provisions

The particulars contained in articles will vary, depending on many circumstances, such as the state or country of incorporation, who is drafting the articles, and the needs and circumstances of the parties. This book is not intended to be a definitive legal reference, but rather to provide general guidelines. For a definitive reference on all of the possibilities, and their various ramifications, you should consult your attorney who can also make specific recommendations to suit your particular situation.

In addition to the issues covered above, typical articles will contain the names and addresses of the Incorporator, the first Director and the Resident or Registered Agent. There may also be provisions pertaining to liability by state law and, in many cases, other issues regarding the relationship between the principals of the corporation. Some states, such as California seldom have articles of more than one page as a way of controlling the volume of material contained in the public record. Corporations in these states will usually cover more of these issues in the bylaws.

Bylaws

While the articles of incorporation are the actual document which brings the corporation into existence, and contain the basic structure of the corporation, the bylaws are much more specific, and contain information as to how the specific players and entities within the corporation will function and interrelate. For example, the articles will ordain a board of directors for the corporation. The bylaws will establish how their meetings will operate, how they will be notified of meetings, and what their specific function in the corporation shall be.

In the same way, bylaws will specifically state what the duties and functions of each officer will be. It is extremely important for anyone who is operating a business within a corporate framework to understand what these requirements and rules are, as they must be followed. Failure to do so may cause severe problems to the corporation and its owners in the event of a lawsuit, or other peril, simply because an adversary will usually examine the corporation's records to determine if you have treated the corporation as a separate entity. If you have not, then a litigating adversary will attempt to have the court set the corporation aside so the adverse party can attack your personal assets. This process is known as piercing the corporate veil.

Some of the issues that are usually covered by the bylaws are procedures for meetings, proxies, stock certificates, what constitutes a quorum in meetings, provisions to allow for written consents, (such as free standing resolutions), the number of directors, the terms of officers, and so on.

The Players in the Corporation

There are four players within the corporation. They are the shareholders, the directors, the officers, and the employees. To fully understand the concept of corporate structure, you need to have a good feel for what these players do and what they don't do. The shareholder is a position, which many people confuse, because of their previous experience with other entities. If you have been either a sole proprietor or a partner, you are used to the idea that the owner of the business is the boss, the one who rules the roost and calls the shots. You maybe used to putting "owner" on your business card, or using that title when signing contracts. If this is the case, be careful with your corporation!

While it is certainly true that the controlling factor in corporate operation is that the person who controls the majority of the voting stock and thereby has control of the corporation, but this control is indirect. In the corporate form of doing business, shareholders are not the people who sign contracts and usually are not the ones who make day-to-day decisions. A look at the history of corporations will reveal why this is so.

Corporations were originally invented as a way to pool assets, limit liability, and provide centralized management. This idea assumes that there will be numerous investors, and several different persons in the management and decision making capacities within the company.

Today, this is typically the case with larger organizations. Publicly traded firms, such as General Motors, are good example of this concept, but this is usually not the case with small and medium sized companies. In fact, there is often only one person who controls the stock and provides all of the decision-making and management functions within a small or medium sized corporation. Such small corporations constitute the backbone of the modern world, providing the greatest amount of growth, jobs, and new products for the economy. They also provide the area of greatest danger for business people who are not entirely clear on the roles that they are playing.

Shareholders exercise their control by electing directors, who are the thinking branch of the corporate structure. Here is where the decisions and policies are actually made. The directors are the ones who oversee the direction that a corporation will take as well as determine what is and what is not to be a corporate act.

To put these directives and decisions into action, the directors elect officers. The officers are the ones who actually sign contracts, negotiate with the world outside of the corporation, and hire employees to do the day-to-day work of the business. If you are in a small corporation where you will perform many or all of these functions, then it is of vital importance that you recognize which function you are performing at any given time and follow recognized procedures for getting the job done. As you can see then, simply using the title of "owner" isn't going to cut it with a corporation and, in fact, is going to invite an adversary to treat you as if you were a sole proprietor. And, since you would be acting like a sole proprietor, you would also be begging to have your corporate veil pierced; the last thing you really want.

As we proceed with the operation of the corporation, you will become more familiar with the differences between the players. For now, remember that no matter how many of these roles you are going to play within your corporation, they are separate and distinct roles.

Corporate Formalities

Corporate formalities are the means by which you document the actions of your corporation and maintain the separation between you and your corporation. Corporate formalities can refer to many things. Signing a document, such as a contract in the corporate form, is an example of a corporate formality. Keeping the corporation in good standing with its state of incorporation is another example. Maintaining the stock ledgers properly would be another. Certainly, keeping your minutes and resolutions up to date would be an example of something crucial in this area, and the issuance of stock is considered by most to be the foremost corporate formality.

Yet, it may seem that all of the things listed above are merely technicalities and that nothing of any real substance is included. Perhaps a person making this case might just have a point. After all, you may not have issued stock certificates, and made entries into your stock ledgers, but the corporation received capital from somewhere. You may not have written up formal minutes and resolutions, but obviously, if the company is operating, decisions were made and carried out. How you sign a contract isn't such a big deal; the fact that the contract was negotiated and executed is what really counts.

Next to whether or not you make the payroll, pay your bills and earn a profit, these little details seem to be nothing more than a nuisance. After all, it is a fact that many small and medium corporations operate successfully for year after year, with dozens or hundreds of happy employees, and thousand paid in taxes and dividends, with little or no attention paid to corporate formalities. As society becomes more and more informal, the little niceties and formalities, seen as the products of a bygone era, seem to drift away into oblivion. Why then fret over formalities?

As long as things go along just fine, formalities are hardly an issue that seems worth the time they take to observe. And then, something happens. Let's use a restaurant example. Years of operation go by. Everything seems great. One day, a customer slips on a freshly mopped floor. This isn't great, but it's really no big thing. After all, there was a yellow caution sign on the floor and nobody was hurt. You fill out an accident report and give it to your insurance company. Then, you comp the unfortunate customer's meal. She is happy, if a little embarrassed, and goes on her way. This may have happened before over the years – not often, but it has happened and nothing ever came of it before. So why worry about it?

Six months go by, still nothing. You forget about the incident. No insurance claims, no phone calls; it's over. Then, one day, while you are in the storeroom counting cases of napkins, one of your employees says that someone is asking for you up front. This always happens when you are doing inventory, and you always have to start counting napkins over again! It's probably somebody who wants to fill out an employment application. Why can't the cashier just give it to the person like they always do? You go up front. The person waiting for you has something in his hand, probably a resume. He looks kind of old to be applying for a position as a dishwasher!

"Hi, can I help you?" you ask.

"Are you John Smith?"

"Yes, I am."

"This is for you," says the process server. You've just been served with a lawsuit.

It seems that the customer who slipped six months ago, and went away unhurt, has been seeing her chiropractor quite regularly for the problem she now has with her back and she is seeking to recover damages. You go back to the office, a little chagrined. Why didn't she just file an insurance claim? You look at the document. It says something about gross negligence and punitive damages. Better call the insurance company.

A few days later, your insurance company informs you that the other party is seeking punitive damages in excess of a million dollars. No problem, you have an umbrella policy that will cover this. The lady from the insurance company tells you that they will be settling the actual damages and the doctor's bills, but that the policy doesn't cover punitive damages and she suggests that you might wish to speak to an attorney.

You do. Your attorney looks into the case and finds out that the plaintiff is requesting a mountain of documents and the first one on the list is your corporate record book. It's empty! A chill goes down your spine. "What do they want that for?" "It's customary in these cases for a plaintiff to examine your corporate records," says your attorney, "because they will often try to pierce through the corporation to get at your personal assets and those of anyone else that has helped you along the way, so that they will be available in case the assets of the corporation are insufficient to satisfy a potential judgment. Don't worry though, because I'm sure that you've kept them up to date. After all, I remember telling you how important they were when we incorporated the business."

You can just picture that empty book sitting on the shelf where it has been for the last five years. "Well, they aren't exactly in order," you reply squeamishly. Your attorney informs you that you might just be in real trouble. You could lose your house, your boat and your kids' college fund. Won't your wife be amused!

Are corporate formalities important? You say, "Ha! Restaurants are a high liability business, my business isn't like that. Nobody slips and falls here! I'm a consultant." Okay, let's try something different. Let's say that you are an Internet consultant. Nobody will sue you (famous last words).

Your Internet consulting firm goes along great for three years. No problems. You notice that business is a little flat, so you increase your advertising. Still though, it stays flat and gets flatter still. Why did you have to go and move to larger offices? What's going on, anyway?

Your bank balance gets smaller and smaller. Where have the customers gone? You miss a rent payment, and then another. Your landlord is getting upset. The only thing left to do is to move to a smaller location on the other side of town to cut your losses.

Your landlord doesn't seem to get it. If you couldn't pay a couple of months' rent, how can that idiot expect you to pay four and a half years of rent in one lump sum? A couple of months go by and you are served with a lawsuit from the landlord. That fool! He knew you were a corporation, why did he sue you and not the corporation? Your attorney looks things over and wonders aloud, "Why did you sign this?" It's in your name; you signed as an individual!

The fact is that, even if you're in a "safe" business, if you don't watch out for the little things, the little things will kill you. It won't be anything dramatic. No eerie music in the background when you mess up, like in the movies. Everything will be normal and fine, until there's a problem. And then jumping off a cliff might look good.

This is the importance of corporate formalities. When you incorporated, you expected to limit your liability. After all, limiting liability is one of the reasons people incorporate these days. But, failing to do business in the corporate format can undo all of that if you don't do things right. That is why corporate formalities are important. The tragedy is that, doing things right really isn't very difficult and doesn't take much time, once you learn how.

Piercing the Corporate Veil

This is a concept, which lurks in the backs of the minds of untold numbers of business people in every corner of America. It is like the IRS; a dangerous, somewhat mysterious peril lurking in the dark, ready to pounce at the worst possible moment. Like the IRS, this concept becomes much less threatening when seen under the bright light of day. And, also just like the IRS, this concept must be given healthy respect. For no matter how confident we may be, no matter how invincible we may think we are, there can be devastating consequences for those who don't do things right.

The whole idea of piercing the corporate veil is based on the alter ego theory. Under this theory, a corporation can be set aside by a court if it is just another self for its owners. In other words, if a court can't tell the difference between you and your corporation, then the court can disregard it. Most textbooks on the subject will say something like this:

The requirements under the alter ego theory are:
1) The corporation must be influenced and governed by the person asserted to be its alter ego.
2) There must be a unity of interest and ownership such that one is inseparable from the other.
3) The facts must be such that adherence to the fiction of a separate entity would, under the circumstances, sanction fraud or promote injustice. The person or persons running and owning the corporation will be deemed its alter ego if their interest, and that of the corporation cannot be separated, and if maintaining the corporate entity would be unjust or create fraud.

Once again, separation is a major issue. What can you do to make the corporation look different than you do? There are many possibilities and, of course, keeping proper and appropriate corporate formalities is a big factor. This is not the only factor, though. Keeping very careful and specific documents relating to transactions between yourself and the corporation is another.

In fact, as hard as it may seem to imagine, one of the most troubling areas for many business people is the area of commingling cash and assets. A sole proprietor can grab some cash from the till and use it to buy groceries on the way home, because the business and the proprietor are the same. Not so with a corporation. A sole proprietor can also grab his business inventory and convert it for personal use. Not so with a corporation.

Everybody is familiar with the concept of the home business. Actually, this sort of business is becoming more and more popular with the growing impact of the Internet, home computers, faxes and all of the other electronics of recent years. A proprietor can easily do business at home. There may be an IRS red flag there, if you aren't careful, but that's about the extent of the problem. A corporation can't just live in your house without some sort of documentation creating a reasonable explanation for it, such as a lease. Without it, you are commingling assets. If you have a lease, or some other form of documentation, then everything is okay.

Another criterion in piercing the corporate veil is under capitalization. A corporation must be capitalized with enough capital to give it a fair and reasonable chance of success. If not, then it doesn't appear to be for real. Unhappily, there is no benchmark figure for how much is enough. Obviously, different businesses require differing amounts of capital to give them a reasonable chance of success. A manufacturer of aircraft engines will require considerably more capitalization than will an Internet consultant, for instance. In your planning, you must give this issue careful consideration. Let's look at some common mistakes and possible solutions for those problems:

Failure to Keep the Corporation in Good standing

This one is so obvious that it's almost embarrassing to mention, and yet, it is alarmingly common. Imagine that you are on the witness stand in a court case in which piercing your corporate veil is at issue, and you are maintaining what a great and viable corporation you own, when the plaintiff's attorney tells you that your corporation has been revoked by your state for failing to pay its annual fees. What are you going to say? You can avoid this disaster by simply making the required filings in your state and paying the required fees.

Failure to Sign Documents in the Corporate Fashion

As reviewed earlier, this can be a major error. It can be avoided by signing in the manner indicated below:

AJAX CORPORATION

By_____

President

In this instance, the person signing the document is clearly and obviously signing on behalf of the corporation, and not on his or her own behalf. No opponent can expect to assert that they thought the contract was with the individual, or that the individual misrepresented the nature of his or her involvement. It is clearly a corporate signature.

Failure to Identify the Business as a Corporation

This error falls closely behind the last one. It is important that people with whom you do business know that they are doing business with a corporation, and not with an individual; especially if they are going to be extending credit. It may well be that they would not have extended the credit to the corporation and actually relied on the fact that they were dealing with you individually. It is much better to clear this up right from the beginning. If you wait until you are involved in litigation with this party, they are likely to devour you in court. If you want to provide a personal guaranty, that's fine, but do it from the beginning to avoid more problems than you ever imagined.

Operate Related Corporations Autonomously

If you have more than one corporation, be sure to operate them one at a time. Each one should have its own meetings, its own records, its own bank accounts, and so on. It's fine if you are a player in all of them, as long as they are operated separately.

In short, most of these things are things that you have heard about over the years. There really is nothing new or earth shattering, and none of these are really that tough, but they can add up to trouble if you aren't careful.

Finally, there is another issue when protection of your corporate veil is considered, and that is at the initial set up of your entity. If you want it to look different than you do, ask yourself these questions:

1. Do you and your corporation have the same address, and can you prove that the corporation has a different one?
2. Since you are not commingling funds, does your corporation have a separate bank account?
3. Since you are not commingling assets, does your corporation have a separate phone line?
4. Since your corporation is a distinct entity, does it have a business license?
5. Since your corporation is not simply your "other self," does it ever do business with anybody but you?

These are five test questions to which you need to be able to answer "yes." Look over your situation carefully to ensure that you haven't made mistakes, or failed to consider something. If you can answer, truthfully and verifiably, with the correct responses and, if you keep proper corporate records, then your corporation should be able to withstand most attacks and, any future adversaries who travel down this road will do so for naught.

In looking at the issue of piecing the corporate veil, several cases stand out as benchmarks for understanding how the courts view the issue. Here, we will briefly discuss three Nevada cases to illustrate what sorts of criteria are typically brought into consideration. For those of you who would like to obtain a full legal opinion from your attorneys on these cases, included are cites. What follows is a brief summary intended for illustrative purposes only and should not be considered a legal opinion.

Rowland v. Lapire
308, 662 P.2nd 1332 Nevada (1983)

Glen and Martin Rowland, officers, directors, and shareholders of the Rowland Corporation, which was the holder of a general contractor's license, was sued by Eugene and Judy Lapire, who obtained a judgment. This action had, among other things, resulted in the piercing of the Rowland Corporation's corporate veil, and the judgment being entered against Glen and Martin Rowland individually. Among the several points, which were contested by the Rowlands when they appealed the case to the Nevada Supreme Court, was that insufficient grounds existed for piercing of their corporation.

Question: Is under capitalization sufficient grounds for asserting the Alter Ego Doctrine?

Decision: No

Opinion: The opinion of the Court held that "in order to apply the alter ego doctrine, the following requirements must be met:

1) the corporation must be influenced and governed by the person asserted to be its alter ego;
2) there must be such unity of interest and ownership that one is inseparable from the other;
3) the facts must be such that adherence to the fiction of a separate entity would, under the circumstances, sanction a fraud or promote injustice."

The corporation was undercapitalized, and at the time of trial it had a negative net worth. The Court's opinion goes on to make several interesting observations: "Although no formal directors or shareholders meetings were ever held, Martin testified that in lieu thereof he personally phoned the directors and shareholders regarding corporate business. No dividends were paid to shareholders, nor did the officers or directors receive salaries. The corporation did not have a minute book, nor is there evidence that any minutes were kept. The corporation did obtain a general contractor's license and a framing contractor's license, both in its name. It also obtained a surety bond in the amount of $5,000. The corporation also obtained Workman's Compensation insurance and transacted business with the Employment Security Department. In addition, there was a corporate checking account."

Finally, the Court held: "Although the evidence does show that the corporation was undercapitalized and that there was little existence separate and apart from Martin and Glen Rowland, we conclude that the evidence is insufficient to support a finding that appellants."

Trident Construction *v.* West Electric, Inc.,
776 P.2d 1239 Nevada (1989)

Trident Construction Corp. in a lower court action had been ordered to pay thirty-eight thousand five hundred forty-one dollars and twenty-five cents plus interest to West Electric, Inc. for work which West, a subcontractor, had completed, but for which they had not been paid in full. In addition to entering a judgment against Trident, the lower court also pierced the corporate veil and entered a judgment against Andrew DeLillo, Sr. and Vincent DeLillo individually holding that they were personally liable for the debts of Trident.

The finding of the lower court, that the DeLillo's were liable personally for the debts of the corporation, revolved around the issue of Vincent DeLillo signing a settlement agreement with West without noting his capacity of signing on behalf of the corporation. The lower court believed that, since he did not indicate his corporate capacity in signing this document, that he had personally guaranteed the document.

QUESTION: Does a signature of a corporate official without a statement acknowledging it was applied on behalf of the corporation indicate a personal guarantee.

DECISION: No.

OPINION: In finding that the DeLillo's were not personally liable for this debt, the upper court said "If the intent to make a corporate contract appears from the acts of the parties and the entire circumstances taken together with the subject matter of the deal, a corporate officer signing in his individual name only does not necessarily show that the person was acting in other than his official capacity for the corporation."

Going further, the court cited the Roland v. Lapire case discussed above. They said, "In Roland versus Lapire this court enunciated the standard of proof for the showing alter-ego based on the allegation of under capitalization. It is incumbent upon the one seeking to pierce the corporate veil to show by a preponderance of the evidence that the financial setup of the corporation is only a sham and caused an injustice. By analogous reasoning, we believe it is incumbent upon the one seeking to extend personal liability to an officer of a corporation for a corporate debt, to show by a preponderance of the evidence that the officer intended to be personally bound and that the creditor was looking to the officer as a guarantor of the debt."

Finally, the court declared, "Vincent DeLillo's failure to indicate his corporate capacity is not substantial evidence demonstrating his intent to be personally liable."

Wyatt *v.* Bowers,
747 P.2d 881 (Nev. 1987)

John Bowers and Frederick Boulware, Jr. sued Ancillary Services Corporation over an equipment lease that had gone bad. They persuaded the District Court to pierce the corporate veil of Ancillary Services Corporation and enter a judgment against Oscar Wyatt, individually, for damages. In taking the case to the Supreme Court, Wyatt asserted that, while he was an investor in Ancillary Services Corporation, he was not its alter ego.

QUESTION: Does merely influencing and governing a corporation mean that the unity and interest is such that the corporation becomes the alter ego of the person influencing and governing it?

DECISION: No.

OPINION: In answering the question the court said, "Ancillary was formed as an investment for Wyatt. Adequate funds were injected into the company for capitalization purposes. Wyatt was neither a director nor an officer of the company. Wyatt's personal funds and assets were never commingled with those possessed by Ancillary. There was no diversion of corporate funds into or out of Ancillary and into the pockets of Wyatt. No evidence can be found in the record, which would indicate that Wyatt treated the corporate assets as his own individual holdings. These factors weigh heavily against the application of the alter-ego doctrine."

"Although it is possible that Wyatt influenced Ancillary operations, it cannot be said that he governed the business."

"The mere fact that officers and directors of Ancillary were confidantes of Wyatt, while relevant, is insufficient without more to show that Ancillary was Wyatt's alter-ego. Moreover, merely influencing and governing a corporation does not necessarily demonstrate the unity of interest and ownership resulting in the requisite inseparability of a corporation and shareholder."

Finally, the court stated, "As noted in the past, corporate cloak will not likely be cast aside."

Polaris Industrial Corporation v. Kaplan
747 P.2d 884 (Nev. 1987)

Polaris was owed money by two different Nevada corporations, both of which had gone out of business. In their suit they asserted that Michael Kaplan and Jerome Kaplan were alter egos of the two corporations. Polaris then presented evidence that indicated that the Kaplan's had systematically used bank counter checks to withdraw funds from the corporate accounts, leaving the corporations unable to pay the note.

QUESTION: Does the siphoning off of corporate funds for personal use constitute a unity of interest and ownership sufficient to pierce the corporate veil?

DECISION: Yes.

OPINION: The court held that there are three general requirements for application of the alter-ego doctrine. "(1) The corporation must be influenced and governed by the person asserted to be the alter-ego; (2) there must be such unity of interest and ownership that one is inseparable from the other; and (3) the facts must be such that adherence to the corporate fiction of a separate entity would, under the circumstances, sanction fraud or promote injustice."

The court went on to explain how it arrived at its decision. "In determining whether a unity of interest exists between the individual and corporation, courts have looked to factors like commingling of funds, under capitalization, unauthorized diversion of funds, treatment of corporate assets as the individual's own, and failure to observe corporate formalities. These facts may indicate the existence of an alter-ego relationship, but are not conclusive. There is no litmus test to determine when the corporate fiction should be disregarded. The result depends on circumstances of the case."

The court noted that Kaplan and his partner Davis had diverted significant amount of funds from their corporation that could have been used to pay their debts. These funds were used for Kaplan's and Davis' personal benefit. In addition, the corporation was found to have paid directly the personal bills of Kaplan and Davis. An auditor, hired by Polaris to audit the corporation's books, determined that, "CRI would have had the funds to pay its debts if the withdrawals had not further limited the capitalization of the corporation."

The court concluded, "We are compelled to recognize that the district court clearly reached a wrong conclusion in determining that Michael Kaplan had not been shown to be an alter ego of IMS and CRI. "Accordingly, we... reverse the judgment as to Michael Kaplan."

ACTS OF THE CORPORATION

"The freedom and happiness of man...are the sole objects of all legitimate government. Oppose with manly firmness any invasions on the rights of the people"

Thomas Jefferson

Acts of the Corporation

Simply stated, a "corporate act" is an action taken by a duly authorized corporate authority of the corporation. Implicit in this concept is the notion that corporate directors are the ones who are charged with doing the thinking of the corporation. Since directors are charged with doing the corporation's thinking, they must then be the ones who can duly authorize an action to be taken. Thus, when the president of the corporation takes a particular action, the "brain" of the corporation must have authorized that action. The brain, or the mind, of the corporation is the Board of Directors.

This is not to say that the chief executive officer, or a company's president, cannot make decisions. In fact, they will usually make a great number of decisions. Yet the president and C.E.O. cannot make unauthorized decisions. Normally, officers such as these are authorized to make day-to-day operational decisions as set forth in the corporation's Bylaws. This is a handy fact, because running a business in which the president must seek the approval of the directors before he or she could buy a box of paper clips, would hardly be an organization that could stand much of a chance of reacting to the rapidly changing marketplace and highly competitive environment in which most businesses operate. Therefore, it becomes readily apparent that some sort of concession must be made so that the theoretical can operate in the face of practical situations. Such an accommodation can be found in the resolutions that the directors will adopt.

Documenting With Resolutions

Any action taken by the directors is taken through documentation known as a resolution. Since actions of the directors are by majority vote, it follows logically that there must be some way of recording these actions. Thus, where the directors get together and take some action, that process will be documented with minutes from their meeting. Yet, as we will see later on, holding a formal meeting of the directors every time an issue arises which requires a decision is a terribly awkward and overly burdensome way of doing business. In most cases, to let the period for notice to run its course would involve waiting periods of ten days before an official meeting could be convened at all. So...some sort of accommodation must be arranged. Such an accommodation is found in the "free standing resolution." Such a resolution can be adopted without holding and noticing a formal meeting. In order for such a resolution to be effective, it must have the signatures of at least a majority of the whole board, and will have the same effect as if a formal meeting were held.

All other things being equal, a free standing resolution can be used for any decision or action appropriate for the directors to take. Consequently, very few formal meetings really need to be held. The question really should be: when would you want to bother with a formal meeting at all? There are really two times when meetings are necessary. First, the annual meeting should be held each year on the appropriate day called for by the bylaws. Second, a meeting should be held when a particularly controversial subject is being considered that is likely to divide the directors. In such a case, it is often wise to hold a meeting, so that evidence can be given that nobody was misled, and that nothing was done behind someone's back. Not only will this lead to more harmony within the management of the company, but it will also cut down on the number of lawsuits resulting from someone who feels left out of things. Let's face it, it's rather difficult to say that you've been "hoodwinked" when you had every opportunity to present your case to the entire group, but they simply disagreed with you.

When to Use Resolutions

When to draft and adopt resolutions depends a great deal on the management style and preferences of the directors. These things will to a large part depend upon the relationship of the directors with the president of the corporation. For example, if there is only one director, and that person is also the president, fewer resolutions will be needed, because the director will be able to delegate must of the decision making process to the president who is in fact the same person.

On the other hand, if there are several directors, and they aren't overly confident that the president will make decisions with which they will agree, then they will probably limit the actions that the president is entitled to take. This is done through a very carefully worded resolution, which closely limits the prerogative of the president, in setting out the policy of the corporation with regard to the regular and ordinary business of the corporation, and how the president is to handle things that normally come up. Then, as things arise which are out of the ordinary, the directors will take a very close hand in directing the president to report on his actions and authorize very narrow and specific actions.

As an example, let's say that the regular business of the corporation is the retail sale of western wear, and that the directors do not wish the president to make too many moves they don't personally approve first. They might adopt a policy resolution that states the normal business activity of the corporation is "to purchase and sell to the public, western apparel." Notice that the president doesn't have the ability to assume that he can wholesale the goods. Then, the resolution may go on to say that the president is authorized to conduct the day-to-day operation of the corporation's business "with the advice and consent of the board of directors." Such a statement would indicate that there is little the president could do without the directors' involvement.

In looking at specific actions, the directors may authorize the president to lease showroom space with a specific number of square feet at a specific price per square foot, and in a certain location, subject to final approval of the directors.

A situation in which the directors may prefer to give the president full latitude will look a little different. In the original policy resolution, the directors might grant the president the authority to transact all business, hire and fire all employees, make loans, borrow, and execute all documents necessary, and so on, without further approval. In the lease example, the directors might authorize the president to "find suitable premises´ and to enter into "whatever lease terms the president, in his best judgment, deems to be in the best interests of the corporation." In the latter case, the board would ratify the decisions the president made at their annual meeting.

The manner in which you choose to proceed will depend largely on the circumstances in which you find yourself. One thing to keep in mind is that if your directors are so lacking in confidence in the officers of your corporation, you should probably be asking why the people who are serving as officers are in those capacities in the first place.

Generally speaking it is not a good idea to confer "honorary titles" to key positions within the corporation. Usually this practice breeds problems. If you are the one who will be running the show, then be the president yourself. Use the other offices as "honorary titles" if you must, but not president (unless your bylaws provide for a C.E.O. who is senior to the president. It should go without saying that the position of director is not the place to put a person who should not be making decisions!

How to Draft Resolutions

Resolutions can take on two forms, within the framework of minutes of a formal meeting, and freestanding resolutions. As meetings will be discussed in a separate section, let's look at freestanding resolutions. There are three parts to a resolution: the preamble, the body, and the authentication. The preamble and the authentication are essentially boilerplate, and should be set up on your word processor as a template. After the heading of the resolution, the preamble should say something like this:

"We, the undersigned, being all or a majority in this, a (state) corporation, having met and considered the matters herein set forth, have unanimously . . . " at this point, you are ready to insert the body of the resolution.

The Core of the Resolution

This is the important portion of the resolution, and is usually not boilerplate. Traditionally, you will skip a space, indent, and inert the word "RESOLVED". After this comes your wording. This wording is often the source of some confusion, because people feel the need to write in "legalese". Be careful about this. While it is true that resolutions are usually written in a formal style, they must be very clear as to their meaning. If you are not comfortable using technical or legal expressions, don't disappear. What you need do here is to be as clear as you possibly can be in expressing exactly what is intended. If you are comfortable with legal jargon, okay. But if you are not, then simply state clearly what you intend, and you will be fine.

The core or body of the corporate resolution also presents an opportunity. In many cases, you will have very specific reasons for what you are doing. State them in the resolution. This can be quite important in certain circumstances, should the resolutions of your corporation come to be examined in court, or in a tax audit. Since these occasions usually result years after the fact, you may not always remember the reason (or business purpose) of a particular action. By placing reasons for actions in the resolution, you will not have to worry about this later. In fact, the business purpose for an action becomes a specific and formally documented part of your records.

Let's consider an example: suppose that you need to travel to Hawaii on business. Some years later the IRS decides to audit your corporation's taxes, and questions your travel deductions. It would be a rather juicy prize for the auditor to disallow all of your many business trips, and to assert that they were, instead, personal vacations, and thus income to you, subject not only to income tax, but to payroll tax as well. This could be quite dangerous if you did a lot of business travel. So here's this trip to Hawaii. The auditor wants to know why you went there. You can't remember, after all it was four years ago, for heaven's sake!

Since you can't demonstrate why you went on business, guess what? This trip, and all of your other business trips are disallowed, and then reallocated as income. What if there was another scenario here? Suppose that the resolution authorizing the trip said:

WHEREAS, this corporation is in the business of selling sport clothing and accessories, and

WHEREAS, the International Sportswear Association is holding its annual sportswear exposition in Honolulu, Hawaii in July of this year, and

WHEREAS, this board considers attendance at this exposition by the President to be of prime importance to this Company, therefore be it

RESOLVED, that the President be and is authorized and instructed to attend the International Sportswear Exposition, in Honolulu, Hawaii on July 10-14 of this year, and be it

FURTHER RESOLVED, that the President be and is hereby instructed to secure contacts of new manufacturers of sportswear which can be added to the product line of this Corporation so that the market share of this Corporation can be increased and maintained, and be it

FURTHER RESOLVED, that the Treasurer be and is instructed to reimburse the President for all reasonable and ordinary expenses associated with this trip, including airfare, hotels, meals, and reasonable incidentals.

Where does this leave the IRS auditor? Assuming that there really was an exposition, he's barking up the wrong tree. Also, if all of your travel was documented the same way, you should come out of this part of the audit safely. There are numerous activities within your corporate operation, which could be benefited by drafting resolutions in this fashion. Also note one other thing: the president in this resolution was not only *authorized* to go, but *instructed* to go. By adding this dimension, the directors are not making the trip a nice little option, but a condition of continued employment. Since the president has been required to attend, there should be no question as to the deduction of reasonable expenses.

Notice that the business reasons for the trip were set off by the word "whereas". This is an indicator that what follows is a reason. What follows the word "resolved" is an action, instruction, or authorization.

Finally, what follows the body of the resolution is the authentication. This consists usually of a date, and then the signatures of at least a majority of the directors. Should you have three directors, for instance, then the signatures of at least two must appear on the resolution.

Where Resolutions are Appropriate

As reviewed above, policy resolutions tend to set the tone for that which comes later. Directors generally call upon the president to handle the daily activities of running the company. Policy resolutions set forth the regular business of the corporation. Policy resolutions should reflect what actions the president may take within this sphere. A policy resolution of this kind might be referred to as a "catch all" resolution.

In many companies the president may do pretty much anything, insofar as regular operations are concerned. Another case where a policy resolution would be advisable is the listing of corporate goals, objectives and plans. This area can be handled in more than one way. The president (or other officer) may be directed to make recommendations in one of these areas. When these recommendations are reported to the directors, they may adopt them, amend them or reject them. If a list of this sort were incorporated into a resolution the report of the president would be ratified and attached to the resolution, making it official policy. The same effect could be accomplished with an amended version of the president's report.

lternatively, directors could draft their own goals, objectives or plans within a resolution. Either way, the officers would have a clear-cut guideline within which they could act without further board action. This is an excellent way to handle marketing plans, financial plans and business plans. When this type of approach is taken, it becomes quite difficult for an adversary to claim that a corporation is a sham later on because the policies and business of the corporation have been duly and properly adopted and formalized. The actions of the officers on behalf of the corporation then become obvious and are set apart from their own personal actions.

Organization

The initial organization of the corporation is of vital importance. There should be a formal organizational meeting of the directors in which they authorize bank accounts, required filings, official forms of stock certificates, corporate seals and so on. The officers of the company are usually adopted or appointed in this initial organizational meeting.

The first time your Board of Directors meet will be the corporation's organizational meeting. In this crucial meeting, you will make many important decisions which will affect your business for years to come, such as adopting bylaws, establishing a fiscal year, possible election of "S" status, opening bank accounts, and many others.

Directors, or the single director, need be in place for the first meeting. If you choose to have more directors than are named in the Articles of Incorporation, then you should appoint them prior to the first meeting, if they are to participate in this meeting. Since there are no shareholders at this point, the Board of Directors can do this by adopting a Consent to Action Appointing Additional Directors prior to the meeting. Note that a Consent to Action is usually an action taken by the shareholders, but in this case, since there are no shareholders, the directors are acting in their place in appointing additional directors.

Most U.S. state statues require a form of notice before a meeting of the directors. The easiest way to accomplish this is by using a *Waiver of Notice*. The waiver allows you to proceed with the business of organizing your corporation without waiting for a notice period (typically ten days). Each director who is in office at the time of the meeting must sign the waiver. When this is accomplished, you are ready to proceed with the meeting.

In the first meeting you should address the following issues:

1. Ratify the pre incorporation actions of the Incorporator and first director.
2. Authorize the corporation to reimburse the person who paid the costs of incorporating.
3. Ratify the appointment of the Registered Agent.
4. Adopt the corporation bylaws.
5. Adopt a corporate seal.
6. Adopt a form of stock certificate.
7. Give authorization for the corporate secretary to make all necessary filings.
8. Elect officers for the first year.
9. If you are going to be an S Corporation, authorize the election of S status.
10. If you are not going to be an S Corporation, adopt a fiscal year.
11. Select a bank, and authorize the opening of a corporate bank account. You will also need to designate the person(s) who will be authorized to sign on the account.
12. Approve the Articles of Incorporation.

Let's discuss these items briefly, to ensure that you are clear on the purpose and the result of each.

Ratification of Pre-Incorporation Actions

First, the ratification of the pre-incorporation actions. It is of supreme importance in the operation of your corporation that you maintain separation between your actions as an individual, and your actions on behalf of the corporation. Ultimately, this could be the difference between having your corporate veil pierced in a lawsuit, and having the corporation protect you from attack. Consequently, we begin the Corporation's life by defining this necessary separation.

Incorporating the company is clearly an important corporate act, yet how could it be done pursuant to prior corporate authorization, if the corporation doesn't exist? Clearly, this is impossible. The answer to the dilemma is the ratification of the actions, after the fact, which has the effect of making them corporate actions, and not your personal actions.

Reimbursement of Costs of Incorporating

The second item on the list follows from the first. The cost of incorporating cannot possibly be paid for out of the Corporation's bank account, since the corporation is not yet formed. Authorizing a reimbursement in the first meeting allows you to shift the costs over to the corporation as a reasonable and ordinary business expense.

Ratification of Resident Agent

The third item is the ratification of the Resident Agent appointment. A Resident Agent for service of process is required before incorporation, yet this appointment must be authorized by the corporation, hence we again ratify it after the fact.

Adoption of the Bylaws

Adoption of bylaws, the fourth item, is one to which you should pay careful attention. You may have purchased a corporation from an incorporating company, in which you received bylaws with your other materials. Before you just accept the boilerplate bylaws without thinking, be sure that you review them and understand them. The corporation bylaws are designed to provide the working rules and regulations for your corporation's activities and internal workings. They set forth the dates and times of the annual meetings of shareholders and directors, the method of notice for these meetings, the abilities of the differing players to make amendments and other decisions. All of these items are important for you to consider at this point, and critical for you to follow later. In order for you to operate the corporation after this time, you will need to have bylaws adopted, so don't put this step off.

Adoption of a Corporate Seal

Fifth is the adoption of a corporate seal. Many states, such as Nevada and Wyoming do not require one at all, but that really doesn't mean that you should simply forgo the seal. It will afford a great deal of authenticity and credibility to corporate documents, which may need to be shown to others if you use it consistently.

Adoption of Stock Certificates

Sixth, is the adoption of stock certificates. This is simply the official designation of a particular form or design which conforms to your state's requirements, and will make it difficult for someone to come along with just any old blank form, and claim it as evidence of ownership. The Seal should be placed on a sample certificate, and included with the minutes of the meeting as an official sample for the corporation's records.

Authorization of Required Filings

Authorizing the corporate Secretary to make all necessary filings will provide the necessary authorization to continue the organization process in compliance with applicable federal, state and local requirements for such things as Employer Identification Numbers, officers' lists, business licenses, and so on.

Election of Officers

The election of officers is certainly important. It may seem hard to imagine, but this step is often overlooked. When corporate service providers are asked to help someone bring their corporate records up to date, the first thing they do is to make a chart showing the shareholders, directors, and officers that show up on the various filings and documents that have been done, and compare them with the annual meetings which have (or have not) been held. The purpose for doing this is to determine if there were officers and directors for the corporation in any given year. Usually, there are years, or many years when the corporation transacted business, and did not have valid officers or directors. Begin correctly and do not fail to omit this important step; elect officers.

Who Should Serve

At this juncture, we need to consider two basic questions: who should serve as director, and who should serve as an officer? Often, business people will have others serve in these capacities although they may have only minor roles in the business. However, as is the case in all phases of corporate organization, you need to carefully consider what the purpose of the corporation is, and who really has a role to play in that purpose. For example, if you are starting up a new corporation to conduct your primary business, who is going to make the important decisions?

People with family businesses frequently appoint their older children to officers' positions. Sometimes, they even appoint them as directors. What a sad day many people experience when their disgruntled adult children figure out that they can fire their parents! Is that really what you want?

Another example along these lines is the person who welcomes his new son-in-law to the family by making him a director or an officer or gives his soon-to-be former son-in-law a large amount of stock. Let's face it, there are enough pitfalls in business without causing your own problems by awarding honorary titles that effectively place someone into a position of authority in your own business. You ought carefully consider what could eventually go wrong in the future before you make such appointments.

If it is your intention to maintain tight control over the business, do not appoint other people to critical positions. Take time to consider what could happen. Then and only then can you be secure in your new undertaking.

Adopt a Fiscal Year

If you are planning to become an S Corporation, you will have to adopt a calendar year. A fiscal year for tax purposes will void your S election. If you are not planning on being an S Corporation, then give some thought to your fiscal year end. Most people choose a calendar year because they are used to calendar years. If you have multiple corporations, however, a fiscal year can be an excellent tax-planning device. If your multiple corporations work together, then if you put them on different fiscal year ends, you can take certain steps to "impoverish" the corporation who's year is about to end.

Let's say that you have two corporations. One operates on a calendar year, (corporation A). The other, (corporation B), has a fiscal year, which ends on June 30. In December, corporation A makes a large cash purchase, or enters into a large deductible services contract from corporation B. When the tax year for corporation A ends at the end of the month, its income for the year may be way down because of the transaction just completed with corporation B. This may have an impact on its taxable income, which is about to be calculated for the year. If this results in corporation A owing less in taxes for the year, would that hurt your feelings? (Most people answer "no" here). Corporation B now has six months to figure out what tax planning it will need before its year ends.

Now consider that corporation B enters into a large cash transaction with corporation A in mid June. If this transaction had the effect of lowering the taxable income of corporation B, just before it had to file its taxes, would you feel bad? (Usually a "no" answer works here too.)

Take some time to think about what your various corporations can do for one another, and when would be advantageous times for them to get together before you choose a calendar year for your corporation's fiscal year end. This is also the right time to get some aggressive tax planning advice. You may discover you are able to save on your corporation's taxes with a strategy like the one outlined below.

If you authorize a particular tax year in your first meeting, and then get with your tax advisor, and wish to change your fiscal year, you can do it, as long as you have not filed your first tax return. The corporation's first tax year must end within one year of the time it first started doing business, and must be filed seventy-five days after that ending. At any time prior to the filing of that first return, you can change your fiscal year, as long as your first fiscal year is not longer than 365 days from the date on which you started doing business. Once the first return is filed by the corporation, the fiscal year can no longer be changed, or at least not without some serious difficulty.

After the first meeting has been completed, the secretary will sign the minutes. It is always a good idea for the directors to sign the minutes as well. This will remove the temptation for them to exercise selective memory later, and is a good idea to get into the habit of doing with each subsequent meeting of the directors and shareholders, even though it is not required.

Issuance of Stock

If following proper corporate formalities is your intention, and it must be for the sake of your corporate health, the issuance of stock, as the principal corporate formality, deserves your careful attention. We have discussed previously considerations involved in choosing shareholders, and some of the issues involved. In this section we undertake the actual procedure for issuing stock, and the manner of recording it in your corporation record book.

To begin with let's address a common question that frequently arises. In many cases there are those who deal with corporations where that corporation is not their principal business and so they say something to the effect of "I don't want to own the stock, but I don't want anybody else to own it, either. Why can't I just not issue any, so I can say that I don't own it?"

Most corporations are vulnerable to attack because they don't follow proper corporate procedure (formalities), they have sloppy records, few resolutions, and little documentation of corporate activities. Plaintiffs' attorneys lick their chops at the prospect of ripping through these corporations to get at shareholders' personal assets. Since proper corporate formalities are a major factor in preventing the piercing of the corporate veil, and the issuance of stock is the major formality that any corporation will deal with, not issuing stock is a serious mistake. The question that usually follows is " how can someone get at my assets if "I" don't own the stock?" The answer is simply that the plaintiff's attorney asserts that you are the *effective or beneficial* owner of the stock, because your fingerprints are all over the corporation. Thus your strategy backfires on you, and, instead of distancing you from the corporation, aids the enemy in getting at your assets. "Do you really have to issue the stock?"Yes, you really should.

Types of Consideration

Stock is issued for cash, property, or services. Cash is fairly obvious as a form of consideration, but property and services will vary in form and substance. Property can take many forms, stock can be issued for tangible assets, such as office equipment, and real estate, or it can include such items as mental property, formulas, copyrights, trademarks, and so on. Services can be such things as actual work for the corporation, longevity, consulting, and service contracts.You may have a special circumstance, which will fit into one of these categories, which isn't mentioned, and yet could certainly be a valid consideration for the issuance of stock.

Issuance of the Stock

The actual issuance of the stock is rather simple. You issue stock by corporate resolution. First you will need a resolution to authorize issuance, and then you will need to draft a resolution issuing a specific number of shares to a specific individual or individuals (or bearer) for a type of consideration, cash, property or services. The resolution need not state how much money is involved, just the particular type of consideration. As an accounting function, you will have an equity account, usual called "paid in capital" on your books which indicates the actual amount of cash, or the cash value of the property or services performed in exchange for the stock.

All states require that corporations maintain a stock ledger as a record of share ownership. Stock ledgers usually are in two steps. First is the Register of Original Certificate Issue, which performs much the same duty as a check register. It allows the secretary to keep track of your numbered certificates, so that at any time, he or she can determine where they are. The register will indicate to whom and when each issued certificate was issued. And when combined with the remaining blank or unused certificates in the record book, it will indicate if any certificates are missing.

The second ledger that you will need to keep is called the "shareholder ledger." The shareholder ledger is a separate ledger for each shareholder which indicates each stock transaction the shareholder has been involved in, and shows a running total of the shares each person owns. It also has the address of the shareholder. The shareholder ledger is what is used in determining who is entitled to vote in shareholder meetings, and how many shares each shareholder is entitled to. The address on the ledger is used for providing notices of meetings to each shareholder.

States will vary on whether or not a copy of the shareholder ledger must be kept by the Resident Agent. In some states, such as Nevada, only a statement stating who is the custodian of the ledger is provided to the Resident Agent. If you are not planning on using Nevada to domicile your corporation you should contact your state's secretary of state to find out what is required in this area.

Changes of the Guard

There are several possibilities in this area. First, there is the fundamental matter of appointing officers. Next, there is the possibility that an officer may resign or be fired. Next, directors need to be appointed, they can resign and need to be replaced, and then, of course, they too can be fired. All of these actions are done through documented means. As most of these actions involve actions of the directors or shareholders, there are resolutions involved. Yet even a resignation requires some sort of instrument, even if the officer quits verbally and stomps off in a huff, refusing to write anything down.

The reasons for the need for documentation should be fairly obvious by this time. In a corporation, everything depends on the roles we are playing at any given moment, and upon our ability to prove (or disprove) it. With a partnership or sole proprietorship, this is not nearly as important, because those entities are synonymous with the individuals involved. Corporations however are different, and anyone can claim to be an officer or director for various nefarious purposes. What we don't always consider is that people can also *deny* their truthful position when they want to wiggle out of something. Thus, not only is such documentation important from the simple perspective of formalities, it is critical for some very practical reasons as well.

Officers

Election or appointment of officers is done by directors. In the annual Board of Director's meeting, they elect the officers for the coming year. Yet, in the event that something goes awry during that time, they may have cause to replace an officer. The procedures are relatively simple.

Resignations come about for a variety of reasons. Let's first of all look at what happens when a resignation is friendly. The Treasurer resigns to pursue his or her dream to travel the world. The Treasurer would then submit a brief letter of resignation (usually given to the president, or it might be addressed to the board or the corporate secretary). The directors get together and draft a resolution accepting the resignation and appointing a new person to fill the unexplored term, or not. The new Treasurer accepts in writing the appointment (as all directors and officers should be required to do) and that is all there is to it.

Things can become a little more complicated in an unfriendly situation. Yet, if the resigning officer gives a written resignation, which is exactly what you want them to do, everything would proceed as noted. However, they may refuse to do so and just leave. In this case, it is of vital importance that the directors adopt a resolution accepting the resignation, which documents exactly how they have come to know about it the officer's resignation, since the person in question didn't sign anything.

Suppose that the Treasurer became disenchanted with the management of the corporation for some reason and walked into the president's office and said, "Take this job and shove it, I'm out here!" The president them informs the directors of the situation, and the directors adopt the following resolution:

WHEREAS, it has come to the attention of this Board that Sam Smith, the Treasurer of this corporation, has given his verbal resignation to the president of the Corporation, and

WHEREAS, the president has reported to this Board that said verbal resignation was given to him on Tuesday, March 5, 1998 at 2:35 p.m., and

WHEREAS, the president's secretary, Mary Jones attested that she overheard the verbal resignation of the Treasurer, therefore be it

RESOLVED, that the resignation of Sam Smith from the post of Treasurer of this Corporation, given to the president on the date and time noted above, be and is hereby accepted effective as of the date and time given.

While this resolution may seem to be longer than absolutely necessary, there is a reason for all of this. First, don't be too shocked if this person who quits in a huff turns around and sues for wrongful termination, asserting that he or she was fired. In that case, all of the official documentation possible will be necessary. Second, you need some sort of record to establish that the position was indeed vacant, so that there will be no question as to the legitimacy of the successor. This approach will work in most situations of this type. It would be followed by a resolution appointing a new Treasurer, either combined with the above resolution, or separately:

RESOLVED, that Harry A. Jackson be and is hereby appointed Treasurer of this Corporation, to fill the vacancy created by the resignation of Sam Smith, such appointment to be effective this date.

What about terminations? Termination of an officer may be done by the board of directors, and in some cases by the shareholders. There is some dispute about the degree of detail that is appropriate on a resolution terminating an officer, with some arguing that the resolution should contain all of the reasons for the action, while others disagree. Those favoring the reasons assert that this is an excellent opportunity to document those just causes for the termination, in the event there should be a lawsuit. Those on the other side argue that listing of reasons, in the event of a suit, could end up being a trap for the company, while not listing them will give the company the ability to surprise the other side with the reasons at the right time. If you are thoroughly confused by all of this, you would do well to talk it over with an attorney who is knowledgeable in employment law. For our purposes, it is sufficient to grasp the need and importance of some sort of resolution to remove an officer. A sample resolution of this type would read something like this:

RESOLVED, that Sam Smith, Treasurer of this Corporation, be and is hereby removed from the office of Treasurer, effective immediately.

This simple language will get the job done. Whether or not you prefer to "whereas" all of the reasons is your call. Normally, the president would be the appropriate person to deliver the news to the unfortunate officer in question. In some cases, you may wish to convene a directors meeting for the purpose of calling in the person to be dismissed but from a pragmatic point of view this is usually less productive.

Hiring and firing of employees is normally handled by the president, or by another person designated to do so, such as someone from human resources. As a rule, the directors would not get involved in personnel matters dealing with employees. However, yours might be an organization where the directors would step in and become involved with a particular position, where the president's authority may have been limited in some area. If this is the case, the directors should act, or at least ratify the termination. Obviously, there could also be a case where the directors disagree with the president and insist that an employee be terminated. In such a case, they should adopt a resolution instructing the president to make the termination.

Directors

This area becomes a little more complicated than dealing with the officers, because we must involve the stockholders. Stockholders in most cases appoint directors. Yet, where there are no stockholders, the directors may appoint as many additional directors as the bylaws permit, by a "consent to action." A consent to action is actually the name of a resolution of the stockholders. However, if there are no shareholders and the directors are acting in their place, they would use a consent rather than a director's resolution. The consent to action uses the exact same format as a resolution, simply substituting the name.

There is another case in which the directors might elect directors, even while there are shareholders, and that is to fill an unexplored term, where a vacancy would have resulted from a termination, resignation or death. This appointment could also be made by the shareholders. So, which is the best course of action – having the directors fill a vacancy, or having the shareholders do it? As a practical matter, this depends upon whether you are a director or a shareholder! Since directors serve at the pleasure of the shareholders, it would be a good idea for the directors not to be overly aggressive in this area.

Procedurally, resignations of directors should be handled in the same way as resignations of officers, with written resignation being submitted and accepted by the shareholders, prior to the appointment of a new director. If your board of directors has not fallen below the minimum number set by the Articles, you aren't required to fill a vacancy.

Termination of a director is another matter. In almost all cases, the directors do not have this authority, so it must be done by the shareholders. Additionally, most state statutes require a super majority of the voting shares of the corporation to remove a director, usually two thirds and sometimes three quarters. While removal of a director can be done either in a meeting or by consent to action, if you have several shareholders, it would be wise to hold a meeting, so that the representation of the necessary percentages of shares can be fully demonstrated. Where there is only one shareholder, this would not be a problem.

Salaries

Officers' salaries and directors' fees are also a matter for resolutions. Because officers are hired by the directors, the specifics of their compensation, including bonuses, benefits and salaries are all determined by the board. As always, it is naturally understood that if there is no resolution, the board has not taken an action. This being the case, a corporation which has officers, benefits for officers and officers' salaries (or no officer salaries for that matter) needs to have documentation. A lack of documentation can make the corporation appear to be an alter ego in some cases, or in others it may appear that the officer(s) in question could be acting improperly. Some corporations also pay fees to directors for attending meetings. These fees are also documented with resolutions.

Purchasing

Resolutions relating to purchasing can be minimal in number, or very numerous, depending on the degree of latitude the directors wish to give to the officers. Normally speaking, since the officers are charged with the responsibility of conducting the day-to-day business of the corporation, they can make normal and necessary purchases without prior or specific Board approval. Yet in some cases, the directors may wish to limit the ability of officers to purchase. This limitation would be a matter of drafting and adopting a resolution. Limitations may be placed on types of purchases, dollar amounts, or most anything that the directors would deem necessary.

Out of the ordinary purchases of significant size should always be approved by the directors. Such purchases would include new phone systems, re-tooling of a plant, purchases of company cars which are not otherwise provided for, real estate purchases, and so on. The rule of thumb would be set by a policy resolution. Policy which allowed for purchases in the ordinary course of regular business would then require by implication, resolutions for unusual purchases. For most small to medium sized companies where the players are more or less the same people in differing roles, this arrangement is the easiest one to handle.

Establishing a Principal Place of Business

It is fair to say that in all cases, the establishing of a principal place of business is neither ordinary or regular in the course of a corporation's activities. It is something which seldom occurs, and may only occur once in the entire history of a company. Thus, an action of the Board is going to be necessary to authorize the move. In fact, it may even require a series of resolutions. Let's say that the corporation has maintained the same location for a number of years, but with the growth of the company, the current location is no longer big enough to get the job done.

The Board may direct the president to look into a possible relocation. That's one resolution. Then the president reports back what he has found out. This sounds like a meeting, doesn't it? Then the board tells the president to enter into negotiations with the landlord. Probably the board will say that they would agree to a certain price, or certain terms. They may say that if the price and terms are met, the president can go ahead and sign. All of this would be done by resolution. Remember that the board's thinking and decisions are the purpose of resolutions.

Once the president concludes successful negotiations and signs the lease. At this point he reports to the board, and the board ratifies the lease. Another resolution. This general process may apply to many different situations if you think about it. Real estate purchases, auto or aircraft purchases, business alliances, and many other scenarios may need to work like this. That is not to say that these steps are somehow required, because they are not. However, things may well work out this way. And if they do, you should have them covered in the corporate records. What if you have only one person holding all of the positions, do you need to have such a lengthy process? The answer is, most likely not. Let's go over the process again with a one person corporation. You as president say to yourself, "Hey, this place isn't big enough any more." So you do some checking, and find that you can move the company to a better location. You talk to the landlord, cut a deal, and sign on the dotted line. Now, back at the office you acting as director look at the deal you signed and say, "Good job. You did the right thing." Your resolution would ratify the new lease. Here's some language that might be useful here:

RESOLVED, that the lease for new corporate offices by and between this Corporation, and so and so, executed on such and such a date, and attached hereto, be and is ratified and approved as if done pursuant to prior authorization.

It should be needless to say that the manner in which you proceed will depend upon the particulars of your situation, yet the principals will apply to many cases.

Financing

Financing is another area where the activities are usually not the normal course of business. Obviously, we are not talking about finance companies here. One factor in this area is that most banks will provide you with a resolution for their protection. You need to ensure that the corporate records contain that resolution. However, all financing is not done through banks. For this reason, you should review your corporation's records to ensure that lending or borrowing money is properly documented.

A special case here is the issue of related party loans. Loans to and from stockholders, directors and officers are of particular import, since they can come under intense scrutiny in tax audits. You should ensure that all such transactions are fully documented, contain reasonable terms, and are entirely arms length. This includes that loans be paid back in a reasonable amount of time.

CHAPTER 7

A CLASSIC U.S. STRATEGY

"Over and over again courts have said that there is nothing sinister in so arranging one's affairs as to keep taxes as low as possible. Everybody does so, rich or poor; and all do right, for nobody owes any public duty to pay more than the law demands: taxes are enforced exactions, not voluntary contributions. To demand more in the name of morals is mere cant."

Judge Learned Hand
Former Chief Justice
U.S. Court of Appeals

The Private Corporation

A private corporation is surely one of the best tools in existence for achieving personal financial objectives. Those that have accumulated assets, or believe that they are on the right track to do so, are generally faced with several issues in common that tend to break down into four broad based categories: privacy issues, asset protection concerns, tax shelter and estate/retirement planning.

In some respects it may be easier for a European to grasp the values inherent in a Nevada strategy than it is for an American. For the average American the concept usually comes as a surprise as we tend to think of the U.S. as one cohesive whole without considering the benefits of using another U.S. state as part of a business strategy. However, there are incredible benefits available for those who "think outside the box" and consider how a multi-state strategy might help them.

We will begin by exploring a tried and tested Nevada strategy that provides benefits to Americans. Although the example set forth below assumes one is from the U.S., if you're not from the states you'll still benefit by learning how it works because much of the information may ultimately apply directly to you, albeit from a slightly different perspective.

A graphical chart depicting the Nevada corporation verses other sample U.S. states is contained within the Appendices. A comparative review of state corporate income tax and franchise tax analysis is also contained within the Appendices.

Overview

The following is a legal business strategy but when you first learn how it works it may seem as though something is wrong. Probably the only thing wrong about what you are about to read is that you haven't yet done it yourself and reaped the benefits. But just because it is not illegal, does that make it ethical? This is a question you must ultimately answer for yourself. But consider the following in light of the fact that virtually every major corporation in the world operates within a strategy that is designed to legally reduce the impact of taxation on their respective companies.

The quotation at the beginning of this chapter by Judge Learned Hand, a former Chief Justice with the U.S. Court of Appeals, is repeated here because it addresses the concept of tax strategies and ethics:

"Over and over again courts have said that there is nothing sinister in so arranging one's affairs as to keep taxes as low as possible. Everybody does so, rich or poor; and all do right, for nobody owes any public duty to pay more than the law demands: taxes are enforced exactions, not voluntary contributions. To demand more in the name of morals is mere cant."

To get your mind wrapped around how an interstate strategy might work for you, let's begin with the end in mind. The principle, in a nutshell, is that you transfer profits or earnings from a high-tax jurisdiction to a jurisdiction where the taxes are lower or non-existent, and in doing so you move assets beyond the grasping hands of predators.

In other words, if you're currently based in any of the forty states that have state income tax, you can shave your state tax bill down to little or nothing. And, if you live and work in a state or territory that does not have a state income tax you'll still come way out ahead in terms of asset protection and probably estate planning as well. Sound too good to be true? It is true, and it is relatively simple, and it works like this. Let us assume you have a business or income from a non-Nevada location where you currently reside, and that your home state has some form of state income tax. The first step in this strategy calls for you to form a corporation in Nevada.

Rearranging Your Finances

With the help of a skilled professional, you so arrange your finances that the business in your home state continually owes money to your Nevada Company — so much so that the business in your home state shows little or no profit. The profits show up in your Nevada Corporation where there is no state income tax and where no one knows you own the company. This is called profit upstreaming. The IRS has another term for this process, they call it income stripping and they don't generally like it. But in the case of a state-to-state strategy, it may have no effect on federal taxes, just state income tax – so the IRS simply doesn't care. Do I have you confused? Read on, things will clear up.

If you already own a company in your home state you then form an additional one in Nevada. The one in your home state conducts daily business and the one in Nevada is a creditor of your operating business. In this way you have the capacity to shift funds out of your home state and to Nevada thus reducing net earnings in your home state. Why is this valuable? You have just saved an amount equal to the state income tax that would have been due from your home state business earnings, minus the costs of maintaining the Nevada Company. You have also gained a significant measure of privacy because the State of Nevada does not provide for shareholder information in any public record.

Asset Protection Characteristics

What may be even better than the savings gained from State tax avoidance in the strategy set forth above, is the asset protection characteristics of this type of program. What does this mean? Predatory litigation, or lawsuits on a commission basis, is uniquely a U.S. phenomenon whose horrible example is now being copied to some degree in other countries. This is bad news for Europeans who have laughed at the ridiculous judgments and blackmailing activities pursued by less scrupulous law firms and their ubiquitous, something-for-nothing clientele. These people seek victims from which to garner high settlement penalties and unfortunately all too often they are successful in the game of legal extortion.

A quick look at the growing predatory litigation phenomena, everywhere present in the United States, pretty much tells the story of why business owners and professionals are worried about the need for asset protection:

> **5%** or less of the world's population reside in the U.S.
> **20%** or thereabouts, of the world economy is U.S.
> **70%** of the world's lawyers reside in the U.S.
> **94%** of the world's lawsuits are in the U.S.

Lawsuits performed on a commission basis are against the law almost everywhere except the U.S. So anyone doing business with an American, be it an individual or legal entity, regardless of where they live and work is not exempt from this risk. Regrettably in North America contingency litigation is a major growth industry and the primary targets are people with assets, business owners, professionals, and publicly traded companies. Actually, predatory lawyers frequently consider anyone with wealth, or anyone expected to develop wealth in the foreseeable future, fair game.

Money and other assets held in a corporation, especially one in a jurisdiction other than where you live and work tends to be immune from many forms of judicial proceedings. This is particularly true if your extra-territorial corporation does not do business in your home state. Provided you are judicious about sharing secrets and don't make an issue of your owning stock in the Nevada company that holds a portion of your assets, no one is able to discern this information from the public record particularly if you implement a privacy strategy in concert with the formation of your Nevada Corporation.

Filing Liens

Taking the process one step further, your Nevada Company can actually file liens against you personally or against business assets held or domiciled in your home state thereby cluttering the public record such that a predator cannot easily identify the source of clear and free assets to grab. This conceptual process has been simplified for the sake of explanation, but to do it right, such that your "corporate veil" cannot be pierced, usually takes the assistance of someone knowledgeable in these matters, one who is prepared to assist with the appropriate documents and implement the needed elements of your personal strategy on your behalf.

To summarize this strategy it boils down to what you gain: tax savings, asset protection, improved financial privacy, and perhaps a host of additional benefits that we shall address in later chapters.

In the final analysis is this a valid business approach for you? You probably don't have enough information yet, but consider that tens of thousands of people throughout the United States have enacted this simple strategy and folks from all over the world use Nevada as a base of operations for everything from personal holding companies to major publicly traded corporations.

More About Nevada

The Nevada Option is a consequence of decisions made by the Founding Fathers of the United States. They decided that individual states should have the right of taxation – in other words the citizens of each state have the right to tax themselves as they see fit. And different states tend to see things differently.

Nevada has chosen to permit gambling. The result is an "industry without smokestacks" that attracts billions of dollars into the state. Nevada gets half its revenue from taxing casino income. As we've already discussed, this means there is no need for personal or corporate income taxes. Nor are there taxes that are common elsewhere, such as franchise taxes, franchise on income, inventory taxes, special intangible taxes, fixed asset taxes, capital stock taxes, chain store taxes, admissions taxes, stock transfer taxes, state inheritance taxes, gift taxes and a host of others peculiar to specific jurisdictions.

The variety of taxation methods between states is part of what makes life interesting in the U.S. For example, on the West Coast of the U.S., (what Easterners call the left coast) the State of Oregon has a long-standing taboo against sales taxes. Every now and then some politician gets the bright idea of asking the voters to approve a sales tax. Not only does it never pass, it is also usually the kiss of death for that politician.

Neighboring states like Washington on Oregon's north border, and California directly to the south, both have high sales taxes — well over 8 percent in some parts of Washington on almost everything you purchase. Not surprisingly, residents of border communities in Washington State (not to be confused with Washington DC which is on the East Coast of the United States) do much of their retail shopping in Oregon, and skip paying the sales tax. The State of Washington says it is wrong for their residents to do this without paying a "use tax" to the state, but revenue officers glumly throw up their hands and acknowledge the problem. People are not stupid, they will drive across a bridge to save 8% on everything they buy!

Oregon benefits with one of the hottest retail markets in the country as wealth crosses state lines from all directions in the quest to avoid paying sales tax. It may seem like Oregon has an unfair advantage over its neighbors, but the price of forgoing a sales tax is a high state income tax – 9.2 percent — as well as some of the highest property taxes in the country. So even though Oregon does not charge sales tax it is still a tax hell for those who live there.

Oregon's high state income tax is surpassed by California's personal income tax. The beneficiary is Nevada, where there is no state income tax. If people will cross state lines to avoid paying 8 percent on the purchase of a television, how much more will they cross state lines to incorporate and save 10 percent of their net earnings?

A Simple Example

A firm I once consulted helped an individual from California who liquidated an asset with no underlying cost basis and received about $1.5 million. Had she paid state income taxes in California it would have cost her about $150,000 right off the top before dealing with federal taxes. With her Nevada Corporation in place, all of that wealth remained in her own hands. That is to say, in the hands of her Nevada Company which she owned. Pardon me a small digression; all this talk of saving state income tax reminds me of Libertarian Jeff Daiell's pithy comment:

"When Barbary Pirates demand a fee for allowing you to do business, it's called "tribute money." When the Mafia demands a fee for allowing you to do business, it's called "the protection racket." When the state demands a fee for allowing you to do business, it's called "income tax."

Nevada is not the first domestic corporate shelter. Delaware has been the home to scores of major corporations — mainly because corporate directors had more control there than the shareholders. But Nevada and Wyoming both improved on Delaware's laws, and made the rules more favorable to both large and small corporations alike.

The most recent incorporation rush started in Nevada on March 13, 1987, when legislation was approved protecting corporate directors and officers from personal liability for acts committed on behalf of the corporation or by the corporation. These regulations were strengthened in legislation passed in 2001 in concert with State filing fee increases. These laws along with more flexible capitalization and maintenance requirements have made Nevada the "incorporation capital of the America," upstaging Delaware which had previously held this honor. Anyone from outside the U.S. seeking to do business in the U.S. should absolutely look to Nevada first.

The Privacy Application

For some, the most appealing aspect of incorporating in Nevada is the respect for privacy. Nevada does not keep the identity of shareholders in the public record. In other words, who owns a corporation is no one's business but the owner. If someone is pursuing your assets and they suspect you might own a related Nevada corporation, they're going to have more hurdles in the discovery process than in most states. A record search, for example, generally ends up at a dead end.

Nevada requires that corporations have at least one officer and one director – but it can be the same individual. There are professionals in Nevada who will function as the officer and director of your company. They are essentially a nominee and will do as instructed, provided that their instructions do not violate the laws under which they operate. These services should be used in conjunction with a corporate headquarters package, which in effect provides a virtual office for the company, which includes a telephone number, someone to answer the phone, a fax number, a mailing address, a bank account, and a trained individual who acts as the director/officer of your corporation.

Nevada nominee officers and directors are frequently lawyers or skilled trust officers who specialize in such matters. A nominee officer is not required to know the shareholders or even know their names. The nominee need only know from whom he or she is to take instructions, and where the list of shareholders is kept — not necessarily who is listed on the shareholder ledger. Only under court order is the whereabouts of a shareholder's list required to be made available. And the shareholder list can be maintained in another country altogether. Can you imagine how frustrated a predatory lawyer in your home state will be when trying to connect you with your Nevada Corporation? Not only can you save taxes, you can also build a strong firewall of privacy to protect hard assets as well as the intangibles that so frequently comprise the real value of private enterprise.

Corporate Headquarters Providers

In addition to the full service corporate headquarters providers, there are companies that offer only resident agent and mail forwarding services.

Full service corporate headquarters programs cost from around $165 per month or approximately $2,000 annually (See Corporate Office Services 775-324-7676 www.nevcorp.com) to a maximum of about $250 per month or $3,000 annually, both include such things as a local city business license, corporate bank account, listed phone number and operator, a physical office address, re-mailing services, and other validations for a legitimate presence in jurisdictions like Nevada or Wyoming.

The slightly more expensive version also includes on-site office use when you or others visit your Nevada or Wyoming office, a contract manager to represent you if someone should want to personally check out your company office, pre-made signage for internal offices, and a first-class shared boardroom facility. (See Laughlin International 775-883-8484, www.laughlininternational.com) These same kinds of services are available in Wyoming, a State that has endeavored to duplicate all the advantages of Nevada and from which the same sample strategy out-lined herein will work effectively. (See Incorporations Today 307-632-3333 www.incorporationstoday.com) For a simple corporation without the strategy, the lowest pricing is available from Val-U-Corp Services, Inc, a legitimate Internet corporate provider, at 775-887-8853, (www.val-u-corp.com)

Other Advantages

Nevada has other advantages over Delaware and all the other U.S. states. Delaware has been too quick to share information with the federal government that Nevada considers private. Delaware also charges a franchise tax in addition to a state income tax. Nevada, on the other hand, has no state income tax (there is a constitutional ban on such a thing), and no corporate income tax, and there is no franchise tax either. Even though the franchise tax in Delaware is slight, it still means annual disclosures, including dates of stockholder meetings, places of business outside the state, and revelation of the number and value of shares issued. Nevada asks for none of this information.

As a matter of policy, the state of Nevada involves itself as little as possible in business and corporate transactions. Shares in a corporation can be sold or transferred with no state taxes. Unlike some states that tax a corporation according to the number of shares issued, Nevada has no tax on corporate shares. Neither is there a succession tax, which is a type of inheritance tax some states require. And stockholders and directors need neither live in Nevada nor hold their meetings in the state. You can hold corporate meetings in your own home or take a tax-deductible trip to Hawaii to do so. Your corporate records can be kept anywhere — your home, India — you decide.

Nevada has nothing to say about what kinds of stock your corporation issues — preferred, common or whatever. Nevada and Wyoming also allow "bearer shares." Share transactions can be anonymous, which means that shares of corporations can change hands with no names attached to them. Neither does Nevada have an inventory tax, a unitary tax, a state inheritance tax or personal income taxes. The lack of inventory tax alone has made Reno, Nevada one of the warehouse and distributions centers of the West Coast. At one time inventory taxes in California drove scores of distribution businesses across their east border to Nevada for financial shelter. Companies like Barnes & Noble where you may well have purchased a copy of this book, maintain a huge distribution center in Reno.

Other advantages to Nevada are that directors can change the bylaws of the corporation without interference from the state. And, there is no initial or minimum capital required to start a corporation. A Nevada corporation can buy shares of its own stock and hold them, transfer them, or sell them. The corporation can use the stock to buy or lease real estate or acquire options for them. Stock can be used to pay for labor or services, and whatever the directors decide these things are worth is essentially beyond anyone's question. (With the exception of the IRS, which tends to question anything they do not immediately understand.)

Nevada does not require tax reports, and it does not share the information it does gather with any of the other states or the federal government. Nevada is the only state that does not share information with the Internal Revenue Service, and frankly it makes the IRS mad. As a matter of fact, the last reported effort of the IRS to get such information from the state was in 1991. They tried repeatedly to get information from Nevada's Department of Taxation, Department of Motor Vehicles, Employment Security, Gaming and Control Board, as well as the Secretary of State's office. They soon learned that for them in Nevada, it's "no dice." If the IRS wants information, the burden of proof is on them to prove they need it on a case-by-case basis. They simply can't go on a fishing expedition ransacking state records trying to find people to harass. Nevada has even backed off joining a consortium of states to share information with one another because it could be a way for the IRS to gain access to information about Nevada corporations indirectly.

Federal Taxes and Your Personal Strategy

If you are an American and you own anything of real value, or you have more than one income source, you should have at least one Nevada or Wyoming entity and perhaps several. The cost to purchase a pre-formed corporation is relatively modest. You can fax, mail, or email a purchase request. Check the Appendices for a list of several qualified sources.

After you've purchased or setup a Nevada or Wyoming corporation you must activate it with the IRS by securing a tax identification number, normally your representative agent will do this but if you do it yourself be certain to declare a fiscal year date different from that of the calendar year.

This action allows you future flexibility in shifting income between your corporation and yourself for any given year. Why is the date of the fiscal year so important? Well, as you likely know, a U.S. person filing a joint federal income tax return as of 2002 can earn up to $45,120 and still only be subject to 15% federal income tax. Your personal corporation is only assessed 15% up to the first $50,000 of net income annually. This means, with some planning you and your corporation can earn up to $95,120 collectively and only be subject to a maximum of 15% federal income tax. And, of course, by keeping your company qualified you eliminate corporate state income tax altogether. Further, many normal purchases you may personally wish to make, such as computers, etc., may not be tax deductible to you as an individual, whereas if purchased through your corporation the entire amount should reduce your taxable income.

Using additional corporations correctly, you can shift income progressively forward into different fiscal periods delaying tax due dates for sometimes years into the future and then settling up by spreading earned income over several corporations thereby not exceeding the lowest federal tax bracket of 15%. However, because of sister company rules this latter strategy has become tedious to accomplish correctly so if this is your plan make sure you are working with a tax lawyer or accountant that understands your objectives clearly at the beginning.

If you don't mind paying a punitive 39.6% federal income tax, PLUS FICA taxes, PLUS Medicare, PLUS State income taxes, the aggregate which generally exceeds more than half your earned income, then you're still going to want to invoke privacy and asset protection strategies if you intend to protect what's left.

Now, before you move boldly ahead with a plan to transfer assets into a Nevada or Wyoming company you need to make sure you're not violating fraudulent transfers laws, the subject of the next chapter.

CHAPTER 8

ASSET TRANSFER COMPLICATIONS

"The truth is rarely pure and never simple."

Oscar Wilde

Overview

Any transfer of assets a debtor makes with the actual or constructive intent to hinder, delay, or defraud a creditor is fraudulent. Likewise, transfers by a debtor for less than a fair and reasonable consideration, where the debtor thereby becomes insolvent and incurs debts beyond a reasonable ability to pay, is generally considered fraudulent under law. In these situations, a creditor will likely have protection afforded by fraudulent conveyance statutes and gain relief from the Court thereby voiding prior transfers to satisfy an outstanding judgment.

The subject material included in this chapter reviews what constitutes a fraudulent transfer and how to avoid making them. The treatment and application of this information may determine just how quickly or how completely you may be able to transfer assets into de-controlled or disconnected corporations, family limited partnerships, or other estate planning structures.

Part of your overall plan may be to protect your estate from possible future creditors while ensuring that taxes are minimized. For those living in highly litigious jurisdictions, namely the United States and its territories, protection from predatory litigation will likely be your highest priority. But regardless of why you have decided to move assets, the laws related to fraudulent transfers should be carefully considered before proceeding.

Laws have been around for centuries that provide protection for those who are forward thinking and avail themselves of mechanisms that legally protect an estate for heirs. For example, in 1998 I attended a lecture in Puerto Rico where a British solicitor presented a workshop on English trust law wherein he set forth a series of 800-year-old precedents. The concepts for moving assets to a safe haven are as old as commerce.

There are laws and legal precedents that have serious consequences for those who transfer assets in an effort to defraud creditors. Fraudulent conveyance laws are generally created to protect creditors from debtors who attempt to hide assets to which a creditor might turn for satisfaction of an outstanding but unpaid obligation.

In many jurisdictions a creditor pursuing a legal claim must first initiate and then win a lawsuit against the debtor before going after assets to satisfy a judgment. However, in some cases after receipt of an enforceable judgment, a creditor may find that the debtor has previously transferred assets. In theory, this transfer may now hinder, delay, or preclude the creditor from satisfying their judgment. The creditor's approach might be to go back to court in an attempt to take advantage of various remedies under the fraudulent conveyance statutes.

If a judgment creditor is able to prove to the Court that a debtor's transfer was fraudulent, the creditor may attach or levy directly upon the property or the assets in the hands of the grantee of the debtor. As an alternative, the creditor may endeavor to have the Court void a given transfer rather than proceed against the grantee. The latter is the way counsel might traditionally proceed against a debtor's assets on behalf of their client.

Fraudulent conveyance statutes provide for provisional remedies to protect creditors' rights, who have not reduced their claim to a civil judgment. Likewise, a potential claimant who does not know the extent of their damages or who merely has a potential conditional claim may legally benefit from these provisions.

When a creditor or claimant discovers or believes that you might have transferred assets in a way that will hinder, delay, or frustrate the collection in satisfaction of a judgment, that creditor may among other remedies, ask the court for provisional relief that includes injunctive relief, restraining orders, attachments, and third party receivership for the assets in dispute.

Intent May Not Be Necessary

There are many circumstances where the unlawful actual intent to defraud is not apparent, may not be easily provable, or is, in fact, not present. There are instances where a debtor may simply gift an asset to a relative, a friend or a person in need for purely charitable purposes. Under the most recent economic times, situations have arisen where a debtor might transfer assets for an amount below fair market value to relieve his or her immediate needs for cash. These examples may be challenged in court as fraudulent transfers without regard to the debtor's subjective or actual intent.

The Statute of Elizabeth was meant to make certain types of transfers voidable. The creditor may ask the Court to void the transfer and put the parties back in the position they were in prior to the transfer.

Statute of Elizabeth Jurisdictions

The law regarding fraudulent conveyances is considered to have begun in England in the year 1570, with the Statute 13 Elizabeth, c.5, referred to as the "Statute of Elizabeth." This statute provided:

- For the avoiding and abolishing of feigned, conveyor and fraudulent gifts, grants, alienations (and) conveyances ... which ... are devised and contrived of malice, fraud, collusion, or guile to the end purpose and intent, to delay, hinder or defraud creditors...
- Provided that this Act ... shall not extend to any interest ... conveyance ... upon good consideration and bona fide law fully conveyed or assured to any person...not having at the time of such conveyance or assurances to them made, any manner of notice or knowledge of such, fraud, or collision...

However, early on, the Courts allowed a creditor to proceed directly against the transferred property.

An example of a court's use of the Statute of Elizabeth drawn from a 1980's case in Nova Scotia, Canada which begins with Justice Hallett setting out the often quoted threefold test necessary to set aside a conveyance:

1. The conveyance was without valuable consideration. It may not be sufficient if the plaintiff proves only that the consideration was somewhat inadequate ...The consideration must be 'good consideration'; so-called meritorious consideration, that is, love and affection, is not valuable consideration and therefore not consideration within the meaning of the *Statute of Elizabeth* ...
2. The grantor had the intention to delay or defeat his creditors. It is not necessary that the creditor exist at the time of the conveyance ... However, the court will impute the intention if the creditors exist at the time of the conveyance provided the conveyance is without consideration and denudes the grantor debtor of substantially all his property that would otherwise be available to satisfy the debt ... Apart from that situation, intention to delay or defeat creditors is a question of fact. The court must look at all the circumstances surrounding the conveyance. The court is entitled to draw reasonable inference from the proven facts to ascertain the intention of the grantor in making the conveyance. Suspicious circumstances surrounding the conveyance require an explanation by the grantor.
3. That the conveyance had the effect of delaying or defeating the creditors. This too is a question of fact. The plaintiff must first obtain a judgment against the debtor prior to commencement of proceedings to set aside the conveyance under the *Statute of Elizabeth* and must on the application to set aside adduce sufficient evidence to enable the court to make a finding that the conveyance had the effect of delaying or defeating the creditors."

Jurisdictions that have not adopted a Uniform Fraudulent Conveyances Act, the Statute of Elizabeth, or its derivative, are few. Regardless of your home country chances are good that either the Statute of Elizabeth, or some derivative thereof, is the active fraudulent transfer legislation. The statute states clearly that any conveyance made with the intent to "hinder, delay, or defraud creditors" is prohibited.

The language of these statutes suggests a debtor's actual intent must be affirmatively proven. Despite the actual language of the statute, Courts have developed case law supporting areas of constructive fraud, which have been labeled Badges of Fraud. A creditor uses these in proving the debtor's actual intent to defraud.

U.S. courts have recognized that fraud may be established without actual intent to defraud. For example, a debtor who makes an outright gift or sells at below market price to a relative and by doing so does not have enough assets to satisfy debt is in jeopardy. This kind of conveyance would almost assuredly be presumed to be with the intent to defraud even though the debtor had no real intentions of doing so. In some jurisdictions if a debtor retains use or control of transferred property, a transfer is presumed fraudulent.

Other jurisdictions require proof of actual fraudulent intent, even if under case law the "Badges of Fraud" may be used to prove the intent to defraud. (Badges of Fraud are reviewed later in this chapter.)

Under traditional statutes, a creditor may ignore the transfer and go directly after the transferred asset in the hands of the transferee. In order to do this, the creditor must be absolutely sure the transfer was a fraudulent conveyance. If the creditor is incorrect, he or she may face a lawsuit from the transferee. More typically, a creditor will have the Court avoid the transfer and then levy upon the asset.

Uniform Fraudulent Conveyance

In the late 1920's, the Uniform Fraudulent Conveyances Act (UFCA) was drafted and circulated among the U.S. states for adoption. Approximately one half of the jurisdictions in the United States have adopted the Uniform Fraudulent Conveyances Act. These include: Arizona, California, Delaware, Idaho, Maryland, Massachusetts, Michigan, Minnesota, Montana, Nevada, New Hampshire, New Mexico, New York, North Dakota, Ohio, Oklahoma, Pennsylvania, South Dakota, Tennessee, Utah, the United States Virgin Islands, Washington, Wisconsin, and Wyoming.

In thee above states the Uniform Fraudulent Conveyances Act is the primary statutory law on fraudulent conveyances. In 1984, there was a new draft promulgated called the Uniform Fraudulent Transfer Act (UFTA). It was intended to repeal and replace the Uniform Fraudulent Conveyances Act.

However, only a few states have adopted this new draft, namely Hawaii, North Dakota and Oregon. Due to the prevailing use of the Uniform Fraudulent Conveyances Act over the UFTA, and its similarity to legislation enacted in other countries of like manner, the discussion that follows will reference the Uniform Fraudulent Conveyances Act, rather than the UFTA. In most cases the outcome will be the same under either statute.

There are two principal sections of the Uniform Fraudulent Conveyances Act that enable creditors to avoid fraudulent conveyances; (1) avoiding transfers due to actual fraud, and (2) avoiding transfers based on what is called "constructive fraud." This approach is consistent with similar legislation around the globe.

Intent

Actual intent fraudulent conveyances are instances in which a creditor has clear proof demonstrating the debtor consciously intended to hinder, delay, or defraud their creditor. Section 7 of the Uniform Fraudulent Conveyance Act addresses actual or intentional fraud in pertinent part as follows:

"Every conveyance made and every obligation incurred with the actual intent, as distinguished from intent presumed in law to hinder, delay or defraud either present or future creditors, is fraudulent as to both present and future creditors."

The Uniform Fraudulent Conveyances Act uses language already set forth under the Statute of Elizabeth. Both require actual intent. It is pertinent that present and future creditors may avoid a transfer as fraudulent under Section 7.

Therefore, if a transfer is made with the intent to defraud someone who is not yet a true creditor, that transfer is still deemed fraudulent. This has been taken further under case law, Masomi Sasaki v. Yana Kai, 56 C.C. 2nd 406, and its progeny, wherein there seems to be precedent for those who become creditors after a transfer, not needing to demonstrate the debtor specifically intended to defraud subsequent creditors or to defraud a particular subsequent creditor, i.e. An actual intent to defraud either a present or future creditor, will give rights under this statute to both.

Evidence of actual intent is rarely readily available to creditors. Difficult or nearly impossible to produce, creditors must rely instead on the "circumstantial evidence" of fraud that developed under the Statute of Elizabeth and frequently referred to as the Badges of Fraud. These are incidental or collateral circumstances that usually accompany a fraudulent transfer, such as an uncharacteristic transfer of assets, transfers to relatives for less than fair market value, unreasonable or insufficient transfer consideration, or transfers still leaving the transferor in possession or control, etc.

Badges of Fraud are not conclusive evidence, but are often considered by the courts to be "circumstantial evidence" of fraud.

Badges of Fraud

1. Insolvency by the transfer.
2. Lack or inadequacy of consideration.
3. Family, friendship, or other close "insider" relationship among the parties.
4. The retention of possession, benefit, or use of the property in question.
5. The existence or threat of litigation.
6. The financial condition of the debtor both before and after the transfer.
7. The existence or cumulative effect of a pattern of transactions or a course of conduct after the onset of financial difficulties.
8. The general chronology of events.
9. The secrecy of the transaction in question.
10. Deviation from the usual method or course of business.

Constructive Fraud

1. A transfer of most or all of a debtor's assets, leaving the transferor with nothing to their name, has been held as a sign of fraudulent intent.
2. Transfers where the transferor has retained possession in the absence of any commercial or business purpose.
3. Transfers for unreasonably low consideration or purport to be more than what the asset is worth.
4. Some courts have held transfer documents that contain the very language "this is a legitimate transaction" would only do so if it were done in contemplation of fraud.
5. The Uniform Fraudulent Conveyances Act has set forth factors under Section 4(b), which should be given consideration in determining whether actual fraud exists. Under current law the factors in Uniform Fraudulent Conveyances Act Section 4(b) are the types of acts considered to be Badges of Fraud.
6. Section 4(b) of the Uniform Fraudulent Conveyances Act reads in pertinent part as follows:

In determining the actual intent under subsection (a)(1), consideration may be given, among other factors, to the fact that:
1. the relationship between the transferor and the transferee was a close one;
2. the transferor retained possession or dominion after the transfer;
3. the transfer was concealed;
4. prior to the transfer a creditor had sued, or was threatening to sue the transferor;
5. the transfer was of substantially all the debtor's assets;

6. the debtor has absconded or has removed or has changed the form of the assets remaining in his possession so as to make the assets less subject to creditor process;

7. the value of the consideration received by the debtor was not reasonably the equivalent to the value of the assets transferred or the amount of the obligation incurred;

8. the debtor was insolvent or heavily in debt or reasonably should have expected to become so indebted;

9. the transfer occurred shortly before or after a substantial debt was incurred.

Proof of the existence of any one of the factors listed above does not in itself constitute prima facie proof that the debtor has made a fraudulent transfer or incurred a fraudulent obligation.

As can be easily seen, these represent "circumstantial evidence," or "badges" of a fraudulent intent. They are not conclusive, nor does any one or combination mean there is actual fraud. It does however; give the Court, and the creditor's attorney, a rational to attempt to convince the Court that the transfers were fraudulent, rather than a family, commercial, or business transaction.

It is generally difficult to prove actual fraud. There is rarely a "smoking gun" type of evidence, and the Badges of Fraud require an extreme amount of research on the part of the creditor. Due to this difficulty, the law has allowed several methods of establishing fraud without any actual intent to defraud. Therefore, the law can determine a transfer was fraudulent irrespective of the actual intent of the transferor.

The Uniform Fraudulent Conveyances Act at Section 4 also contains the principal provisions regarding "constructive fraud."

Section 4 reads in pertinent part as follows:

"Every conveyance made and every obligation incurred by a person who is or will be thereby rendered insolvent is fraudulent as to creditors without regard to his actual intent, if the conveyance is made or the obligation is incurred without a fair consideration."

The legal theory behind the idea of "constructive fraud," or allowing a transfer to be deemed fraudulent irrespective the proven intent of the transferor, is someone who knows they have no money, has or will be incurring new debt, yet transfers assets out of their ownership, "should" know the transferred asset is the only thing of value the creditor would be able to attach if the debt, was not paid. Since the transferor "should" have known that result of their action, the law therefore will deem the transfer was a constructive fraud.

An Example

The law would probably deem as fraudulent, the gifts or transfers of property of an insolvent person to their child, while not receiving any or adequate consideration in exchange. Therefore, if a debtor transfers away property without receiving a reasonably adequate commercial exchange in return, it would be determined that it is so prejudicial to the creditor, who under equitable law owns the property. The law will avoid the transfer in order to give the creditor a remedy, irrespective of the actual intent or thoughtfulness of the debtor.

The Uniform Fraudulent Conveyances Act presents three "presumed-in-law or "constructive fraud" transfers. All three address a person who is insolvent, will soon become insolvent due to the transfer of the extent of the transfer, or is near insolvent, while not receiving reasonable or adequate consideration for the asset transferred.

The three categories of constructive fraudulent transfers under the Uniform Fraudulent Conveyances Act are:

1. Transfers by an insolvent for less than fair consideration, or for less than a reasonably equivalent exchange.
2. Transfers for less than fair consideration by a businessperson without retaining sufficient capital to meet the likely future needs of that business.
3. Transfers for less than fair consideration by anyone, businessperson or consumer, without retaining enough property to meet his likely future debts as they become due.

The majority of litigation by creditors or by a bankruptcy trustee regarding fraudulent transfer involves one of these three "presumed-in-law" or "constructive fraud" premises for the transfers similar to as set forth in the above court excerpt from Nova Scotia.

Fair Consideration

The law regarding Constructive Fraudulent transfers determines the standard of fair consideration or reasonably equivalent exchange. Under this standard however, the transferor need not receive the exact market value of the property. The law usually allows for something less than fair market value. The law has allowed a certain amount of flexibility due to actual market conditions. People often sell property for less than fair market value, due to the necessity of quick cash, or because they have incorrectly valued the property, or have sold to a buyer who has out negotiated them. Due to these realities of a free-market society, the standard is still a debatable point.

Under several notable Court cases, the bench mark for "fair consideration or reasonably equivalent exchange" has been determined to be at least 70% or more of the fair market value, the Court is likely to determine that fair consideration was not had and would rule a constructive fraud had taken place.

This 70% rule is merely a guideline. There are instances that may make it "reasonable," under specific circumstances, to sell a property for less than the 70%, and the Courts have so held.

Affirmative Defenses

Both the Uniform Fraudulent Conveyances Act and the Federal Bankruptcy Code provide a defense for good faith transferees who give value.

The Bankruptcy Code at Section 548 (c) provides as follows:

"Except to the extent that a transfer or obligation voidable under this section is voidable under Sections 544, 545, or 547 of this title, a transferee or obligee of such a transfer or obligation that takes place for value and in good faith has a lien on or may retain any interest transferred or may enforce any obligation incurred, as the case may be, to the extent that such transferee or obligee gave value to the debtor in exchange for such transfer or obligation."

The Uniform Fraudulent Conveyances Act considers a conveyance made for "fair consideration" when either (1) in exchange for the debtor's conveyance, "as a fair equivalent therefore, and in good faith, property is conveyed or an antecedent debt is satisfied" or (2) the debtor's conveyance is received in good faith to secure a present advance or antecedent debt in amount not disproportionately small as compared with the value of the property, or obligations obtained.

Good Faith Buyer

To successfully avoid a transfer as fraudulent and obtain the transferred asset to satisfy their judgment, a creditor must prove the debtor's fraudulent intent (whether actual or constructive), and the transferees, the person acquiring the asset purchased in "bad faith," attempt to avoid their obligations to their creditor.

Under the Uniform Fraudulent Conveyances Act at Section 9, a person acquiring an asset, has total protection under the law if they acted in good faith and pay reasonable or equivalent value. If the debtor had actual fraud as the bases for the transfer and it was easily proven, the creditor or the bankruptcy trustee will not be able to avoid or take the transferred asset from the person who has purchased in "good faith." They would be protected from attack.

The Uniform Fraudulent Conveyances Act at Section 9, requires the "good faith purchaser" to meet the following three requirements:

1. He or she takes the property in good faith.

2. He or she takes the property without knowledge of the fraud that the creditor is seeking to perpetrate.
3. He or she is given fair consideration – that is, a reasonable equivalent exchange for the property received.

If any of the above three elements in the test of the bona fide purchaser is not met, they will not have the protection of the Uniform Fraudulent Conveyances Act. Under this rule a person purchasing for fair market value, having knowledge the transfer of the asset would delay, hinder, frustrate or preclude a creditor of the transferor, then the transferee will not be deemed a good faith or "bona fide" purchaser. The transferred asset would be attachable by the creditor or bankruptcy trustee.

Inadequate Consideration

What if the opposite of the above situation exists, where the person acquiring the asset does so in total good faith and with no knowledge of any creditors? They negotiate paying significantly less that the fair market value, even below the 70% test mark. The principal cases in this area show the law requires the asset to be delivered to the creditor. It is only delivered pursuant to a lien in the purchaser's favor in the amount of the actual consideration the purchaser gave for the asset. This is not fair market value or its replacement value. In essence, the law will protect the purchaser's out of pocket expense of the purchase. The Courts consider total protection of one who negotiates to the exclusion of a creditor's rights would be too unfair. Therefore, at the sale of the property for fair market value, the Courts would deliver the purchase amount to the transferee. The remainder would go toward satisfying the creditor's judgment.

Issues Checklist

1. Act when your "legal seas are calm." Whether or not a transfer was in contemplation of a creditor's claim against you is the main focus of a fraudulent transfer claim. It is therefore paramount to "judgment proof" your assets in advance of legal or financial difficulties.

2. If possible, avoid dealing with close family members, as such transactions are naturally vulnerable to attack. Transfers to trusted advisors or business associates are less likely to be challenged.

3. Maintain paper trails to support your transaction. As you know with corporations, to keep that entity legally formed the "formalities" must be maintained. This habit should be kept up in all your asset structures. In areas subject to an inquiry it is wise to have supporting documentation, showing capitalization or consideration exchanges.

4. If you owe monies to a friend or relative, have the debt formalized in writing or a promissory note. No matter how bonafide the transaction, reconstruction is difficult and time consuming, with pertinent facts being forgotten.

5. To gain maximum protection in forming asset protect structures, have reasons other than asset protection for the transaction. If the asset protection structure is being set up at the same time as the rest of your estate plan, it is estate planning. If it is being set up when you start to do investing overseas, it is global positioning for better access to your investments. If gifts are made to relatives at special occasions the gift is for other reasons than merely sheltering assets. Timing is important.

6. Seek advice from professional counselors. Advice from your attorney to transfer your assets to your spouse for estate planning purposes or for tax purposes can help negate the inference of fraudulent intent on your part.

7. Numerous transfers are less likely to be challenged. The Courts are less likely to overturn transfers of different assets, to different persons, that are made at different times, for different reasons. Likewise, regular or consistent transfers will support the most recent transfer as normal and not intended to defraud the recent creditor.

8. Never attempt to conceal assets from known creditors or while in a bankruptcy proceeding. Such activity is dealt with harshly and may "unravel," what you have done prior to such activity, and had done legally. There is a subtle, yet distinct difference between lawful asset protection and privacy, and unlawful asset conceal- ment. Follow your attorney's advice to be able to defend the actions you take.

9. State statutes of limitations for fraudulent conveyances are usually from three to six years. In Federal bankruptcy Court, the Court's trustee is limited under Section 548 of the Bankruptcy Code from setting aside transfers "made or incurred on or within one year" from filing the bankruptcy petition. The trustee does have the option of proceeding under State law to gain the benefit of a longer statute of limitation.

10. Don't wait. Even if your legal circumstances are not as calm as you might like, you can do some planning and asset transfers. And,

although a legal structure put in place now may not protect you entirely from a potential creditor you are faced with currently, getting started could protect you against future and yet unknown creditors.

11. Do not rely on the "economic sense" of your creditor. Creditors generally pursue cost-effective means of collecting debts, which is good from an asset protection perspective. However, it would be unwise to believe that a fraudulent transfer will protect your assets simply because it will not make economic sense for your creditor to continue. Whereas it is true that to pursue this type of claim is typically expensive and time consuming, the penalties of fraudulent conveyance are a risk you should not be willing to take.

SECTION III

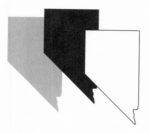

The Hows

Asset Protection: Analysis of a Strategy
Case Studies & Tax Reduction
Taking Money Out of Your Corporation
Taxation and Multiple Corporations
Alternative Considerations

ASSET PROTECTION: ANALYSIS OF A STRATEGY

*"If you want to be successful, find someone who has achieved
the results you want and copy what they do and you'll achieve
the same results."*

Anthony Robbins

A Sad Tale

Jack was a Veteran who served in the armed forces during the Second World War. He served in the European theater, and was wounded shortly after the D-day landings. His wounds were so severe that he had to have his right leg amputated, and spent many months in a hospital before he could return home. When he arrived his family and friends were horrified at his appearance, not only had he lost his leg, his face and hands had been disfigured with burns caused by an explosion.

That wasn't really the worst of it, because once they got over his changed appearance, they realized that his personality had changed as well. The innocent boy who had enlisted to save the world from tyranny had been exposed to the horrors of war in a very real and personal way. Not only would he require dozens of surgeries, but for years he would wake up at night in a cold sweat screaming as he dreamed of the horrors about which he couldn't speak. Jack spent years in a darkness that nobody around him could quite understand. There was one thing about Jack, however, that was becoming the center of his personality, as he healed from his psychological wounds. He was the proudest veteran you have ever seen. He was proud of his service, proud of his contribution, and proud to be an American.

In the early 1950's, he realized that his life was wasting away, and he took what little cash he had and decided to go into business. It would have been much easier for Jack to have simply gotten a job, but what could a disabled Veteran do? There was no Americans With Disabilities Act in the 1950's. And to top off his disability, his appearance made him undesirable to most employers. So, Jack went into the distribution business. He started small at first, working in his parents' garage, but he was utterly determined to succeed. After a couple of years, he was able to go out and rent a small warehouse and hire an employee.

As the years went by, Jack made a success of himself. His business grew larger, and everyone marveled at his success in spite of all of the odds being against him. Jack remained the proudest Vet you could imagine, and he always said that one day, he would have a facility where he could fly a huge American flag to show his pride. By the 1980's, Jack got his wish. His business had grown to the point where he could afford to install a huge flagpole out front by the main street, and the flag was flown with pride. On a spring day in 1990, Jack, who was about to retire, noticed that a sudden storm was brewing. He asked a couple of his workers to take the flag down before the rain started. As they were doing so, the wind whipped up. They struggled with the flag in the sudden strong wind. A passing motorist saw their predicament and stopped to help. As the motorist was holding one end of the huge flag, a sudden gust caught the flag and violently ripped into it, throwing the motorist into the air. He landed a few feet away on his back. He was immediately in pain, and Jack called an ambulance.

Jack contacted the man, and filed an insurance claim. No problem, insurance would cover all of the man's bills. Unfortunately for Jack, however, the man's friends convinced him that he should contact an attorney, just to make sure that he was protected. The attorney convinced the man that Jack had been negligent, because he should have known that flying a very large flag would be dangerous. Jack, and other zealots like him, need to be taught that they cannot fly large flags. It is a threat to those around them.

In the inevitable lawsuit, the man who stopped to help take down the flag claimed not only his doctor bill, which amounted to a few hundred dollars that Jack's insurance had offered to pay, he claimed five million dollars in punitive damages, to teach Jack a lesson. Everybody told Jack that since this claim was ridiculous, he had nothing to worry about, but "everybody" wasn't on the Jury. This was in the post Vietnam era when many people held serious anti-American sentiments and couldn't understand why anyone would fly a flag to begin with. The jury awarded the full amount. Jack was utterly heartbroken. Nevertheless, he should be protected; after all he did have a ten million dollar umbrella policy.

It was only a few days later when Jack got the biggest shock of all. His insurance covered the few hundred dollars of the claimants doctor bills all right. But the five million was punitive damages. His insurance excluded punitive damages. He lost his business, he lost his retirement, and on the day they auctioned off his house and furnishings, Jack put a bullet through his head.

This story would be sad enough if it was only fiction, but it isn't fiction. It's all too true, and stories just like it are all too common. In the words of former President Clinton: "It makes you proud to be an American, doesn't it?"

The Legal Reality

Its no wonder that more and more people are taking steps to protect their assets. But, what can we really do to protect ourselves from run-away juries, predator lawyers, and a sometimes misdirected government agency? What exactly is asset protection? Is it legal? Is it moral?

To begin with, let's look at what asset protection truly means. Asset protection is the lawful process by which a person or entity makes its (or their) assets difficult for a creditor to attach. Often, this involves setting up roadblocks to discourage people from wanting to attack. The idea here is to take steps to reduce your vulnerability and make you less of a target. Let's face it; there are those of the general public that believe business people are all rich and ruthless individuals, those who gain obscene profits by cheating ordinary people.

Frankly its no wonder some have arrived at this conclusion if they've ever attended classes taught by extremist professors who've never worked outside the protected environment of the campus, or they've read much of the yellow journalism presented to us as facts in the news media. So a litigant's reasoning might go something like this: everybody knows that business people are evil, cheating no goods, right? If someone has more than someone else, it's not fair, right? The reasoning proceeds in this vein and pretty soon they've convinced themselves that they are on a holy mission by simply separating you from your net worth. But, perhaps the largest problem of all is that jurists tend to be government employees, teachers, and the unemployed. They may be wonderful individuals but they simply do not understand what it means to be in business for yourself. Studies have demonstrated time and again that those who are consumed with busy schedules request exemption from jury duty and are almost always granted their request. In other words, only rarely are there business owners or accomplished professionals on a jury to provide some balance. So…simply by being in business, you become a target and the deck is stacked against you.

It's one thing to be a perceived target, but quite another to be a target in actuality. Consider what happens when someone goes into an attorney's office to discuss a typical suit. Take Jill, who was involved in an auto accident. Her car was damaged, she was a little shaken up, and sore the next day. At the urging of her boyfriend, she called an attorney they had seen advertised on TV, and soon had an appointment. What had caught her boyfriend's attention was that the ad said that there was no charge for the initial consultation, and that if a case had merit, you could go to court at no charge at all.

When Jill went to see the attorney three days after the accident, he asked her some questions about what had happened, and made a copy of the accident report. Then he told Jill that he would look into the merits of the case, and get back with her in a week. At her next appointment, Jill was thrilled to hear the attorney thought that she really had a great case. The other motorist had seriously erred, and Jill's chances of recovery were very promising. In fact, Jill was told that she had been damaged way more than she had realized at first. The attorney was so nice, he even suggested that she see a Chiropractor to make sure everything was all right, and lo and behold, the nice man the attorney referred her to found that she had sustained a potentially serious neck injury that would have to be treated immediately to prevent lasting complications.

Jill's boyfriend was delighted that he had suggested this attorney, because he had earned major points. Jill was thrilled, because she certainly didn't need a lasting injury, and she didn't need to come up with any money for either the attorney or the doctor, and could expect to receive a tidy little sum for herself, after all was said and done.

On the other side of this case, Claire realized that she shouldn't have changed lanes when she did. She hadn't seen Jill's car though, she really hadn't. That night, she and her husband had talked it all over, and she felt much better. This, after all, is what insurance is for, right? They would take care of everything. Her agent had said so. Claire had almost forgotten the whole thing when one day her assistant told her that there was someone in the outer office who had something for her. It was Jill's lawsuit. Jill was suing for a quarter of a million dollars! How could this be? That was even more than her insurance limit. She could loose her house and her business. What had happened, Jill's car didn't have more that a couple of thousand dollars in damage, and Jill wasn't hurt...

A Lawsuit's Merit

Here's the part that neither Claire nor Jill knew. After Jill had left the attorney's office, the attorney contacted an asset search company. The asset search people had run a routine check on Claire, and found out that she had a home, a business, and signed on several bank accounts, and that she was worth about a quarter million dollars. When Jill's attorney received the report, he realized that the case had "merit" and was ready to take it on a contingency fee basis, meaning that Jill needed to put up no money, and the attorney would keep a substantial percentage of the collected amounts from the judgment after court. Of course, he would also deduct the costs incurred, including those of the Chiropractor. Jill would receive the rest. Even though Claire's insurance only covered fifty thousand dollars, Jill and her attorney could proceed with a larger suit, because there was money to collect from Claire.

Let's take another look at this case. Suppose Jill's attorney had discovered in the asset search that Claire had nothing unencumbered or available to take. She had no home, no business, no bank accounts, and nothing else, except for her insurance. How much "merit" would the case have had then? Enough for the attorney to take it on a contingency? Hardly. An insurance settlement would have looked much better at that point. In the first instance, Claire was a target. In the second, Claire was not an attractive target. Asset protection is all about being a poor target for law-suits.

What Asset Protection Is Not

Before we continue, let's take a moment to discuss what asset protection is not. Asset protection is not about defrauding people. It is not about skipping out on your bills or other obligations. It is not about cheating, and it is not about taxes. Any ethical business person realizes that he or she must pay their bills, fulfill their other obligations, and pay their taxes. If an ethical person or business damages someone, then they will not only need to compensate the damaged party, but they should also want to do so. Integrity demands it. Decency demands it. If you are someone who takes pride in accomplishment and doing your best, you will have no problem with this concept. This is precisely what insurance policies are all about, compensating people who are damaged and making them whole again.

Sadly, there are not only people in this world who wish to get away without taking care of their obligations, there are also people who desire to profit inappropriately from a claim. They see opportunity in filing claims, in claiming damage that was not incurred, and telling lies in court. They file frivolous lawsuits because they realize that someone will settle, because it's less expensive than fighting. They prey on the unsuspecting, or on those who have something to lose. Such people have plenty of help. Attorneys sometimes wonder why their profession is held in such low regard, yet those who have been the victims of unscrupulous lawyers who make fortunes abusing the legal system know full well why they these feelings are pervasive and powerfully felt.

The Morality Issue

Of course, politics enters the scene, as it always does when money is involved. Trial lawyers make billions in encouraging such claims. They are huge contributors to political campaigns, and have influence well in excess of their numbers in the legislative halls of America. Tort reform never seems o get out of committee time and again, and for those of us who are targets, there is no relief in sight. So who is immoral, the person who seeks to protect what he or she has worked so hard to develop, or the one who seeks to take it away with a frivolous claim? You be the judge. Who is unethical, the one who seeks to limit liability, or the one who adds millions in punitive damage claims to a small injury? Again, you be the judge. Who is in the wrong, the one who seeks to protect his or her livelihood, or the unscrupulous attorney who seeks to enrich himself by inflicting ruin on other people?

The whole concept of asset protection is to level the playing field when liability claims arise. The playing field needs to be leveled, because there are no contingency fees for defendants. There is also no "loser pays" style of system in the United States, like there is in all of the other industrialized nations. In other words, if someone sues and loses, they should pay the legal costs for your defense. Why isn't this the case in America? Because trial lawyers would loose money as there would be considerably fewer lawsuits. That's why trial lawyers are so aggressive in the political arena; they are simply promoting more opportunities for litigation. What happens if you are sued, anyway?

A Quick Sketch

First you contact defense counsel, who must file an answer to the complaint, usually within thirty days. Never mind the fact that the plaintiff may have taken a year to file, you must respond in a month. Your attorney isn't going to work on a contingency, because there isn't going to be a collection. Your attorney needs an upfront retainer to get started, $10,000, $20,000, and in my case once $250,000! That of course is money you must pay right now. Thereafter, each month you'll need to pay more. What if you don't have the money? That's an easy answer; you'll lose the case. What if you don't respond? You lose the case. After you initially respond, the issue may, and usually does, drag out for several years, which in turn requires you to pay out more and more money each and every month to keep your attorney on the job. What if you decide to quit paying? You loose.

Eventually a trial date is set and not postponed. More money, more agony, more worry. Then, let's say you win, and you don't lose everything to the plaintiff, you're out tens of thousands of dollars, perhaps hundreds of thousands. How much can you recover from the plaintiff? Nothing. What about your mental anguish? Can you sue? Of course not. What has the plaintiff lost? Not one cent. Who was the winner? Your lawyer. Is this justice? Yes, in America, this is justice!

Don't Be a Target

It would be difficult to imagine that anyone who reads this will not see why the playing field needs to be leveled. But how? The answer is simple. Don't be a target. The way to not be a target is also simple. Be poor! This may seem silly, but when was the last time you picked up the paper and read about a multi-million dollar judgment against a homeless person? Yet every day you can pick up a paper and read about such judgments against millionaires, and the reason is that a homeless person doesn't have anything to take. They don't have enough in the way of assets to start the wheels of justice turning against them!

The obvious problem here is that you don't want to be poor. In fact, that may be precisely why you pursued your business career or went into business in the first place. Consider this story. In the early 1990's it was widely reported that Donald Trump was experiencing financial difficulty.

Apparently he had made a killing in real estate in the 80's, but with the recession that had hit in the early 90's, the tide had turned. A reporter asked him at that time how much he was worth, and to the amazement of the reporter, Trump pointed to a homeless man across the street, and said that he was worth a hundred million less than the homeless man. Looking back on things, which one would you rather be, the homeless person, or Donald Trump? Trump lived pretty well during that time, as everyone knows. He was worth less than the homeless man because Trump was in debt. Judging from the newspaper accounts, Trump still had plenty of walking around money, though!

Think back to Jill and Claire. In the second scenario, an asset search revealed that Claire had no assets. What would happen if she had both assets and secured debt? Let's revisit the first scenario, where Claire had a house, a business and bank accounts. Suppose that an asset search revealed a house mortgaged to the hilt, and business mortgaged to the hilt, and bank accounts with first position liens filed against them. Jill's attorney would have looked at the report, and found no "merit" to the case because there was nothing to collect, because the existing creditors would have to be paid from Claire's assets before Jill and her attorney could see a dime, and if Claire was mortgaged to the extent of wiping out her equity there would be nothing left. Yet Claire would still have the house, business and accounts. In fact, Claire would be just like Donald Trump, only with smaller numbers. This is an example of leveling the playing field. Poor Jill would have to "settle" for being compensated for the damages she really had incurred, and wouldn't have had the opportunity to make a profit from an accident. That is one form of asset protection.

Incorporating for Asset Protection

Incorporating a business is another form of asset protection, because by incorporating, you place a non-person in the line of fire. Remember Jack? He had a very serious problem because someone sued his business and obtained a life ruining judgment against him. Could his situation have been different? Consider what may have happened had Jack been incorporated. The plaintiff's suit would most likely have been against the business, and not against Jack personally, as a sole proprietor. The judgment would not have reached Jack's personal assets in that case, and although the situation would still have been very bad, at least Jack would not have lost his home and all of his personal assets.

Corporations can provide additional benefits and protection as well. To see this more completely, you need to understand that a corporation is not only an artificial person, but is very much like a citizen. No, it can't vote. But it can do just about everything else. In fact, a corporation is a citizen of the state in which it is incorporated. Thus, a corporation that is incorporated in the state of Wisconsin is a citizen of the state of Wisconsin.

If it travels to Minnesota, it is a visitor there, and if it decides to conduct its business in Minnesota, it must follow the laws of Minnesota while it is there, but it can return to Wisconsin at any time, and deal with Minnesota no further.

If you think about it, this is really no different that you as a natural person, being a citizen of the nation in which you were born. If you were born in the United States, then you are a citizen of the United States. If you travel to Morocco, you must follow the laws of Morocco while you are there, yet when you return to America, your connection with Morocco is over. During the time you are in Morocco, you still retain your US citizenship, and have all of the rights and privileges of US citizenship, and the same is true of a corporation.

If a corporation is formed in Nevada, and it travels to another state, it is still a Nevada corporation with all of the rights and privileges associated with it. There are some terms associated with this, which will be helpful for you to become familiar with. A corporation is a "domestic corporation" in the state in which it is incorporated, a "foreign corporation" in a state other than the state in which it was incorporated, and a corporation formed in another country is called an "offshore corporation".

Since corporations retain their citizenship when they travel, and state laws regarding corporations vary, it stands to reason the laws in some states are more favorable for corporations than laws in other states. These states are called "preferred" states. Preferred states can offer many advantages for businesses, low taxes, enhanced privacy, less red tape, and more.

Poverty, The Road to Asset Protection

As we briefly saw in the case of Jill and Claire, "poverty" can be significant asset protection technique, at least on the surface. If Claire had no assets to take away, Jill had little incentive to proceed with a lawsuit. If Jill were to proceed anyway, she could make Claire's life somewhat miserable, but she would not be able to recover anything if Claire didn't have it to take. But how is this helpful, after all, isn't the whole point of being in business to accumulate assets and net worth?

Let's look at another example. Sean wanted to go into business, so he did some research and discovered that he could open a small retail store in his hometown. He got all of his cash together, formed a corporation, and rented some space in a small strip mall. He realized that he was running low on cash, so he went to the bank to get a loan. His banker agreed to make a loan of $50,000 to Sean's corporation, if Sean would personally guarantee the note. Of course, Sean was only too happy to do so, so everything was fine. Sean got his money, bought display shelves and inventory, and opened for business. The bank took all of Sean's fixtures and inventory for collateral to secure the loan, and filed a UCC-1 Financing Statement against the assets. So far, so good.

Everything went along just fine for about six months. Sean's store was reasonably successful, and Sean was very pleased. One day, Chris came in to the store, but slipped and fell. As would be expected, Chris sought out an attorney to file a lawsuit. The attorney discovered that there wasn't much "merit" to the case, because the bank was first in line for Sean's assets, because of the loan, and the UCC filing. With the bank already in line as a secured creditor against all of the assets of the store, what could Chris take? What could Chris' attorney use to ensure payment of a contingency fee? Nothing, because the bank would have to be paid in full before anybody else could receive a cent from Sean's assets, and there just weren't enough assets to go around.

Being Judgment Proof

Business people refer to this situation as being "judgment proof". Sean was judgment proof for any creditor other than the bank. The bank was still in a good position to be paid, though, but as long as Sean made his payments to the bank, he had little to worry about. In a situation such as this, Chris would probably need to seek relief from Sean's insurance. Chris is compensated for the injury sustained in the fall, Sean stays in business, and everyone is as happy as can be. The only flaw in the situation has already been identified, and that is the need for Sean to make the monthly payments. If Sean doesn't, the bank takes everything, and the ballgame is over for Sean's business.

What makes this concept work, is not just the fact that the bank made a loan to Sean, and it's not just that the bank has collateral. What makes this work is that the bank filed a UCC-1 Financing Statement. By doing so, the bank has "priority of lien" over any subsequent claims. Priority of lien means that the bank must be paid in full before any other creditors who come along after the bank's UCC-1. Priority is not a new concept. It is what happens whenever you finance a house and the finance company requires a mortgage or deed of trust on the property. By recording this instrument, the bank or finance company puts the world on notice that they have a collateral interest in the property. The result is that anyone can find out about the interest, and if anyone wants to lend you money against that house, they will know that they are in line after the bank or finance company. The same holds true for a judgment. The judgment creditor would be in second position behind your lender, and can't be paid until the lender is paid in full.

There can be any number of people in line, but the rule is that the first one to file, is the first one paid, the second to file is the second paid, and so on. It is for this reason that interest rates are typically higher for second and third mortgages than they are for first mortgages. If the property were ever auctioned off to pay debts, it will be more and more difficult for lenders to recover their money the farther down the list they are.

A potential plaintiff would be well advised to know where they might find themselves in line before they get a judgment, if they are really sure that they want to be paid.

The UCC-1 Concept

Notice that in this example, Sean's bank filed a UCC-1 financing statement, rather than a mortgage or deed of trust. This is because Sean's business had "personal property" and not real estate. There are two types of property, real property (real estate) and personal property. Personal property is everything that is not real estate. This would include inventory, furniture, art, jewelry, cash, account's receivable and so on. When dealing with real estate, a lender will file either a mortgage or a deed of trust, depending on the state where the property is located. When dealing with personal property, you file a UCC-1 financing statement. If this is new to you, you can think of a UCC-1 as a mortgage for personal property.

When the mortgage, deed of trust, and/or UCC-1 is filed, we would say that the creditor has "perfected" his security interest in the assets of the debtor. Perfecting a security interest is what establishes priority of lien, and is a critical step to take if someone wants to have that place in line secure. Even though a lender may have a valid promissory note, and a security agreement, which describes the collateral for the repayment of the note, if his security interest is not perfected, by filing the necessary document on the public record, they don't have a place in line if subsequent debts come along. This is a very crucial fact to remember as we continue our discussion!

What would happen if, instead of the bank having made the loan to Sean's business, Sean had a preferred state corporation that made the loan? First Sean's preferred state corporation negotiates with Sean's home state corporation about the loan amount and repayment terms. Next, when they agree, Sean signs a promissory note for the loan. Third, Sean's preferred state corporation wants collateral for repayment of the note, just like a bank would. Sean must sign a security agreement that sets forth the description of the collateral, and the provisions in case of a default. Then, the preferred state corporation insists that Sean sign a UCC-1 on behalf of his home state corporation. Then and only then does the lending corporation write Sean's home state corporation a check, and it files the UCC-1 in the Sean's home state.

At this point, reenter Chris. When Chris is looking to sue Sean's business, the outcome would be the same as if Sean had borrowed from the bank, because the preferred state corporation did exactly the same things that the bank did, and has the same rights that the bank had. The difference in the second situation is that if Sean had difficulty making his monthly payments, he would probably have had a much easier time dealing with his corporation than he would have in dealing with the bank!

The Strategy Summary

Let's take names out of the picture, and look at the above scenario in conceptual terms. You have a business in your home state. You incorporate that business for all of the reasons we have already covered. Let's call the home state corporation Red, Inc. Then, you establish a corporation in a preferred state; let's say in tax-free Nevada, called Warbucks Nevada, Inc. Warbucks and Red, Inc. get together and agree that Warbucks will loan money to Red, Inc. in the amount of $100,000. Red, Inc. signs a note, a security agreement and a UCC-1, which Warbucks files in Red, Inc.'s home state. Let's say that the interest on the note is 24%, because this is a difficult loan to get, and because it is at 100% loan to value. Since Nevada has no usury laws, the interest rate can be at whatever rate the parties agree.

Now that this has been accomplished, what happens if someone wants to file a suit against Red, Inc.? They find out that Red, Inc. is heavily indebted to Warbucks, and there are no assets from which to recover a judgment. The attorney isn't particularly interested in a contingency fee, and the plaintiff has to lay out real cash to get the suit moving. Once again, it is quite likely that the plaintiff will quickly decide to settle for what real damages and not bother to pursue punitive damages. But let's say that he doesn't, and goes on with a suit, and is awarded a judgment. He calls you at Red, Inc. and demands to be paid. You tell him that he can just have the whole corporation, because it is hopelessly in debt to this company in Nevada, who just called its note. Probably the next thing you will hear is a dial tone!

What if you had this structure, but there was never a lawsuit? Red, Inc. must pay interest to Warbucks on the loan it received at the rate of 24% interest. On $100,000 that would be $24,000 per year based on a simple interest calculation. If your home state has an income tax that is based on net income, the interest paid by Red, Inc. to Warbucks would be deductible in your home state, and taxable in Nevada. Since Nevada has no income tax, the interest you pay to Warbucks would reduce your state income tax, and be earned state income tax free in Nevada, allowing you to significantly reduce the income taxes you pay to your home state, as an added benefit to protecting your business assets.

The strategy herein reviewed is commonly called the "Warbucks – Red, Inc." strategy, or sometimes an interstate commerce strategy, or perhaps a multi-jurisdictional strategy, but regardless of what you call it, it really works. This type of strategy is generally able to save your assets and reduce your state income taxes as an added benefit. Yet there is one more detail to be covered here. If Warbucks is really sharp, and they must be if you are calling the shots, then what kind of note would they require from Red, Inc.?

Demand Promissory Note

There are many types of promissory notes, but one in particular is perfect for the Warbucks – Red, Inc. strategy, and that is a demand promissory note. A demand note is due upon demand of the borrower. It may have monthly, quarterly, semi-annual or annual interest payments, but the principal is not due until Warbucks says it's due. Thus, you are not building up equity, leaving assets available to other subsequent creditors. In addition, it can be called on short notice, when Red, Inc. will not be able to repay, forcing Warbucks to seize the assets. How disappointing for the judgment creditor and his greedy attorney.

The strategy outlined above is one of the most powerful business tools that exist for asset protection purposes. Yet, it must be used carefully. If you wait until a lawsuit has already been filed to get started, you will have waited too long. This is a strategy that must be established while your legal seas are calm, when there are no judgment creditors, no lawsuits in play, or none clearly on the horizon.

The law does not allow you to set up any structure that has as its purpose the obstruction, delay or hindrance of a legitimate creditor. Thus, if someone is owed by Red, Inc., they need to be paid. However, if there is no creditor, no claim, or potential claim, then Red, Inc. can do whatever it wants. If someone comes along later, then they may proceed against Red, Inc. with their eyes wide open, and take their chances. In such a case, you have effectively evened the playing field and moved to encourage your claimant to accept compensation for real and reasonable damages, and not astronomical, ridiculous and devastating judgments.

CASE STUDIES AND TAX REDUCTION

"There are numerous legal and ethical devices that can be used to protect the assets of those in every income bracket. If you have anything of material value you simply cannot afford to lose, know this, your assets are at risk in today's litigious and over taxed society and they should be protected."

Aaron Young
CEO Laughlin Int'l

Case Study #1

The Situation: An East Coast consultant named John, living in a high tax location, desired to limit his liability exposure and reduce his state income taxes. John's clients were large corporations who hired him to train their management employees in employee relations. Because of the nature of the business, John needed to update his presentation materials regularly to reflect changes in regulations and laws. His training consisted of in-house training presentations, including workbooks and videotapes. John's main concern was that he and his firm could be held liable in the event one of his trainees took an action that resulted in litigation against one of his clients. John's objective: protect his business and personal assets and lower his home state taxes.

The Strategy: Since John needed to regularly update his materials, John established a Nevada corporation to research and develop his training materials. Since he had four different training programs, John would contract with the Nevada corporation to produce those materials, one program at a time. First, his home state firm contracted for one of the training programs for the following year. The price for the production of the program was $125,000. Of this amount $25,000 was paid up front, and the balance was carried on a one year, interest only note, secured by the assets of his operating home state firm. Included in the contract were a set number of workbooks and tapes. Orders for those training materials would involve an extra charge. Next, John's firm entered into similar agreements for the production of the other three training programs, at the same price and terms for each one.

Because there would be significant additional purchases of training materials from the Nevada corporation, the Nevada corporation extended a line of credit to John's firm in the amount of $100,000. Because the assets of John's firm were not sufficient to cover an additional hundred

thousand dollars, John signed a personal guaranty, and offered his residence as additional collateral for the note.

In the next year, John's firm was pleased with the work of the Nevada corporation, and once again contracted with it to produce its materials. At the end of each one year contract, John's firm paid the respective notes in full, and entered into the new arrangement for the following year.

The Result: John's business and personal assets were encumbered to his Nevada corporation, resulting in John's firm, as well as John himself, being an unattractive lawsuit target. John was able to reduce his home state income taxes significantly be deducting in excess of $500,000 per year in his home state, and earning it in tax-free Nevada. When a potential lawsuit did arise, John's opponent decided against a suit, and settled for a small amount, because there were no assets from which to finance unnecessary litigation.

Case Study #2

The Situation: Maria, a software developer, had a new software product, which was destined to make her a great deal of money. Before she even had the final version finished, she had orders from several large companies that she knew would only be the tip of the iceberg. Concerned that she could be at risk in the event of litigation, Maria wanted to protect her fledgling software business, while also ensuring that her children would be provided for in the event she passed away unexpectedly. Finally, she was interested in reducing her state income taxes as much as she possibly could.

The Strategy: In order to make her new software firm as unattractive for lawsuits as possible, Maria needed its assets, meager now, but very shortly to be quite significant, encumbered. Yet her Nevada Warbucks corporation was new, and lacked the capital necessary to make a loan. The newly copyrighted software which would be the basis of her software firm was copyrighted by Maria, who developed it. Since Maria was also concerned about providing for her heirs, she formed a family limited partnership, and a family security trust for the benefit of her heirs. She contributed the software copyright to the family limited partnership in exchange for a general partnership interest. The family limited partnership contributed the software copyright to Warbucks, which in turn sold the copyright to her home state firm for $500,000. Obviously the home state firm didn't have that kind of cash, so it executed a note in favor of Warbucks, and put its assets, both those it had at the time, and those it would acquire later, up as collateral to secure the note to Warbucks.

The Result: Maria retained control of both Warbucks and the family limited partnership. She also succeeded in encumbering the assets of her home state software company, which soon became very successful. She also succeeded in reducing state income taxes, because the home state company was able to deduct the interest payments it made to Warbucks. Because this was an installment sale, Warbucks paid taxes on the interest, and on the principal paid by the home state company for the purchase amount as it was paid, and the principal was paid very slowly. In short, Maria was able to accomplish all of her objectives.

Case Study #3

The Situation: Bob, a surgeon, was fed up with Medicare billing hassles. His office staff had to spend a great deal of time dealing with the red tape and endless forms. He was so fed up, that he, like many other doctors, was seriously considering not taking new Medicare patients. As a last resort, he did some investigating, and found out that there are companies that handle Medicare billing for doctor clients, but they are expensive. One of his associates joked that Medicare billing companies were so costly that Bob should start his own billing service.

After laughing this off initially, Bob though that maybe that wasn't such a bad idea. He could set up a Nevada corporation to do his billing, charge his own office for the service, and earn money in tax free Nevada, while deducting it in California, his home state. When he put pencil to paper, it was worth doing.

The Strategy: Bob established a Nevada corporation, based in Nevada, and hired a nominee to be the officers. He then set up a small office in California, and formed a new California corporation there. His medical practice hired the Nevada corporation to do its Medicare billing. The Nevada corporation subcontracted with the new California corporation to provide office support in the billing process. Bob's office staff that was dedicated to Medicare billing were terminated by the medical practice, and hired to work for the California corporation, in its own separate office. As a subcontractor, the California corporation charged the Nevada corporation just enough money to cover its expenses, while the Nevada corporation charged Bob's medical practice enough to make a healthy profit, even with the cost of the subcontractor.

The Result: Bob's medical practice, a professional corporation in California, paid taxes at the personal service corporation rate, of a flat 36%. This amount was greatly reduced by contracting with the Nevada corporation for billing services. Since the new California corporation made little profit, it never paid above the minimum 15%, giving Bob a savings of 21% on the taxes it paid. The Nevada corporation, which did no business in California, earned a hefty profit in tax free Nevada, where it paid taxes at less that the PSC rate on the Federal side, and no state income tax, realizing a significant savings for Bob. After several months, a few of Bob's associates asked Bob if they could hire his company to do their billing as well, and Bob realized a whole new profit center. As this new business grew, Bob soon realized that he could earn more money by doing Medicare billing and insurance billing for other doctors, with better hours and dramatically less stress and liability that he could as a surgeon, and he quit his medical practice altogether to spend more time with his family.

Case Study #4

The Situation: Hank is a used car dealer in Texas. His used car dealership, incorporated in Texas, offers financing to anyone, no questions asked. His corporation buys low priced used cars from new car dealerships that take them in as trade-ins at low wholesale prices, and then sells them to first time buyers. These first time buyers pay a third to a half down, and then Hank's dealership finances the balance for twelve months at high interest rates. This type of used car dealership, called a "buy here – pay here lot" can be very profitable, with fairly low risk of default, because in the event of a default, the dealership repossesses the car, and repeats the process. In addition, interest rates are often in excess of 30%. Hank was concerned about two things. First, used car dealers find themselves in lawsuits frequently, and second, his taxes were becoming quite hefty and he was looking for ways to reduce them.

The Strategy: Hank took all of the extra cash he could lay his hands on; including proceeds from the sale of some real estate, as well a second mortgage on his home, and decided to set up a finance company and an estate plan. The finance company (Warbucks) was incorporated in Nevada, with nominee officers. Hank took his cash, and contributed it to his family limited partnership in exchange for his general partnership interest. The family limited partnership then used the cash to buy the stock of the finance company.

The finance company then entered into an agreement with Hank's car lot to provide financing for new inventory. They agreed that the lot would use this money to buy used cars, and when they were sold with financing, the lot would keep the down payment, and then assign the notes to the finance company, who would then release the car which had been collateral, and agree to lend more money for new purchases.

The Result: Because of the lending relationship, Hank's inventory was encumbered by the Nevada finance company, making the used car dealership an unattractive target. Next, with the dealership keeping the down payments from sales, but assigning the notes to the finance company to obtain new financing, the profit of the dealership dropped significantly, which the Nevada finance company was in a position to make the main portion of the profits in tax free Nevada. Hank saved on both state and Federal taxes because of the income splitting from one to two taxpayers, and he later began doing financing under similar terms for two start up used car lots owned by friends. Hank was successful in accomplishing his goals.

Case Study #5

The Situation: Paula and Janet are attorneys in California. They have a unique business, at least for a couple of lawyers. They are in the business of establishing, managing and operating medical clinics. The way they do it is to find a doctor who wants a job, and incorporate a professional medical corporation for the doctor. The doctor works regular hours in the clinic, gets a paycheck of Friday and spends the weekend at home. The doctor also owns the stock of the clinic, because only a doctor can own stock in a professional medical corporation. Paula and Janet, however make all of the investment, run the offices and are forced to trust that the doctor will not "go south" on them. Their dilemma was how to open more clinics, and maintain control of the doctors?

The Strategy: Paula and Janet had some rather difficult problems. Not only controlling the doctors, but liability protection and tax planning were issues to tackle. They formed a new California corporation to perform management services for medical clinics. This management corporation would hire all non-professional staff, provide all equipment, manage all office functions, and lease all office premises. Paula was the owner and officer of this corporation.

The management corporation need money to do this, so Janet formed a Nevada corporation to act as finance company for the management company. The Nevada corporation loaned money to the California management company, taking all of its assets as collateral. The management company entered into agreements with the current, and all future medical clinics to provide the services mentioned earlier. To ensure that it received timely payment, the management company required the medical clinics to provide their assets as collateral. The only assets that the clinics would have were their receivables, which had to remain in the ownership of the professional corporation under medical licensing regulations in California.

The Result: The fees that the management company charged the clinics left little if any profit in those companies after the doctor's salary was covered, leaving little income in the Professional Service Corporation's rate. The doctor, if he or she decided to cheat the attorneys who had set them up in business, would have nothing to take, because the only asset of the clinics was their receivables, which were liened by the management company. The management company held real assets, and was in a potentially difficult liability position, but all if its assets were encumbered by the Nevada corporation. Much of the management company's income also had to be paid to the Nevada corporation in the form of interest on its loans, where the income would be earned state tax-free. As this structure unfolded, it became so successful that Paula and Janet opened twelve more clinics, and left the practice of law to operate their business full time. All of their objectives had been accomplished.

Tax Savings Through Incorporation

As pointed out previously, incorporating can produce tax savings, because corporations are taxpayers with their own tax rates and schedule of deductible expenses. In addition, splitting income streams to multiple taxpayers can also result in tax savings. Let's now take a more in depth look at how corporations can result in tax savings, within the law. Over the next few pages are several charts, which illustrate personal versus corporate tax rates. Take a few minutes to review them, and you will realize that by incorporating a sole proprietorship or a partnership, you can achieve some serious savings, even if nothing other than the tax tales changed. Yet this doesn't even take into account the fact that corporations have many more deductions than individuals do. For instance, a corporation can deduct 100% of the amounts it pays for insurance provided to employees, but can you as an individual... no, you can't. A corporation can also write off the interest it pays on loans. An individual can write of mortgage interest only. (See charts in Appendices)

After reviewing these charts, you can see that a corporation pays the lowest 15% tax rate on net income up to $50,000 while single taxpayers can only go up to $23,350., and married couples filing jointly only pay 15% up to $39.000. On the highest end, corporations have a maximum rate of 35%, while individuals go up to 39.6%, so that even without the extra deductions, corporations usually will save money over sole proprietorships and partnerships.

There is more to consider, as well. By incorporating a sole proprietorship you are beginning to employ income splitting into your tax planning. Income splitting means that you take an income stream, and split it between more than one taxpayer. If you have a sole proprietorship, the income it generates passes through to your personal return, where it is added to any other income that either you or your spouse may have. If you incorporate, only the portion that you pay to yourself as salary is reported on your personal tax return, after being deducted by your corporation, leaving a lower amount of taxable income on both your personal return, and on your business tax return, which tends to keep both you and your corporation in a lower tax bracket.

There are numerous ways to achieve tax savings with a corporation. While this is not primarily a book on taxes, we will discuss some of the better known ways to save money with a corporation in the next few pages. Each of these possibilities is easy to implement, and useful for everyone, or nearly everyone.

Medical Reimbursement Plans

As the costs of medical care continue to skyrocket, and more and more health insurance plans cover less and less, for higher and higher costs, the Medical Reimbursement Plan (MRP) can be a great way to balance the scales in your favor. As an individual, you can only deduct medical costs if they exceed 7.5% of adjusted gross income. If your adjusted gross income is $40,000 the first $3,000 you pay in medical expenses is not deductible. However, if you have a corporation with an MRP, that same $3,000 would be paid tax free, and the corporation could receive a 100% write off for it. You see, with an MRP, the corporation can cover uninsured expenses, and the payment is not considered income to you.

In order to qualify, an MRP must be formally adopted by your corporation's Board of Directors, and it must be primarily for the benefit of the corporation's employees. Of course, you can be an employee of your corporation. The MRP can be very flexible, since there are no minimum or maximum payments allocated to any particular period, and there are no premiums to be paid because an MRP is not an insurance plan.

There are "off the shelf" plans, which are readily available, or you can consult with an attorney or benefit consultant in setting one into motion. Thus not only are they flexible, but easy to set up. Surplus earnings of the corporation can be placed into the MRP to avoid dividends liability, thus providing an excellent way to do your tax planning, since there are currently no limitations on contributions. Any excess funds not used by employees continue to accumulate, and the plan can be terminated at any time by giving written notice to the employees.

In addition to the flexibility in set up, an MRP can provide very interesting benefits. The funds can be applied to any service or product that a doctor or health specialist recommends that will improve employee health. For example, an employee received reimbursement for a clarinet, and lessons for a child whose orthodontist recommended it to correct an overbite. (Revenue Ruling 92-210)

Other interesting rulings include an employee whose wife was susceptible to nasal infections. Their house had shingle siding that harbored mold and dust that her doctor believed cause her irritation. The siding was replaced by MRP funds, entirely deductible to the corporation. Another instance was the costly removal of paint containing lead, which could be a danger to children, and recommended by a doctor. Another employee's wife was paralyzed in an accident, and the MRP paid for the installation of an elevator in their home. Another case involved a woman who lost her hair while undergoing treatment for cancer. The MRP paid for wigs, and a hair transplant. In short, an MRP can provide much broader coverage than an insurance policy, while providing a shelter for earned, undistributed income for the corporation.

There are special requirements for maintaining an MRP. Since they are a form of self-insured health plans, they must be non-discriminatory. This means that they must not discriminate in favor of "highly compensated employees", who are now defined as employees who:

Are among the five highest paid officers of the company;
Own more than 10% of the company; and
Are among the highest paid 25% of all of the employees and officers.

In addition, the MRP must benefit:

70% or more of all employees; and
80% or more of all employees who are eligible to participate

Employees who need not be considered when making the above calculations include those:

With less than three years of service;
Under 25 years of age;
With part time or seasonal jobs;
Who are non-resident aliens; or
Employees who are Union members

Section 1244 Stock

Section 1244 stock is qualified for ordinary loss treatment under Section 1244 of the Internal Revenue Code. It is estimated that 90% of the corporations formed in the United States automatically qualify for Section 1244 stock treatment. In the past, when you incorporated, you had to have a written plan to realize the benefits of and be qualified under Section 1244, but that is no longer true

If you own stock in a corporation that is qualified under Section 1244 and it goes under, regardless of whether you realize a loss when you sell the stock or the stock becomes totally worthless, you are entitled to take an "ordinary" loss deduction for the value of the stock up to certain levels. This is very beneficial because you would realize an ordinary, rather than a capital loss, should the stock become worthless. A capital loss means that you can only deduct $1,500 ($3,000 if married filing a joint return) and any excess loss over that level would have to be carried forward to use in future years.

While there is a dollar ceiling on the amount of ordinary loss you can deduct, according to Section 1244, it is much better than a capital loss. If you lose money on a sale of stock, or the stock becomes totally worthless, you are entitled to a loss deduction up to $50,000 if you file a single return, and up to $100,000 if you file a joint return, provided you really lose the $100,000.

As noted above, it is estimated that 90% of the stock issuances by private corporations automatically qualify for Section 1244 stock treatment, thus 10% do not qualify, because there are some prerequisites. First, the stock must be a common stock in a domestic corporation. There is no favorable Section 1244 treatment if you invest in a corporation formed in a foreign country (offshore corporations). Furthermore, the stock you buy must be common stock. However, preferred stock issued after July 18, 1984, can also qualify for Section 1244 treatment. There are also requirements such that shares must have been issued for money or for property other than stock or securities. This means that you cannot acquire stock in exchange for other stock or securities.

Promoter's stock for services (sometimes called "promotional stock") will not qualify for Section 1244 treatment. Services rendered are not "money or other property." The promoters have never received compensation for, and have never paid taxes on, the services rendered. Therefore, the tax laws don't allow a promoter to claim an ordinary loss, or any deduction, for promotional shares issued to him or her.

To be eligible for Section 1244 stock treatment, during the 5-year period immediately before the date the stock became worthless or the date you sold the stock at a loss, the business must have been primarily engaged in an active trade or business. It appears that the corporation should not have derived more than 50% of its gross receipts from passive income, which are largely considered to be sources such as royalties, rents, dividends, interest, or gains from the exchange of stock or securities. Since most businesses derive well over 50% of their income from an active trade or business, this requirement does not usually pose a problem.

The final requirement for favorable Section 1244 treatment is that the dollar value of your stock issuance must be small. More precisely, at the time of issuance of the stock in question, the total capitalization raised cannot exceed one million dollars. Generally, this means that Section 1244 is only available to smaller corporations.

In conclusion, if you or your investors find yourselves with up to $100,000 of worthless stock, it may well be of consolation to know that it was Section 1244 stock and that you are entitled to an ordinary loss deduction. One other thing – you must be one of the original recipients. Stock acquired from another individual does not qualify under Section 1244.

Stock Dividends in a Corporation

One of the most effective ways, and perhaps the only way to receive exclusions from gross income of stock dividends, is by having your corporation own the stock and receive the dividends. A corporation is entitled to a deduction from its gross income for the dividends it receives from domestic corporations for which it owns an interest. If your corporation owns less than 20% of the stock of the corporation paying dividends, the exclusion is 70% of the dividends that are received, leaving only 30% of what is actually received as taxable.

If your corporation receives dividends but owns at least 20% of the shares of another corporation, but less than 80%, the exclusion increases to 80% of the dividends received. In other words, you only pay tax on 20% of the dividends received. Finally, if the dividends are paid to the corporation that owns 80% or more of the shares of the paying corporation, the deduction is 100%. As you can see, this is a huge benefit for anyone who owns dividend-producing stock. This little known wealth shelter can increase your yield substantially.

You've now learned to reduce your federal income tax on dividends received by 70% or more, but why stop there. You can totally eliminate your state income taxes on dividends by basing your corporation in Tax-Free Nevada. Just have your Nevada corporation own the stock of another corporation and receive dividends on that stock. Since Nevada has no state income tax, your Nevada corporation pays no state income tax on the dividends it receives. What a savings this can be when you plan your corporate strategies! Your yield just increased again!

There are some limitations on the deductions. Shares of the paying company must be held for at least 45 days before the recipient is eligible for the deduction. If the stock is cumulative preferred stock, and the recipient gets more than 366 days' dividends, the stock must be held at least 91 days in order for the deduction to be allowed. If dividends are considered "extraordinary" dividends, the deduction is allowed, but the taxpayer is required to reduce his or her basis in the stock by the non-taxed amount of the dividend. When does a dividend fall into this special category? It usually happens when the dividend exceeds 10% of the Shareholder's adjusted basis in the stock. It can also apply if the dividend is greater than 10% of the fair market value of the stock just before the date of the declaration of the dividend, and if the taxpayer has not held the stock for more than two years prior to the date of declaration of the dividend.

There are other limitations or restrictions on the above type of dividends received. However, if you are an investor and expect to buy stock for the dividends, you might just consider purchasing them through your corporation. If you can qualify for the special treatment, the advantage may just be worth the extra effort.

Note: If you want to use a corporation only for this purpose, consider electing S-Corporation status. The dividend received exclusion still applies, but you won't need to worry about your corporation being classified as a personal holding company.

Start-Up Expenses

Getting a new business off the ground can be a complicated task. Anyone considering such an undertaking should know that how they choose to treat pre-opening expenses might well determine how successfully they minimize taxation and maximize profits downstream. Tax strategy must be employed from the start in a way, which will allow maximum profits in a company's early struggling years. Three situations should be considered, each with its own distinct tax consequences. You may:

1. Start a completely new venture. (Pre-opening expenses generally are not deductible. They must be capitalized and written off over a period of five years.)

2. Expand an existing business. (Related costs may be deducted on a current basis.)

3. Organize your business venture as a corporation. (This is particularly important for a high-risk venture. Being incorporated allows pre-opening expenses to be de-ducted as ordinary losses if you must abandon your business before it becomes profitable.)

Exactly what can be classed as pre-opening expense? Following are three general categories with examples.

Inquiry expenses occur as you investigate and evaluate your potential business before actually going ahead with it. Items such as the costs of feasibility studies (marketing surveys, potential locations, surveys of the costs and availability of materials, labor and transportation), travel expenses, salaries and professional fees are all included as investigating expenses.
NOTE: If your venture is an investment rather than a managed business, you cannot amortize these expenses.
Organizing expenses occur after you decide to start your business but before the business actually is organized. Items such as fees for incorporating, preparing charters, bylaws and minutes, legal fees, and the costs of organizational meetings for Shareholders and Directors are included. These expenses can be amortized over no less than five years after the date your business begins to operate.
NOTE: Costs involved in issuing stock (such as those involved in printing a prospectus) may not be amortized or deducted.
Starting expenses occur after you decide to establish your business, but before the business is fully operational. Expenses incurred while hiring and/or training and while designing the product(s), including salaries, travel costs, and phone calls made by those working during the start-up process, are part of starting costs. The cost of depreciable property is not a starting cost.

For many tax benefits, a key question involves the time when the business began its operations. Two differing views on this question are widely held. One holds a business doesn't begin until it produces income, and allows no deductions before this time. The second says business starts when it can make money, even though no money has yet been made. (You may have had trouble lining up sales for a new product line, etc.) Your conservative or liberal stand will determine your view. The IRS will probably be contesting cases reviewed by the courts regarding tax fights in this area.

So what can you do to exercise care when organizing your company? Follow these seven steps.

1. **ANALYZE:** See if you can expand a business or if you really need to start a new company. Expansion costs (both inquiry and starting costs) can be deducted as they are incurred.

2. **DETERMINE:** What date did your business actually start operating?   This determines whether you may amortize or expense the costs involved.

3. **PREPARE:** If you may abandon your venture before it is operational, consider incorporating. Forming a corporation allows you to deduct any pre-opening expenses as a loss.

4. **CONSIDER:** You can abandon your business within the first five years after it   has started. Expenses still not amortized at time of abandonment can be classified as a loss.

5. **REMEMBER:** Tax laws are varied and complex. Go to a good consultant before you finalize any plans. His strategy may be an invaluable aid to you as you consider the tax consequences of opening, expanding or incorporating your business.

6. **EXPANSIONS:** When considering expansion, take into consideration the hazards, risks and liabilities your new venture will bring to your existing business. Would it be wiser to insulate the new venture from your existing business by incorporating? If you incorporate the new venture, it is all you risk.

7. **DEDUCTIBLE EXPENSES:** Consider causing another entity to do immediate business with your new venture and thus produce income immediately, once and for all settling the question with the IRS as to whether your expenses are deductible.

Avoiding Double Taxation
Many will say, sure corporations pay less tax up to $110,656 in net

taxable income but the income that corporations receive is double-taxed, so this benefit is really no benefit at all. This is actually a true statement, assuming you do everything wrong. If you form a corporation, earn income in it, take advantage of only a handful of deductions available to it, take advantage of no fringe benefits, and declare all income that the corporation receives as a dividend to the Shareholders, then it may be true.

Let's take a look at what happens when you do a few things right.

People who say the income a corporation receives is double-taxed assume that the corporation is a "C" corporation and that its Shareholders are going to take all of the earned income out in the form of dividends. A "C" corporation pays taxes separate and apart from its shareholders and so it must file a return in addition to its individual shareholders. An "S" corporation does not pay taxes at all, but instead the individual shareholders pay their share of the company's earnings at the individual tax rates as if all the earnings were simply personal income.

When a regular or "C" corporation earns money, it pays taxes on its net income. When it pays a dividend to its Shareholders, it cannot deduct that dividend. However, when a Shareholder receives a dividend, he or she must pay tax on it. That means that the same income was taxed once at the corporate level and then taxed again at the individual level. This costs a lot of money and is only a last resort for taking money out of a corporation and a not-very-smart way to go.

There is no law that says a corporation must distribute its profits out to its Shareholders in the form of dividends, although many people seem to think otherwise. Your corporation does not have to declare a dividend. The corporation can simply retain the earnings in the corporation. That way the money is only taxed once. Plus, since a corporation pays less tax on its income up to $110,656 net per year, the income is not only taxed once, it is taxed once and pays less than you would if you earned the money personally in the first place.

Furthermore, the corporation has many more deductions available to it than does an individual. So, a corporation can earn much more than an individual and still pay less tax.

Maybe you've heard your accountant say that there is a limitation on how much money a corporation can retain without declaring a dividend. Well, yes and no. The corporation can retain up to $250,000 without ever having to declare a dividend. Many people will tell you that when it reaches $250,000 of retained income that it has to declare a dividend, but that is not true. The corporation can retain far in excess of $250,000 provided it is retaining that income for growth and has a corporate resolution to that effect, and the point of being in business in the first place is to grow.

*In California, at the state income tax level, a corporation electing to be treated as an S-Corporation does pay a 2.5% state income tax at the corporate level.

You see, people operate under the assumption that they have to take money out of their corporation, and this just isn't true. When you have a corporation, you have a corporate checkbook as well. It is just as easy to write a check on the corporation as it is to write one out of your personal checkbook and many things that a person wants to write a check for are actually business expenses. The corporation can buy a car, pay medical expenses, provide for the individual's retirement, and buy real estate. The corporation can do all that and then buy an airplane if it so chooses.

If you do need to take money out of the corporation, one method is to simply have the corporation lend you the money. You may have lent the corporation some money when you first started out and then the corporation can pay you interest payments. In the case of the corporation lending *you* money, there is no tax. Of course, you would have to pay the corporation interest on any money you borrow and the corporation would have to claim that as taxable income, but the tax effects are usually minimal. With the lower corporate tax rates and higher corporate deductions, you still have quite a tax benefit.

If you lent money to the corporation when you started out and the corporation is paying you interest, yes, that interest is income to you that is taxable. But it is deductible to the corporation, so that you're only taxed once on that money – effectively eliminating double taxation. Further, corporate money paid to you as a payment on the principal amount you lent it is not income to you.

Also, the corporation is probably going to pay you a salary of some sort. That salary is an expense to the corporation and is income to you. It is not double taxed except to the extent that the corporation and you must contribute 7.65% in Social Security taxes, and the corporation's contribution is a deductible payroll tax expense on the corporation's books. The rest is only taxed once, and again, the tax benefits that the corporation has far more than make up for the Social Security tax.

So there you have it. First, there's no law that says the corporation has to declare a dividend to begin with. Second, you probably don't need to take that much money out of the corporation. Third, if you do need to take money out of your corporation, there are much better ways than dividends. As you can see, double taxation is really an overblown problem. In fact, in most closely held corporations, it is no problem at all.

"There are a variety of different taxes — income taxes,
sales taxes, corporate profit taxes, property taxes, and so
forth. All of them have one thing in common. They take
spending away from those taxed."

Roger N. Waud

Get The Money

Many business people face a common problem today: How ought
they safely take money out of their closely-held companies for their own
support while keeping the business healthy financially? There are many
ways to do this because tax laws let you spread income among family
members in a lower tax bracket. These are ways you can legally avoid high
bracket taxes.

Often the easiest and quickest way for a successful businessperson to
save tax dollars is to incorporate. How does incorporating help save tax
dollars? Following, are some examples:

Corporate tax rates are generally lower than corresponding individual rates; therefore, you may save on taxes by directing much of your
income into your corporation.

A salary for services is the most obvious way to receive money from
your corporation. The payment to you by the corporation is deductible to
the corporation. Be careful, though, that you don't take too much out as
salary. If your salary is questioned by the IRS and found to be unreasonable for the tasks you perform and for the overall income of the corporation, deductibility of the salary may be denied. You will still receive the
same amount of income, but the corporation may not be able to deduct
the payments. So as far as the corporation is concerned, it will be a dividend payment and will not be deductible to the corporation.

One way to get around the unreasonableness issue is to take a smaller
salary and provide for bonuses, both short and long-term, based on company profitability. You should have an employment contract that sets out
the terms of your employment, benefits, vacation, salary, bonuses, etc. –
particularly if you are a shareholder.

Current qualifying fringe benefits are tax free to the corporation's
employees, but they are deductible expenses for the corporation. Health,

disability and life insurance, tuition help for students, special executive training, and travel to conventions are only a few fringes with helpful tax benefits for both the corporation and its employees. Instead of getting a paycheck and buying such services with after-tax dollars, you're receiving these services with before-tax dollars. The payments are tax deductible by the corporation and are not included in your income. Also, company automobiles, airplanes, and other qualifying expenditures.

Utilize the benefits of deferred fringe benefits. The corporation can claim a deduction for its contribution to a pension or profit-sharing plan, while you receive the funds in a tax-deferred trust for your retirement.

Leasing, not purchasing, may save you tax dollars. A family partnership may purchase property and lease it to the corporation at a fair price. The corporation deducts the rent it pays to the partnership as a business expense. The structure of the partnership is also important. Taxpayers in higher brackets should own the largest partnership interest if the partnership reports a loss, while those in lower brackets should be own a greater interest if the partnership realizes taxable income.

A corporation with prior earnings, a promising future, and no plan to invest its earnings may choose to file an S-Corporation election. This passes any gain or loss directly to individual taxpayers and avoids the double taxation otherwise encountered by a corporation and its shareholders.

Another concept is to have your spouse and children on the payroll. Their pay must be reasonable for the work performed, but this can be easily accomplished. Often, even young children can do office cleaning and janitorial duties, run errands, answer telephones, etc. Almost certainly, their tax rates are going to be less than yours, and you won't have to give the kids an allowance.

Tax Savings Through Family Employment

By incorporation of a family business and employing family members, taxpayers can reduce their tax bite. *But Wait, There's More!* The incorporated family business can save even more tax dollars by employing family members while they build an investment vehicle for their children.

Following are two tables showing the different tax consequences for a family with two children under the ages of 18 running a small business.

The business earns $150,000 and nets $75,000 after expenses but before federal taxes. Both examples have $10,000 in itemized deductions. Table 1 shows that there are no tax consequences for the employed children, who each receive $6,250 a year; $2,000 of which is placed in an IRA.

Table 1
EACH CHILD'S 1040 FORM

	Family Business 1 (Proprietorship)	Family Business 2 (Corporation)
Wages	$0	$6,250
IRA	$0	$2,000
Standard Deduction	$0	$4,250
TAXABLE INCOME	$0	$ 0

Table 2 shows the contrasting tax effects of the two different approaches. As president of the corporation, the father (who is married) pays himself a salary of $18,000 a year. (In this case we assume that the corporation is an S-Corporation.)

Table 2
PARENTS' FORM 1040

	Family Business 1 (Proprietorship)	Family Business 2 (Incorporated)
Wages		$ 18,000
Schedule C	$ 75,000	
Schedule E		
(Form 1120S K-1)		75,000
Less: Personal Salary		(18,000)
Child No. 1		(6,250)
Child No. 2		(6,250)
Corporate Payroll Taxes	_____	(2,493)
Adjusted Gross Income	75,000	60,007
Less 50% Self Employment Tax	(5,738)	
Less: Itemized Deductions	(10,000)	(10,000)
Exemptions (4 x $2,800)	(11,200)	(11,200)
Taxable Income (Form 1040)	48,062	38,807
Income Tax	7,757	5,821
Self-Employment Tax	11,475	
Corporate Payroll Taxes		2,493
W-2 - S.S./Medicare Tax Withheld	_____	1,377
TOTAL TAXES	$ 19,232	$ 9,691

A quick glance at the bottom line shows that the incorporated family business ends up with a tax bill $9,541 less than the proprietorship. In addition, the children will see their IRAs grow untaxed. The children, of course, would be expected to use their salaries to pay for their general expenses; expenses that otherwise would come out of their parents' after-tax income pocket.

NOTE: The Economic Growth and Tax Relief Reconciliation Act of 2001 has been passed into law. It will be phased in over the next five years, and in general, individual tax rates will be reduced gradually over the period. The illustration above, which was calculated under previous law, would still show substantial (although not equivalent) savings under the new legislation. The example is prepared solely for illustration purposes as to the possible structures and strategies available.

Expense Reimbursements

An expense account from your closely-held corporation can be a great perk because the corporation reimburses you for business expenses. It is able to write them off without the problems you would have claiming unreimbursed business expenses, and you don't have to report the reimbursement as income. You just need to be sure to follow the rules the IRS has about expense plans.

If a corporation agrees to pay an employee a set amount of reimbursable compensation, regardless of whether the expenses are actually incurred, then such payments will be considered part of the employee's compensation and are subject to withholding and employment taxes. There are some obvious drawbacks to this method.

An arrangement for providing a per-day allowance for travel expenses that is computed on the basis of number of hours worked, and miles traveled is satisfactory, but only if:

1. The per day allowance was paid separately and identified as such when paid to the employee; or

2. The per day allowance was commonly used in the industry in which the employee works.

If an employee is paid more on a per-day basis than is considered substantiated by the IRS, then these excess payments will be considered part of the employee's income. The payments will be treated as part of the employee's pay and subject to withholding. Probably the best thing you can use is an "accountable plan", which is a plan for expense reimbursement that allows the corporation to advance you money for expenses, just so long as you account for the use of that money on legitimate business expenses. Any advance payments exceeding the employee's actual expenses must be subject to withholding no later than the first payroll period following the period during which the actual expenses were incurred.

The IRS has also ruled that reimbursements paid under an accountable plan do not need to be reported on the employee's W-2 form. However, if the employee does not use an accountable plan, then the amounts paid must be reported as wages or other compensation on the W-2 form.

Travel Expenses

To take a deduction for business-related travel, a taxpayer must ordinarily keep detailed records showing the amount of each separate expense for the travel, meals and lodging. In addition to the taxpayer's records of the expenditures, a receipt or canceled check is required for any travel expense greater than $25.

The business standard mileage rate may be used for any car which has been depreciated using the straight-line depreciation, but may not be used if the auto has previously been depreciated using a method other than straight-line depreciation.

Often, the business traveler feels as though he or she is spending more time keeping travel records than traveling or making money. The year begins with the best of intentions, and the records are maintained meticulously for a while. As the year goes on, the drudgery of this record keeping wears down the taxpayer and the best-laid plan deteriorates into an occasional, if ever, practice. Come tax time, the CPA is faced with the sad task of telling the client that what isn't recorded should not be deducted.

An alternative to this heavy record-keeping burden is to use the per diem method. Under this system, the taxpayer can ignore the requirements that everything must be fully substantiated. He or she can instead, claim a travel deduction based upon the amount the IRS allows, which is the same rate the federal government pays to its employees while they are traveling.

These rates vary, depending on the costs of travel in various areas. The traveler uses the government rate for the area in which he is staying. Perhaps, you may not be able to claim as large of a deduction as if you had documented every item, but in the end you certainly will have a larger overall deduction for the year than if you had kept careless records.

There are two principal requirements necessary to implement the per diem method. First, you must make sure to use the correct per-diem rate for the area in which you are traveling. If you would rather not keep track of the per diem rates for each of the localities, a simplified system called the "high-low method" may be used that includes meals and lodging. The combined lodging, meals and incidental expense "high" rate is currently $201 per day ($159 for lodging only) and $124 per day ($90 for lodging only) for all other locations. The Federal meals and entertainment rate is $42 for a high-cost locality and $34 for any other locality within the continental United States. The government publishes a list of selected high cost localities for which the "high" rate may be used. All other localities use the "low" rate. High cost localities are usually updated in March of each year. The second important requirement is that the traveler must be prepared to prove the business purposes of the trip and its time and place.

If you are disciplined enough to maintain the necessary records, and if your actual costs are higher than these figures, then you might achieve a better result if you go with the actual-cost approach. If record keeping is not your forte, however, this alternative may yield a greater deduction.

Check with your CPA to determine which method might produce the greatest benefit.

Car mileage is another type of expense that can be deducted. For 2000, business travelers using cars can either claim an expense of 32.5 cents per mile or claim the business portion of their actual costs. The choice again hinges on how well the traveler keeps records of expenses. The 32.5 cents includes all costs associated with running a car; fuel, maintenance and depreciation. The rate applies to all business miles. The business portion of tolls and parking fees may be deducted, in addition to the standard mileage rate.

For cars owned by businesses and used by employees, the business is allowed to depreciate the full cost basis of the automobile. If the employee uses the car part of the time for his or her personal use, the value of the usage of the automobile is a taxable fringe benefit to that employee. This value may be calculated under one of three acceptable methods:

1. Annual Lease Value Method: An annual lease value based upon tables published by the IRS. The values are based on the auto's fair market value when it is first made available to the employee.

2. Cents Per Mile: If the auto has a fair market value that does not exceed the maximum recovery deductions allowable for the first five years after the auto is placed in service, the value may be determined by multiplying the personal miles by the standard mileage rate.

3. General Valuation Method: If the special methods above are not used, then a lease value is determined by reference to the lease of a comparable vehicle to a third party in the same geographic area.

Auto Loan Interest Deductible

While loan interest for auto loans is no longer deductible for personal property, loans on cars purchased by corporations is deductible. Obviously, for owners of small corporations, such car loans should be taken out in the name of the corporation for full tax deductibility.

Deducting the Cost of Living

Many business people are engaged in a business activity that forces them to combine work with everyday living accommodations. Certain occupations require a specific dwelling location for an employee, or require employees to take meals on the premises. The value of any meals or lodging furnished to an employee *for the convenience of the employer*, are excluded from the gross income of the employee. In the case of meals, they must be furnished on the business premises of the employer. In the case of lodging, the employee is required to accept such lodging as a condition of employment on the business premises of the employer.

Be aware, that Section 280A denies a home office deduction for expenses attributable to the rental by an employee of any portion of this home to an employer if the employee uses the rental portion to perform services for the employer.

Three Tests for Deductibility of Living Expenses:

1. Expenses must be furnished on the employer's premises: in other words, you must live on corporate premises.

2. Lodging must be furnished for the convenience of the employers; it must be necessary to the employer that the employee lives on the premises.

3. The employee must be required to accept the lodging as part of the condition of employment. The employee has no option but to accept the housing if he or she wishes to accept and keep the job.

Clear-cut examples of deductible living expenses are in the hotel and catering industry. If the corporation runs a ski resort, for example, then the corporation will almost certainly need a 24-hour-a-day on-site manager and therefore, provide lodging at the resort. The company inserts a clause in its letter of employment to the resort manager stating that he must live on site as a condition of employment. In such cases all living expenses are deductible to the corporation.

Living expenses are defined to include such things as heat, electricity, gas, water, sewer services, garbage service, etc.

There are numerous cases and rulings that define what constitutes "convenience of the employer" to live on the business premises. Unfortunately, most of these cases are directed to rank and file employees and are not relevant to highly compensated management or employees.

Four Tests of Deductibility for Meals:

1. Meals are supplied to employees who must be available for emergencies or on-call.

2. Individuals who work in a restaurant may receive meals that are deductible to the corporation and not taxable as income for the employee.

3. Meals furnished to employees who are restricted to a short lunch period and cannot reasonably be expected to eat elsewhere.

4. If there are insufficient dining facilities in the area and the meals are made   available to the majority of the employees.

Commuting To Temporary Work Sites

The IRS has ruled that a taxpayer with a regular place of business can deduct daily transportation costs incurred traveling between the residence and temporary work locations. This means that the taxpayer who has one or more regular places of business and who travels to a temporary work site may now deduct his business travel costs.

However, travel expenses from the taxpayer's home directly to several regular places of business are considered to be commuting expenses and are not deductible. Travel expenses for traveling between several work sites are fully deductible.

The IRS defines a temporary place of business as a location at which the taxpayer performs services on an irregular or short-term basis. These deductions are claimed as a miscellaneous itemized deduction on Schedule A of the 1040 tax form and, therefore, must total more than 2% of the taxpayer's adjusted gross income before having any impact on the bottom line.

Here's to Your Good Health!

Are you convinced health is important? Good, because so are the people at many major corporations. Good employee health improves attendance, reduces insurance claims and reduces accidents. Healthy people look better and get along better, and healthy people perform better too. Because of this, big corporations invest in weight programs, diet programs, quit-smoking programs, health and country club memberships, massages and exercise equipment. Some even incur the construction cost of building their own facilities. As a general rule, the fair market value of any athletic facility that is on premises and is operated by the employer substantially for its employees or their spouses and dependent children, is excluded for income and employment tax purposes.

Research and Experimentation

A Texas district court has ruled that there is no limit to the amount a corporation can spend on research and experimentation, including the traditional research and development expenses.

The IRS had sought to claim that there was a test for reasonableness that a corporation must pass for its R&E spending, but the court sided with the corporation in its claim that R&E expenditures were not subject to such a standard.

The Court noted that on one hand it could be claimed that no R&E expenditure could be considered reasonable unless it resulted in the development of a viable product. But it also noted that it could just as convincingly be argued that all R&E spending could be considered reasonable in that it added to the fund of knowledge, even if it never resulted in a product.

The court decided that since no test of reasonableness was justified, there should be no limits on the amount that a corporation spent on R&E. The Court noted that it is a requirement that the expenditure must not be for the purpose of tax avoidance and that actual research must take place. Only costs of laboratory research carried on by the taxpayer or by a third party for a taxpayer are deductible. Product testing and market research costs are not considered R&E expenses. The company may elect to currently deduct the costs of a project or to amortize them over a period of not less than 60 months.

Alternatively, the taxpayer may claim a credit for incremental research expenses. A credit is calculated based on qualified research expenses paid or incurred for the tax year in excess of the taxpayer's base amount for that tax year plus basic research payments to a qualified organization. Startup ventures also qualify for this credit but under a different base amount formula. An alternative incremental credit regime is available. The credit applies to qualified research expenses paid or incurred after June 30, 1996 and before July 1, 2004. Thus, the research credit will terminate for research expenses paid or incurred after June 30, 2004. The credit is generally equal to 20% of the qualifying amount.

TAXATION AND MULTIPLE CORPORATIONS

"Nothing is more familiar in taxation than the imposition of a tax upon a class, or upon individuals, who enjoy no direct benefit from its expenditure, and who are not responsible for the condition to be remedied."

> Harlan F. Stone
> Former Chief Justice
> U.S. Supreme Court

Tax Advantages of Multiple Corporations

If the ownership of multiple corporations can be structured so separate corporations are not considered part of a "Controlled Group", there can be significant tax advantages to using multiple corporations. Take a look at the following comparison.

Multiple Use of Graduated Corporate Tax Rates:

Corporate tax rates currently are:

Tax Rate:	Taxable Income Over:	But Less Than:
15%	$ 0	$50,000
25%	50,000	75,000
34%	75,000	100,000
39%	100,000	335,000
34%	335,000	10,000,000
35%	10,000,000	15,000,000
38%	15,000,000	18,333,333
35%	18,333,333	_____

Corporations that are members of a controlled group must share one set of the above tax rates.

Multiple corporations that are not members of a Controlled Group benefit from the lower 15% and 25% tax rates on the first $75,000 of taxable income for each corporation, rather than one corporation with income over $75,000 taxed at the higher rates. One simple way to get this benefit is to have two corporations, one owned 100% by you and one owned 100% by your spouse. (See Section 2.)

On the first $100,000 of taxable income, savings from the lower 15% and 25% tax brackets (referred to as the surtax exemption) is $11,750.

1. **Accumulated Earnings Tax Credit (AETC):** Multiple corporations that are not members of a "Controlled Group" each have their own $250,000 accumulated earnings tax credit ($150,000 for personal service corporations) as opposed to only one $250,000 credit per controlled group. The AETC applies to a regular C-Corporation's accumulated earnings, not needed for business expansion purposes, which may be maintained in the corporation without being distributed to the shareholders as dividends.

2. **Alternative Multiple Tax Credit:** Multiple corporations that are not members of a "Controlled Group" are each allowed their own $40,000 exemption in calculating a minimum corporate tax.

3. **Environmental Tax Credit:** Multiple corporations that are not members of a "Controlled Group" are each allowed their own $2,000,000 environmental tax credit. The environmental tax is .12% on earnings over $2,000,000.

4. **Election to Expense Certain Depreciable Assets–Section 179:** Multiple corporations that are not members of a "Controlled Group" are each allowed their own $20,000 limitation amount for purposes of expending personal depreciable property in the year of acquisition.

5. **Other Tax Advantages of Multiple Corporations:**
   a. The ability to use different year ends and different accounting methods (cash or accrual), whereas, one corporation with different business divisions must use the same method for all divisions;
   b. The ability to more easily dispose of a business segment operated as a separate corporation, and, in certain cases, be able to effect a tax-free disposition of a business segment operated as a separate corporation in a tax-free reorganization;
   c. The ability to separate foreign from domestic-source income and, in some cases, avoid double taxation;
   d. To allow Section 1244 ordinary loss treatment, as opposed to restricted capital loss treatment, on up to $100,000 of stock invested in a segment of a business separately incorporated, that has no more than $1,000,000 on total stock investment; and
   e. The ability to set up a separate Subchapter S "Brother" corporation to make start-up losses from a new enterprise a current tax benefit to the individual shareholders on their personal tax returns, instead of being required to carry the corporation losses forward until future profit exists so that the

tax benefit can be utilized.

Tax Planning with Multiple Corporations

Having a group of corporations that isn't considered a 'controlled' group is great! You can save big tax dollars and it doesn't always mean you cannot control them. Confused? It is probably easier to understand what a controlled group is not rather than determining what it is, so here are several examples of what would not constitute a controlled group:

1. You own 100% of one corporation and your spouse owns 100% of another corporation. You and your wife manage your respective corporations separately. These two corporations are not a controlled group.

2. You own 49% of one corporation and your child over 21 years of age owns the balance. You own 100% of another corporation. The two corporations are not part of a controlled group.

3. You own 79% of one corporation and your brother (or sister) owns 21%. You own 100% of another corporation. The two corporations are not part of a controlled group. However, you do have control over both.

4. You own 79% of one corporation, you are at least 21 years old and your parents own 21%. You own 100% of another corporation. The two corporations are not part of a controlled group, however you do have control over both.

5. You own 79% of one corporation and a totally unrelated third party owns 21%. You own 100% of another corporation. The two corporations are not part of a controlled group, however you do have control over both.

Think about the possibilities here. These structures can put dollars in your pocket!

There are basically two types of controlled groups. One is a parent-subsidiary controlled group. The other is a brother-sister controlled group.

Parent-Subsidiary Controlled Group

A parent-subsidiary controlled group exists where one or more corporations, through a chain of ownership, own at least 80% of the stock and value of another corporation.

Brother–Sister Controlled Group

A brother–sister controlled group consists of two or more corporations in which:

1. Five or fewer persons (individuals, estates, or trusts) own at least 80% of the voting stock or value of shares of each corporation; and

2. These five or fewer persons own more than 50% of the voting stock or value of shares of each corporation, considering a particular person's stock only to the extent that it is owned with regard to each corporation.

Stock Attribution Rules for a Brother–Sister Controlled Group

In applying the above two tests for a brother–sister controlled group you are considered to own:

1. Stock owned by your spouse, in a corporation in which you also own stock or take part in management.
2. Stock owned by your children under age 21.
3. Stock owned by your children over age 21 and grandchildren, if you own more than 50% of the value and voting power of the stock in the corporation.
4. Stock owned by your parents, if you are under 21 years of age.
5. Stock owned by your parents or grandparents, if you own more than 50% of the value and voting power of the corporation's stock.
6. Stock held by a trust, estate, partnership or corporation in which you own a 5% or more interest.
7. Stock on which you hold an option.

Note that stock owned by a brother, sister, or in-law is not considered owned by a shareholder through attribution, nor is stock owned by children over 21, or parents of children who are over 21, if the person in question does not own more than 50% of the stock of the second corporation.

Disadvantages of a Controlled Group

You only get one helping of tax breaks, no matter how many corporations you own, if they are part of a controlled group. They are, therefore, not so much "disadvantages" as they are a restriction on "seconds."

Multiple corporations that are members of a Controlled Group must allocate the lower tax brackets, accumulated earnings tax credit, etc., (items 1 through 5 above under Tax Advantages of Multiple Corporations), so that the controlled group members, in total receive only one each of the above listed tax benefits.

For example, corporations "A" and "B" which are members of a Controlled Group must allocate the lower 15% tax rate bracket so that "A" receives only $25,000 of taxable income at 15%, and "B" receives only $25,000 of taxable income at 15%, instead of $50,000 apiece. The next $12,500 in taxable income of each controlled group member is then taxed at 25%. The subsequent $12,500 is taxed at 34%, and $50,000 to $167,500 for each corporation is taxed at 39%. Each succeeding bracket is split in the same manner.

Likewise, members of a Controlled Group receive only one $250,000 Accumulated Earnings Tax Credit ($15,000 for professional service corporations) to be allocated among the controlled group corporate members, one Alternative Minimum Tax Credit, one Environmental Tax Credit, and one Section 179 election.

Examples of a Brother–Sister Controlled Group

The following example assumes Shareholders "A," "B," "C" and "D" are unrelated taxpayers in regard to the above-listed stock ownership attribution rules.

Remember that "B," "C" and "D" can be brothers, sisters, adult children, parents of adult children, or in-laws and will not be considered to be related per the stock ownership attribution rules, because neither "B," "C" or "D" owns at least 80% of either corporation, and more than 50% of the other.

However, since "A" owns at least 80% of Corporation 1 and more than 50% of Corporation 2, "A" would be deemed by attribution to also own the stock of his adult children and his parents.

The complications and necessary planning considerations of Multiple Corporations, and Controlled Groups can be complex and dependent on the facts of each situation. So remember, when setting up your corporate empire, professional tax advice is recommended.

Example 1
PERCENT OF STOCK OWNERSHIP

Shareholders	CORP 1	CORP 2	Percent of Identical Ownership
A	80%	60%	60%
B	20%	20%	20%
C	0%	10%	0%
D	0%	10%	0%
TOTAL	100%	100%	80%

Because the identical ownership column is greater than 50%, and Shareholders "A" and "B" own at least 80% of both entities, corporations 1 and 2 are a Brother/Sister Controlled Group, subject to the limited tax benefits of a Controlled Group.

Example 2
Consider stock ownership adjusted as follows:

PERCENT OF STOCK OWNERSHIP

Shareholders	CORP 1	CORP 2	Percent of Identical Ownership
A	80%	29%	29%
B	20%	20%	20%
C	0%	26%	0%
D	0%	25%	0%
TOTAL	100%	100%	49%

Corporations 1 and 2 are not part of a Brother/Sister Controlled Group. Even though the greater than 50% identical ownership test is met; the same shareholders that meet the 50% test must also meet the 80% test. Since Shareholders "A" and "B" do not control at least 80% of Corporation 2 (Vogel Fertilizer vs. U.S., a Supreme Court tax case) the 80% test is not met. Therefore, Corporations 1 and 2 are not a controlled group, and both corporations are entitled to their own and separate surtax exemptions, accumulated earnings tax credit, alternative minimum tax credit, environmental tax credit, and section 179 election.

Doing Business At Arms Length
It is essential that owners of multiple corporations doing business with each other transact business at arm's length, on normal commercial terms. Otherwise the IRS may invoke the dreaded Section 482 and treat all members of a controlled group as one corporation, with all the ensuing tax consequences.

Section 482 applies to "Controlled Groups," which for the purposes of this section, is loosely defined and can mean "any type of control, direct or indirect. It is the reality of the control which is decisive, not its form or mode of exercise." Even worse, there is a "presumption of control if income and deductions are arbitrarily shifted". In other words, if two or more companies act like a controlled group, they are a controlled group.

What the Section says is that if a controlled group manipulates its component companies (not just corporations but any business form) in such a way that either "the (federal) taxable income is understated" or "the true income is obscured," the District Director may intervene "and determine the true taxable income". The Director can consolidate the results of the controlled group and assess tax based on that consolidation (even if the

different companies have different fiscal years).

The fundamental basis for judging whether Section 482 applies and in what manner it should be invoked is "arm's length" transactions—transactions that would occur between unrelated third parties. The more members of a controlled group interact like unrelated third parties, the less likely that Section 482 applies.

Section 482 is usually invoked under two circumstances:

1. When there is a significant element of tax avoidance or evasion.

2. When there is a sharp separation of the expenses of producing gain from the gain itself. (For example, if profit is shifted from one company to another to take advantage of accumulated losses of the second company.)

If Section 482 is invoked, the District Director may reallocate income from interest on loans based on an arm's-length rate of interest, taking into account "amount, duration, security, credit standing of borrower, and prevailing interest rates."

The Safe Haven interest rate is not less than the Federal Rate and not greater than 130% of the Federal Rate. (There are different Federal Rates for loans: short, up to 5 years; medium, 5 to 10 years; long-term, 10 years or more. The rate is based on the Treasury Bill Rate and is adjusted quarterly.)

Section 482 verses Warbucks/Red, Inc.

Section 482 should not affect the Warbucks/Red, Inc. strategy (in which a corporation in Nevada lends money to a corporation in another state with corporation tax) as long as the net effect on the Federal tax liability is the same. However, if a corporation owner tries to get too clever and uses that strategy, with a few added wrinkles, to avoid Federal taxes, and charge an unrealistic rate of interest, then Section 482 may be invoked.

S-Corporations

An S-Corporation is a regular corporation whose shareholders elect to qualify it under Section 1361 to Section 1379 of the Internal Revenue Code. A common misconception is that there is something special or extra to be done in "forming" an S-Corporation. That is not true. An S-Corporation is just like any other corporation at the outset. It is a regular corporation that later files an election with the IRS to become an S-Corporation.

For example, a newly formed corporation shell may remain a regular corporation, or you, the shareholder(s), may convert it or elect to qualify it as an S-Corporation under the IRS Code.

An S-Corporation is one that pays no income tax. It is exempt from paying income tax by virtue of its S-Corporation status. Instead of the corporation paying tax, the profit or loss of the corporation flows through to the individual shareholders' personal tax returns in the pro rata amount of their stock ownership in the corporation.

Those who have not had experience working with S-Corporations usually believe that there is some complicated procedure to go through or some mysterious red tape that must be coped with to become or qualify as an S-Corporation. That is simply wrong.

Those qualifications for S-Status are as follows:

1. For tax years beginning after 1996, an S-Corporation may have up to 75 Shareholders, with a husband and wife being counted as one, regardless of the manner in which their shares are owned. The estate of a deceased spouse and the surviving spouse are to be treated as one shareholder.

2. The shareholders must be individuals, estates, or certain types of trusts, not corporations or partnerships. However, a partnership can hold S-Corporation stock as a nominee for an eligible shareholder. The Small Business Protection Act of 1996 [hereinafter 1996 Act] has added a number of eligible trusts to aid estate planning for S-Corporations, as well as tax exempt organizations that may participate with S-Corporations (e.g., QSST, ESBT, 401(a) qualified retirement plan trust, 501(c) (3) charitable organizations). The requirements for creating these shareholders are quite technical and if you have a need to operate with one, you should contact a CPA or attorney to assist you.

3. There can be only one class of stock. Dividend and liquidation rights must be equal. However, straight debt is not a second class of stock. Also, voting rights in the one class of stock may be different.

4. There must be no nonresident alien shareholders

5. The corporation must be a domestic corporation.

6. If an S-Corporation has no C-Corporation earnings and profits left over from its C-Corporation years, its entire income can come

from passive income—dividends, interest, rents, royalties, annuities, or securities gains. A corporation with C-Corporation earnings and profits will lose its qualification if it has earnings and profits at the end of each of three years, and its passive income equals more than 25% of its gross receipts in each of those years.

The election must be timely and proper. The corporation must file IRS Form 2553. The election can be made at any time during the preceding taxable year or at any time during the first 75 days of the beginning of the taxable year for which the election is intended. If not filed within 75 days, it will be effective for the following year. The shareholders, who are all required to consent, are those who hold stock on any day during the period the corporation was eligible to make the election.

If you want to get technical (as the law can be that way), then your S-Corporation election must be made before the 15th day of the third month in the first tax year of the corporation (in English; 75 days). Since you must file within 75 days from the beginning of the corporation's tax year, you can probably see that it is very important to know when, according to the law, the first taxable year of the corporation begins. The first month of the corporation's initial taxable year begins at the time that the corporation issues stock, acquires assets, or begins doing business; whichever comes first.

Therefore, you can wait longer than 75 days after the date of incorporation if you have done absolutely nothing with your corporation. In other words, if you have purchased a newly-formed corporation shell, you really have 75 days from the date that you issue the stock to the shareholders, commence doing business, or from the date the corporation acquires assets. Prior to that time, you cannot have done any business as a corporation. You cannot have transferred any assets to your corporation. If you even so much as open a corporate bank account with $10, this avenue is not available to you. Note that this does not mean that your corporation cannot elect "S" status—it simply means that your corporation cannot elect S-Corporation status for that current tax year—it can be treated as an S-Corporation for the next tax year. If you have an existing corporation, as opposed to a new one, you can elect S-Corporation status within 75 days after the beginning of each corporate tax year.

The 1986 Tax Reform Act made some changes to S-Corporations and to the eligible tax years they must use and to the conversion of regular C-Corporations to S-Corporations. The 1986 tax act excepted S-Corporations from certain restrictions placed upon the use of the cash accounting method for regular corporations with gross receipts of over $5,000,000. It also made certain changes as to how income is classified when it is passed to shareholders, as to whether it is passive or active.

The regulations closely resemble the rules that apply to partnerships.

The shareholders report on their individual returns, their respective share of the current taxable income of the corporation. This income, in the hands of the shareholders, is classified in one of three ways: Active, passive or portfolio.

If the shareholder "materially participates" in the business, that shareholder's income is active income. If the shareholder doesn't "materially participate" in the business, then his income is considered to be passive income. [A brief word as to the meaning of "material participation". A taxpayer is said to be materially participating if he or she is involved in the business activity, on a regular, continuous and substantial basis.] Any rental income is considered to be passive income regardless of whether the owner materially participates in the activity or not and it retains its character when passed through the conduit from the corporation to the shareholder. Income such as interest, dividends, etc., is classified as portfolio income (S-Corporation dividends are excepted) and it retains its character when passed through the conduit from the S-Corporation to the shareholder.

Except for S-Corporations that were formerly C-Corporations, and may have previous Earnings and Profits, the treatment of distributions from S-Corporations, whether cash or property, is precisely the same as the distribution from partnerships. Distributions first reduce basis to zero. If they exceed basis, they are taxed as capital gains income. There are specific changeover regulations for corporations that were S-Corporations in prior years. There are also specific regulations for corporations that have Earnings and Profits for any reason. A regular "C" corporation with assets or earnings that wishes to elect "S" status after 1986 may be subject to a so-called "built-in gains" tax placed upon the "recognized gain" on the disposition of certain assets within a defined "recognition period." If you need more information regarding this, you should contact a CPA or attorney.

Many people have heard that S-Corporations are the best entity to adopt for tax purposes. Of course, no business exists solely for the purpose of avoiding tax, but any business trying to make a profit can lose money.

Let's talk about how you as an S-Corporation shareholder, can claim a deduction for business losses.

1. First, of course, obtain a complete corporation package.

2. Then, direct the corporation to acquire for business use, various business assets such as a company car or an airplane, for example. These expenditures are necessary to the conduct and pursuit of the corporation's business in the judgment of the corporation's management, as reflected in the corporate record book in the form of resolutions or minutes. That judgment may be good or bad and

it may be successful or unsuccessful. It may be profitable or unprofitable, and it may go on for a number of years. The corporation continues to try and make a profit. If it is unprofitable, and the corporation loses money, this loss under S-Corporation status passes through as a direct deduction to your personal 1040 federal income tax return, up to the amount you have invested in the corporation!

3. There are many other expenses the corporation will obviously have which may in turn result in a bigger loss to the corporation and a bigger personal tax deduction for you. Some examples are; office rent, telephone bills, travel expense, and various other deductions.

4. By now you are probably thinking, "That's all great, but where does this newly-formed corporation get the money for these expenses and assets in the first place?" That is very simple, too.

   You use the money that you normally would have spent for those items to purchase stock in the corporation. That money is not taxable to the corporation and it is money you have invested in the corporation that the corporation can use to purchase the assets we talked about in Step 1.

   You buy stock in the corporation, which furnishes funds for the corporation's payment of expenses that we have discussed. If the corporation loses money, then that loss becomes a deduction for you, instead of being deferred until the corporation makes a profit against which the loss can be offset

5. Under tax regulations, the deduction you claim from the S-Corporation cannot exceed the investment (basis) you have in the ownership (stock) of the S-Corporation. So, we suggest that you put money into the corporation by an equity investment instead of loaning money to the corporation.

6. In many instances, a Nevada S-Corporation is not even required to qualify or register in many states so long as it is simply trying to get into business, as described above. This can avoid regulatory fees and paperwork.

   For example, under this S-Corporation procedure, your corporation can move you across the nation. The moving expense can become a tax deduction for you instead of a deferred loss to the corporation.

   By the same plan, lawyer and legal expenses can often be

handled through the corporation as a corporate expense instead of a personal expense and, therefore, become a personal tax deduction.

Fringe benefits paid to shareholders of an S-Corporation receive special treatment. For example, if these benefits are paid to owners of more than 2% of the shares, the cost of the benefits is deductible to the S-Corporation and included in the 2% or more shareholder's income, unless a Code provision allows exclusion of the benefit. In 2001, a shareholder is permitted to deduct 60% of the cost of the health insurance premiums paid on his or her behalf. These limits increase to 70 % for 2002 and for 2003, and thereafter, the rate is 100 percent of the cost.

This list of ideas could go on and on, but we hope these concepts will stimulate your thinking and show you how to operate an S-Corporation. Keep in mind that under S-Corporation status, the corporation is NOT taxed. In the event that the corporation has a profit, that profit is passed through to your 1040 personal tax return just like the loss discussed above. This eliminates double taxation on dividends. Otherwise, dividends would be taxed first, at the corporate level and second, when the individual receives them from the corporation.

No Profit Benefits

Here is the story of Mr. and Mrs. John Doe, who tried and failed and still came out ahead. This is an illustration of the merits and advantages that could result from conducting your activities within the framework of a Nevada S-Corporation. You will constantly discover and develop new advantages from the myriad of possible variations and ramifications as you manage and run your own corporation; be it large or small. You will find it usually gets better as you go along. The point is, you have to start, and the time to do that is NOW!

Mr. and Mrs. John Doe got smart. They decided to form a Nevada S-Corporation with the idea in mind of selling pictures painted at home by Mrs. Doe, who at the time was a homemaker. Keep in mind that she was already at home, tending the little Does and keeping a good home for Mr. Doe. Mr. Doe was a good, hard-working, ambitious man. Inflation had driven up their cost of living, the price of food, clothing, gas—everything had gone up faster than he could increase his paycheck.

Mr. Doe was a bit of an entrepreneur at heart. He was determined to better provide for his family. Mrs. Doe was not working and had difficulty, under the circumstances, obtaining work. So to them, their little picture painting business seemed like a good idea. They became entrepreneurs and started their small business. They kept books and properly paid Federal Social Security (FICA), state unemployment insurance, state workman's accident compensation insurance, etc.

Mr. Doe claimed enough dependents in this particular case so that NO income tax withholding was necessary. They had no money to start with (permissible under Nevada law). So, how did the corporation get enough money to pay Mrs. Doe?

Mr. Doe took all of his paycheck each week and purchased stock in the corporation. The money that Mr. Doe put into the corporation is classified as paid-in capital. The total contributions made by shareholders to a corporation, whether in exchange for stock or otherwise, are treated as paid-in capital. These contributions are, therefore, not taxable income to the corporation. The corporation took the money with which Mr. Doe purchased stock and paid Mrs. Doe, along with the various employer/employee insurance contributions required. Mrs. Doe, in turn, used her earnings (the same money that Mr. Doe earned and invested) to support the Doe family.

NOTE: Mrs. Doe could have been paid all or in part by the issuance of stock, promissory notes or other instruments from the corporation so long as the employer/employee employment taxes were paid in cash. The effect of this can be to:

1) Decrease the investment capital required;
2) Conserve cash flow; and
3) Increase her protection and the amount of benefits payable to her under the various coverages in the event she should become eligible for any benefits.

(Consider the protection and cash benefits Mrs. Doe could have from State Industrial Insurance or Workman's Compensation if she were temporarily or permanently disabled on the job.)

Their intentions were good and they valiantly tried. Mrs. Doe painted pictures for the corporation and the corporation tried to market and sell the pictures. During this period, Mrs. Doe even became pregnant and had a baby without affecting her employment. (The corporation graciously gave her time off with pay to have the baby.)

At the end of the year of trying diligently to succeed, the corporation had sold only a few pictures to relatives and friends and certainly had NO profit. In fact, as a result of this failure and other bad judgments and circumstances, the corporation had lost all the money Mr. Doe had invested. The corporate loss predominately amounted to all of the money the corporation had spent in wages paid to Mrs. Doe. Therefore, the corporation finally made a good decision and put Mrs. Doe on lay-off status due to the lack of sales. Mrs. Doe, whose occupation was Corporate Secretary and Picture Painter, could not find other employment consistent with her occupation. Therefore, she correctly filed for and collected the unemployment benefits to which she was legally entitled and for which the corporation had been compelled to pay during her period of employment. The end result was that the family gained several thousand dollars in legal employment benefits as a result of conducting this activity within a proper corporate structure.

It also happened that Mr. and Mrs. Doe were able to deduct the corporate loss (to the extent of their investment) from their other individual earnings and they legally saved a considerable amount of income taxes. In fact, Mr. Doe got a nice, fat refund check from the friendly IRS for the federal income taxes withheld by his employer.

The corporation then became dormant for a year or so. This was no big deal, because it only cost them a couple of hundred dollars per year, including their Resident Agent fees, to maintain their corporation in good standing.

After the dormant year or so, the corporation decided to try again. (They were already incorporated and did not have to incorporate again.) Try again they did! The corporation decided to rehire Mrs. Doe. Regretfully, the same failure resulted, but once again the Does came out many thousands of dollars ahead, by the same set of circumstances. In fact, as a result, the Doe family prospered.

Again after a period of dormancy and inactivity, the corporation decided to try again. The third time's a charm! This time the corporation finally found a market for its pictures. Like all good entrepreneurs, they finally made it, and made it big! The Does now have paid executives to run their company and they are paid directors of the corporation. They live happily and comfortably on the dividends and earnings paid to them from the corporation, plus many other outstanding fringe benefits they enjoy from the corporation.

Note that even in apparent failure, the Doe family profited substantially. You, too, can be as smart and innovative as the Does. This is a case in point that it pays to try—that when you try, you can lose and still win—that it pays to incorporate!

Although, the unemployment insurance system took somewhat of a beating for a couple of years, the Doe corporation has been compelled to pay in so much as a result of its success that even the insurance system recovered and has realized a profit on the Does' efforts and their resulting contributions to society. They say that this is what insurance is for; to help when the chips are down.

Social Security (FICA) Taxes and the S-Corporation

As a rule, whenever an employer pays salary or wages to an employee, the employer and the employee both must pay Social Security tax (FICA). For example, as of 2000, the employer and the employee must contribute 7.65% each on all wages up to a certain maximum salary or wage, which is the legal tax base.

By implementing a somewhat aggressive strategy, the S-Corporation can be used to reduce the payment of Social Security tax. This strategy is workable because of the distinction between a "dividend" and "salary ".

An S-Corporation is no less a corporation because of its S-Corporation election. Insofar as the employer/employee relationship is concerned, it is treated just like a regular corporation. The employer (your corporation) can decide whether to pay you, a shareholder and officer, a dividend or a salary. FICA tax is due and payable on salary and wages. No FICA tax is withheld or paid in connection with payment of a dividend. Be aware, however, that if the shareholder/employee performs substantial services, reasonable compensation must be paid by the corporation. Let us assume that your S-Corporation makes $30,000 in a given year. "Reasonable compensation" may be $6,000 for the year. The remaining $24,000 could be paid as a dividend. This way, the FICA tax is paid on only the $6,000, and not the entire $30,000. (Or—you may wish to borrow the $24,000. This will be tax deferred, if handled right.)

There could be some drawbacks here if your corporation is planning to adopt, or has already implemented a pension or profit-sharing plan. Consider your options and proceed with the best strategy for you. Remember, the amount you usually contribute to your pension plan may be a percentage of your salary or wages, not of your dividends.

Retirement, Social Security and Your Nevada Corporation

In all probability, you have a relative or friend who may reap benefits from some of the possibilities in the following explanation. For the most part, Social Security is a bureaucratic rip-off! Retirees should be adequately recompensed when one considers a legitimate return on the dollars invested. After all, Social Security is not welfare. Retirees paid into the system for all the years they were employed.

For 1997, the amount of income a person, between age 65 and 69, drawing Social Security benefits can earn, without having those Social Security benefits reduced, is $13,500 per year. Thereafter, for every $3.00 in reportable income earned above the $13,500, benefits are reduced by $1.00. As anyone knows, $13,500 in this day and age is a wholly inadequate amount to live on. The earnings limit is $8,640 for persons under 65 and the benefit reduction is $1.00 for every $2.00 over the earnings limit. Earnings in or after the month you reach age 70 do not affect your Social Security Benefits.

NOTE: The earnings limits are changed by Congress every year, beginning in January so check for updated earnings limits every year to help your tax planning.

There is a secret, magic word in the above—reportable. Reportable income includes commissions, wages, fees, vacation and/or severance pay, tips, when they exceed $20 per month, etc. These must be reported annually to the Social Security Administration on HEW Form 777.

The above is simple enough, and there is a simple, legal, intelligent solution to the problem. The solution is to have income that is not required to be reported. Income that need not be reported includes pensions, veterans benefits, royalties, rental income from real estate, gifts and inheritances, capital gains, annuity income, interest on savings and investment income in the form of dividends. This last one, dividends, deserves closer study! Therein lies a little bit of the end of the rainbow: the opportunity to kill two birds with one stone; to make money and still be entitled to your hard-earned and well-deserved Social Security benefits.

What is the answer? It is simple, easy, economical and affordable. Create an S-Corporation.

Establish a corporation and have your corporation negotiate a contract on a fee basis with your former employer or others. Run your business in the usual manner, deducting costs from receipts to get net earnings. You and the other shareholders receive the net earnings, not as wages, but as dividends. You will still have to pay tax on the dividend income, but it does not reduce your monthly Social Security benefit. No matter how much money you make.

There are hundreds of thousands of retirees who could use this completely legal means to better their life.

Qualified Personal Service Corporations

A Qualified Personal Service Corporation (or a QPIC) is a corporation whose principal activity is the performance of personal services that are substantially performed by employees who own more than 10% of the outstanding stock. This is a classification that you'll want to avoid, if possible. The tax liability associated with a QPIC is burdensome. We'll elaborate later, but first, what is a Qualified Personal Service Corporation?

There are two tests that determine whether a corporation is a QPIC: a Function test, and an Ownership test. These are tests you'll want your corporation to flunk.

Function Test: The function test is met if substantially all (95% based on compensation costs) of a corporation's activities involve the performance of services in the fields of health and veterinary services, law, engineering (including surveying and mapping), architecture, accounting, actuarial science, performing arts or consulting.

Ownership Test: Specifically, this test requires that at least 95% of the value of the corporation's stock must be owned directly (or indirectly through one or more partnerships that does not have a corporation as a partner, S-Corporations, or qualified PSCs that are not tax shelters) by 1) current or retired employees; 2) the estates of current or retired employees;

or 3) persons who acquired the stock by reason of the death of such employees (but only for a 24-month period that begins on the date of the death of such employees).

In order to pass the test, the employees owning stock must perform services for the corporation in connection with activities involving one of the fields above. Indirect holdings through a trust are taken into account. For purposes of applying the ownership test, community property laws are disregarded, and stock owned by an ESOP or a pension plan is considered to be owned by the beneficiaries of the plan.

At the election of the common parent of an affiliated group, all members of the group may be treated as a single entity if 90% or more of the activities of such group involve the performance of services in the same qualified field. Stock is considered to be held indirectly by a person to the extent that he or she owns an interest in a partnership, S-Corporation, or Qualified Personal Service Corporation that owns such stock. For purposes of applying the ownership test, stock attribution rules, other than those already mentioned above, are to be ignored. The ownership test would not be considered to be met if non-employee children owned more than 5% of the stock, despite the fact that their father might be an employee of the corporation.

If the corporation meets both of the above tests, then it is considered to be a Qualified Personal Service Corporation.

With one notable exception, status as a QPSC is not beneficial. A QPSC is exempt from the rule denying the cash method of accounting to corporations with more than $5 million in gross revenues. Now, the downside of QPIC status:

1. Loss of the benefit of lower graduated corporate tax rates; all taxable income is taxed at the rate of 35%;

2. Allows the IRS to reallocate income and deductions between the corporation and employee-owner where QPSC is formed for tax avoidance motive;

3. Generally requires the corporation to have a calendar year;

4. Limits loss deductions to the investment amount at risk; and

5. Limits deductions for passive losses.

Tips About QPSC Status

The chain of stock ownership by attribution under Code Section 318 is only as strong as its weakest link. Severing the weakest link by having the employee-owner own 10% or less of the stock, with the balance owned by in-laws, brothers, sisters or individuals as listed above, will escape status as a Qualified Personal Service Corporation. Or, conversely, see that non-employee owners own more than 90%, or see that certain employees not connected to personal service activities own more than 90%. Also, if 80% or more of the corporation's compensation costs are paid to non-owner employees, who also perform services, then the corporation is not a Qualified Personal Service Corporation. Since S-Corporations are not subject to PQSC provisions, an S-Corporation election will terminate status as a Qualified Personal Service Corporation as well.

Personal Holding Company

In 1934 the Personal Holding Company surtax provisions were added to the Internal Revenue Code. Wealthy individuals who placed their stocks, bonds, and other investments into controlled corporations to take advantage of the corporate tax brackets, which were lower than the highest individual tax brackets at that time, were referred to as "incorporated pocketbooks."

Put simply, a Personal Holding Company is a regular C-Corporation, not an S-Corporation in which five or fewer individuals own more than 50% of the stock which derives more than 60% of its income from Personal Holding Company Income sources as described below.

By Internal Revenue Code definition, a C-Corporation is a Personal Holding Company if it meets the following tests:

1. If at any time during the last half of the tax year more than 50% in value of the outstanding stock is owned, directly or indirectly, by or for not more than five individuals (including stock ownership by attribution under code section 544, which includes stock owned by brothers, sisters, spouse, grandchildren, and partners. Unlike Code Section 318, or QPSCs, PHC attribution rules include all lineal descendants, ancestors, and brothers and sisters), and,
2. At least 60 percent of adjusted ordinary income for the tax year is "Personal Holding Company Income."

Personal Holding Income

As distinguished from an operating company's normal operating income and capital gains, Personal Holding Company Income includes:

1. Dividends, interest, and royalties (many exemptions apply here if interest or royalties are the primary trade or business of the corporation);

2. Rents, unless rents are greater than 50% of adjusted gross income, and a 10% test is met regarding dividends received. (If there are no dividends, then there is no problem—your corporation is not a personal holding company);

3. Mineral, oil, and gas royalties, unless similar 50% and 10% tests are met as in (2) above (again, if you have no dividends, you have no worry);

4. Copyright royalties, unless similar 50% and 10% tests are met (again, no dividends, no problem);

5. Produced-film rents;

6. Payments received from a 25% or greater shareholder for the use of personal property;

7. Payments received from personal service contracts for services performed by a 25% or greater shareholder, who is specifically named in the service contract by the other party to the contract, and whose services are   so specialized that no other person or substitute can be named to perform the services on behalf of the corporation;

8. Income derived from loan interest (unless a small business lending company exemption is met as could be the case for the "Warbucks" strategy. This exemption applies if generally the corporation has qualifying business expenses equal to at least 15% of the first $500,000. The company must receive 60% or more of its income from an active and regular lending or financing business. No more than 20% of its ordinary gross income can be from sources such as dividends, rents, royalties and so forth; or,

9. Any gain derived from the sale of any interest in an estate or trust.

Disadvantages of Personal Holding Company Status
The penalty for being classified, as a PHC is a 39.6% additional sur-tax over and above the normal corporate tax rates on "Undistributed Personal Holding Company Income".

Is There a Way Out of PHC Status?
Your first line of defense here, if you think you have a problem, is to try to meet an exemption. This is usually a good possibility if your business

is in copyrights, oil or gas royalties, making loans, renting real or personal property or providing personal services. Secondly, there are strategy options that you have available to "get out of the pickle."

Tips to Avoid PHC Status

1. Consider an S-Corporation election, since an S-Corporation is not subject to PHC tax provisions or, use an LLC instead of a corporation.

2. Reduce the amount of PHC income below 60%. For instance, dividend income can be reduced by investing only in growth stocks instead of yield stocks. Interest income can be reduced through shifting investments to exempt state and municipal obligations.

3. Increase operating income above 40%.

4. When using personal service contracts, avoid naming a 25% or greater shareholder as the individual to perform the service. If this is still not possible, add a provision to the service contract that allows the corporation to name a substitute providing the named employee-owner cannot perform the service.

5. If possible, spread ownership among at least 11 unrelated shareholders so no five shareholders own greater than 50%.

6. Structure your affairs to meet an exemption if income is derived from royalties or interest.

Many unenlightened attorneys and CPAs that do not fully understand corporate strategy options are highly distraught over passive income and the personal holding corporation trap. This should not be a problem with adequate planning. Particularly, if the shareholders involved have enough business savvy to implement a specific corporate strategy when necessary. This strategy is a simple one involving two corporations.

The tactic is that whenever you are approaching an undesirable percentage of passive income (60%), make sure that the other corporation does some business with the passive income corporation.

Purchase certain items or services through or from it, in order to alter the passive income percentage. This way, you are pumping active income into the corporation. Pump enough active income into the corporation so that it is no longer in danger of being classified as a personal holding corporation.

Let's say the other corporation purchases $50,000 worth of items and services from the passive income corporation. That means $50,000 has gone from the other corporation to the passive income corporation. Now the passive corporation will purchase certain items and services from the other corporation.

The other corporation has its $50,000 back in the bank. The passive income corporation is no longer a PHC because it has enough active business to alter the critical percentage. The entire transaction was a wash. There are no other taxable consequences or liabilities.

If Personal Holding Company status cannot be avoided, the penalty can be avoided by reducing taxable income to zero or below by increasing expense deductions that can include salaries to employee-owners. Also, don't forget perks like pensions and medical reimbursement plans.

Foreign Nationals

So you're thinking, "This is really quite an idea, but I don't understand what it has to do with me. After all, I am a foreign citizen, and not a resident or citizen of the United States, let alone Nevada!" That may be true, however, under Nevada law, you don't have to be a resident of Nevada or a citizen of the United States to own and operate a Nevada corporation.

The important point to remember is that when you own a Nevada corporation, the corporation exists as a separate entity. You can live in another state in the United States, or in Canada, Germany, England, Spain, Nigeria, Australia, Japan, China, Taiwan or any country in the world. It is the corporation which conforms to the requirements of the state in which it resides. And Nevada, you will find, is the state with the benefits to protect you and your corporation.

Non-U.S. Citizens Welcome in Nevada

Effective July 1, 1981, the Nevada Legislature made a very important change in its corporate law. Nevada corporate owners and operators are no longer required to be United States citizens. That's good news for you, if it applies.

Why would you want to have your own corporation in the United States? You would want it to protect your profits, to increase your assets, and to save your money. To do with your money as you please, with as much control over its disbursement as possible. Remember, anybody can buy a corporation in Nevada and make it work for them, inexpensively, easily, legitimately and ethically.

You buy a Nevada corporation, already formed, and have it do contracted, real work with your foreign business. For example, the corporation can contract to do services such as research and development, accounting, advertising, copyright service, etc. Use the corporation for consulting services. Buy options, real estate and other property from your Nevada corporation.

Perhaps you have an engineering company. Buy a ready-made corporation in Nevada. Use the corporation to do the research and development needed for your foreign company. Contract with the Nevada corporation for the services. Your Nevada corporation will bill the foreign corporation roughly what the foreign corporation's yearly profit would be for the services rendered. This procedure transfers the profit or earnings from the foreign company to your Nevada corporation.

You project a $50,000 profit in your foreign company. Your Nevada corporation will bill the company approximately $50,000 for advertising and marketing services, for example. Now, the $50,000 is in Nevada, where there is no state corporate or franchise tax. There is no capital stock tax, no succession tax or stock transfer fees or taxes. The business in your home country didn't make a profit for that year so you probably won't pay taxes to your home government.

By owning a legitimate, legal United States corporation, you have also gained a measure of U.S. citizenship through your corporation—sort of a "remote control" citizenship, one could say. Remember, the corporation is a citizen of the state in which it is founded and is subject to the laws and provisions of that state. You could choose to be employed in the United States if you wish. Through your corporation, you have access to the benefits of any U.S. citizen.

In a sense, now you have dual citizenship, the best of two countries by merit of your U.S. corporation. The doors to financial freedom and creativity are all yours.

There are minimal disclosure and reporting requirements. Shareholders and owners of Nevada corporations are anonymous and not a matter of public record. Nevada is reaching out its arms to corporations, inviting them to be at home in Nevada.

Additional Benefits of a Nevada Corporation

Tax savings are only one among many benefits you may enjoy as an owner and operator of your own Nevada corporation.

More and more people are finding that a nice, secure, operating office in Nevada is a valuable alternative to have at your command for a wide variety of situations that may arise. Be prepared; have that alternate ace in the hole, another base, a welcome haven in a troubled world and economy. It pays, not only in profit but also in security and peace of mind

Visa Enhancement

Once you have purchased your U.S. corporation, you may become elibible for an L-Visa under that status of an intracompany transferee.

As an executive or manager of your corporation, you will have to fulfill three requirements to qualify for the L–Visa:

1. Document that you are an executive or manager of the foreign affiliate where you reside.

2. Document that you are needed by your U.S. corporate affiliate.

3. Document your experience related to corporate needs.

"You cannot bring about prosperity by discouraging thrift. You cannot strengthen the weak by weakening the strong. You cannot help the wage earner by pulling down the wage payer. You cannot further the brotherhood of man by encouraging class hatred. You cannot help the poor by destroying the rich. You cannot keep out of trouble by spending more than you earn. You cannot build character and courage by taking away man's initiative and independence. You cannot help men permanently by doing for them what thy could and should do for themselves."

Abraham Lincoln

Business Verses Personal Asset Protection

Up to this point, we have only considered a strategy dealing with the protection of assets related to your home company or business. Your home state business, the one with the exposure, I refer to throughout this text as "Red, Inc." There are, however, situations where you may not wish to incorporate. And, even though incorporating your home state business is a very important step in protecting assets, if you are in a circumstance where this is inappropriate, you can still have protection from your private Nevada or Wyoming corporation, which throughout this text is referred to as "Warbucks."

The same principles apply to you as they do your home state company. Simply insert yourself in the place of Red, Inc., in the various illustrations you have reviewed and in most cases you will be able to achieve the same result of significantly improving asset protection. Generally, one will want to protect both their business assets and their personal assets. So, you ought to be thinking about some other things you can do.

Suppose you were concerned that not only your home state corporation could be sued, but that such an event would also include you personally. As you know, in most situations where a corporation borrows money, a lender will require a personal guaranty from the corporation's owner or principal. Very often, the lender will also require that the guarantor put up additional collateral for such a loan, very often the person's home. Warbucks in your situation may do the same thing. By requiring you to sign a personal guaranty and add additional collateral, and then filing a UCC-1 against you personally, as well as recording a deed of trust or mortgage against your real estate, you would find yourself in the same position as Red, Inc., judgment proof.

The strategy we have looked at thus far assumes that Warbucks has the cash available to fund a loan to Red, Inc. A transaction of this nature needs to be funded, because if it is not, the encumbrances against Red, Inc. are not likely to withstand scrutiny. What happens, then, if Warbucks doesn't have the cash necessary to make this situation work? Debt can be created by more than just a cash loan. Anything of value can be used to provide consideration for a note. Some possibilities are, advertising services, marketing services, mental property, purchasing, contract rights, real or personal property, or lines of credit, to name a few.

Can Warbucks perform a service for Red, Inc.? Does Warbucks have something to sell? These are a couple of the questions that you would need to explore to find alternatives to cash consideration. Let's look at a couple of examples to get things rolling. First, suppose that Red, Inc. is accustomed to doing a considerable amount of advertising. What would happen if Red, Inc. were to contract with Warbucks to handle its advertising for the next five years. Suppose that Red, Inc. spends $25,000. on advertising now, and plans on expanding its efforts. It hires Warbucks to handle the future advertising. Warbucks agrees to take care of everything for $50,000. per year, inclusive of hard costs and Warbucks' fees. A five-year contract at $50,000. per year would total $250,000. for the contract. Warbucks wants to be paid up front, but Red, Inc. lacks the cash right now, so Warbucks agrees to accept a down payment and a note for the rest at 18% interest. The result is that you are now ready to begin the strategy. Of course, Warbucks will be the one that actually contracts the advertising for Red, Inc., Red, Inc. pays the money to Warbucks to cover the hard cost, Warbucks pays the vendor, and there is consideration for the note. Warbucks earns a profit in tax-free Nevada, and Red, Inc. generates deductible expenses back home.

Protecting Mental Property

Mental property can consist of many things, copyrights, patents, recipes, formulas and so on. If Warbucks has this sort of mental property, and Red, Inc. needs it, there is no reason that Warbucks couldn't sell it to Red, Inc. Let's say that Red, Inc. is in the business of producing resins and epoxies, and it needs a formula that Warbucks owns. Red, Inc. offers to purchase the formula, or the rights to use the formula from Warbucks. They agree on a price of $100,000, but Red, Inc. doesn't have that kind of cash. Warbucks agrees to take a note at 21% interest. You probably get the idea!

The same thing can work for almost anything of value. In the section on case studies, we will look at many different possibilities in greater detail. What you need to understand at this juncture is that the Warbucks – Red, Inc. strategy can be put into effect even if Warbucks doesn't have the cash to make a loan.

Is Warbucks a Real Corporation

Before we continue further, we need to examine whether your Nevada or Wyoming private corporation, "Warbucks" is a real company under law. In other words, is this merely a sham or a shell game? Warbucks as a validly existing Nevada or Wyoming corporation needs to have certain things in place before it can pass the acid test of absolute legitimacy.

Suppose that you were investigating Warbucks to determine if it is a force to be reckoned with in a possible lawsuit against Red, Inc. You have discovered that Red, Inc. is encumbered to Warbucks, and if you can't get past the encumbrance, then you see no reason to proceed with a suit. If you were in this position, what would you look for?

The most elementary thing you would probably look at would be its address. Does it have one? You find an address listed on the UCC-1 that it filed against Red, Inc.'s assets. Is it a real address, or is it a post office box? If it's not a real, physical address, you may be curious to check further. Next, you wonder what would happen if you called its offices, so you call information for the city listed in the address to get a phone number. If there is no phone number, you will begin to smell blood, but you get one. You might then call the number wondering if it will be answered. If it is an answering machine, things won't look too good for Warbucks, but when you call, a receptionist answers in the corporate name and asks how your call should be directed. Bad news for you. Then you call the city offices to see if Warbucks has a city business license, after all, how could a legal operation not have a business license? The city gives you a license number. More bad news.

At this point, you need to take a quick break from your investigating and consider what you have found. If laymen could figure these simple steps out, it would seem rational to assume that a professional investigator would figure it out. Does Warbucks have these bases covered? If so, then it has passed several tests. If not, it has a problem. A professional investigator may also be able to find out whether or not it has a bank account, as well. Your Nevada company really needs to have a bank account if it is an operating business entity and doing business. Over the years, courts have looked at many things when trying to figure out if a corporation is "real". From these many cases, the following five tests have emerged as critical ones that your corporation must not fail:

1. An actual business address, and the documentation to prove it
2. A telephone listed in the corporation's name
3. A business license
4. A corporate bank account
5. Transactions with unrelated parties

These are the same five things discussed above. If a corporation has these things, then it will usually be considered to be operating legitimately. If Warbucks is supposed to be doing business in Nevada or Wyoming, then it needs to meet these tests in the correct state, and not in your home state.

In the event that someone checks further into the corporation, there are certain operational questions that need to be addressed as well. Most of these are covered in the sub-chapter, piercing the corporate veil, and others are listed below:

Validations
 1. Keep personal and corporate funds separate
 2. Document all transactions with the corporation
 3. Never commingle assets such as inventory or property between yourself and your corporation, or between related corporations
 4. Make sure to sign documents in the corporate name
 5. Remember to operate corporation's autonomously
 6. Keep separate corporate record books if you have more than one corporation
 7. Keep separate accounts if you have more than one corporation
 8. Hold separate corporate meetings if you have more than one corporation
 9. Remember to identify your business as a corporation.
 10. Make sure that creditors know they are dealing with a corporation
 11. Use the corporate name wherever and whenever you use the business name
 12. Keep your corporation renewed and in good standing
 13. Pay corporate annual filings on time
 14. Never dissolve a corporation with debts
 15. Ensure that your corporation is properly capitalized, with enough capitalization to give it a reasonable chance to succeed

Once your Warbucks corporation has covered these considerations, then you can rest assured that it is real, legitimate and will help you in your strategy.

At this juncture, there are some additional questions that need to be considered, such as who should be the officers and directors, and who should own the stock.

Initial Officers and Directors
You have lots of choices beginning with you, your spouse, an adult son or daughter, a relative, friend or business associate. There is another

factor to consider, and that is privacy. How much privacy do you want or need to achieve is a question that you will need to consider before making a decision.

Financial privacy is something that most Americans assumed in the past, but as has been discussed already, it is no longer a fact of modern life. Whether or not you should care about it is another question. Who needs to know your business? Where Warbucks is concerned, would it be more to your advantage to have another person show on the public record as the officer and director? In most cases the answer is yes. This is because a quick search on the Internet will show anybody who is looking that you are the officer of Warbucks, and that is likely to lead to questions from a potential opponent who would like to sweep Warbucks out of the picture to take your assets. Having another person, unrelated to you, will often take this sort of attack away. In such a case, privacy can be an important consideration. When you file a UCC-1, do you want to be the one to sign for both corporations? Again, the answer is probably not. Thus, you would be well advised to have different people listed as officers and directors of Warbucks than are listed for Red, Inc. Another possibility for the officers and directors for Warbucks would be your attorney, or a professional nominee.

Professional nominees are people who serve in various capacities for you, with a binding contract that sets forth what they will and will not do, and who can direct their actions. They enable you to retain control of the corporation, without serving in the offices yourself.

The next matter for your consideration will be who should own Warbucks. Once again, you can own the stock yourself. However, in most cases this is not the best way to proceed, because if you are sued yourself, you could loose the stock of Warbucks, and end up loosing everything. Some other possibilities would be to have a relative own the stock, a friend, a business associate, use bearer shares, use encrypted stock, or use another entity, such as a limited partnership. Again, each has its advantages and disadvantages, but you need to consider how you will maintain control of Warbucks. Can you control your relatives, and do you want them knowing your business? How about friends and associates?

For most situations, the use of a limited partnership makes a tremendous amount of sense, because they are easy to control, you can be protected against loosing your interest, and they can also be used as an effective estate planning tool. From the case studies in Chapter 10, you can see how others have successfully used them to own Warbucks.

Bearer shares and encrypted shares, on the other hand, usually create more problems than they are worth. Bearer shares are available to Nevada corporations, and are stocks that are issued to the bearer, not to a specific individual or entity. In effect, they are like cash, essentially non-traceable. Whoever holds them physically owns them. If you loose a bearer certificate and someone else finds it, they own your stock, and there is nothing that you can do about it. This should be enough to avoid their use. However, some persist, because they believe that they can put the certificate away somewhere, like in a safe deposit box, and say under oath that they don't own them. The fact is, that in a case like this they do own them and saying otherwise under oath is a crime.

Encrypted shares are share certificates, which are electronically encrypted so that no one can view them without the correct software and key. They are normally regular registered shares issued to an individual or entity. Like bearer shares, they are often used by people who believe that they will have the ability to lie about stock ownership without getting caught. This practice is not recommended. There are simply too many legitimate methods of holding stock to even consider such things.

In the next section, we will discuss several special situations, which will assist you in understanding how the Warbucks – Red, Inc. strategy can be modified to fit special circumstances. As you read this section, be thinking about which of these things may apply to your situation, and how you might apply them.

Using Assets as Capital Contributions Without Owning Stock

This is a common situation, which can be easily overcome by anyone who wants to follow these simple steps. A capital contribution is made when something of value is transferred to a corporation in exchange for its stock. It is a tax neutral transaction, and provides the basis of ownership, allowing you to retain control of the corporation. Such an asset can be anything of value, including cash, mental property, real estate, equipment, motor vehicles, or whatever. Here is how to accomplish the transfer without owning stock in Warbucks.

First, incorporate your Nevada corporation. Second, form a limited partnership. This in most cases will be a family limited partnership, with you and potentially your spouse as general partners, and your adult children or a family security trust as limited partner. By using a family security trust, you can maintain the estate planning benefits of the partnership without directly involving your children in the partnership, creating gift tax implications, or confusion regarding a controlled group.

Next, contribute the asset to the partnership in exchange for your interest as a general partner. Now, you have "paid" for your control position in the partnership. Then, have the partnership contribute the asset to the corporation in exchange for the corporation's stock. The partnership ends up as the stockholder of the corporation. You are the general partner of the partnership, with full management authority over the partnership. As a result, you are also the one who, on behalf of the partnership, will vote the corporation's stock. This is controlling the corporation without owning it. Finally, you also have an estate plan set up for the benefit of your heirs.

Asset Protection for Licensed Professionals

Licensed professionals have a more difficult time separating their business liabilities from their personal liabilities than perhaps do non-licensed business people, because they cannot simply incorporate out from under their business liability that derives from their licensed profession. However, they can still have asset protection using the Warbucks – Red, Inc. strategy format. In their case, they can encumber their personal assets through a personal guaranty of Red, Inc.'s loan and provide additional assets for collateral. By doing so, while they may still face liability, they are less attractive targets because their assets are not available to judgment creditors who come along later.

Using Lines of Credit

A line of credit can be useful in the implementation of the Warbucks strategy when no other option is available. It has one drawback that will need to be understood in advance, and that is that it will not completely stand up in the collection phase of a lawsuit. It will, however provide your first line of defense, which is making you an unattractive target.

In using this tool, first realize that a line of credit is an agreement to lend money up to a certain amount, usually in irregular installments called advances. If the line of credit is $100,000 for example, the lender will lend up to that amount in advances that can be requested by the borrower over time and as needed. As each advance is made, it begins to accrue interest. The unadvanced portion does not accrue interest. However, in some cases, a line of credit will contain provisions that require up front fees, often set up as a percentage of the credit limit. These fees may be paid in cash, or be allowed to become advances on the credit line and subject to interest. If you had a million dollar credit line containing a set up fee and annual facilities fee of 2% each, you would owe Warbucks $40,000. at the inception of the note, giving Warbucks cash to advance back to Red, Inc., or simply allow the fees to become advances on the credit line. Either way, you will begin to pay interest to Warbucks, providing Warbucks a pool of cash to advance to Red, Inc. later on, which in turn will increase the amount of interest to be paid.

Over a period of time, you can extend the entire amount of the credit line, which will work to your benefit, should the worst come. It is important to cause as much use of the credit line as possible, because the portion of the credit line that is not advanced is the portion that will not stand if someone is trying to take your assets. If you have 30% of your credit line advanced, a judgment creditor could take equity in your assets amounting to the other 70% of the credit line.

The saving grace of the structure is that the encumbrances that would be found in an asset search would cover the entire line of credit, whether advanced or not. This fact may be quite familiar to you if you have a home equity line from a bank. They file a deed of trust or mortgage against your home for the entire amount of the home equity line at the time of the note, before any advances are taken, and Warbucks would do no less. The opposition is not entitled to know about the details of the credit line and how much has been advanced until after a judgment is rendered, and a debtor's exam is under way, usually a process requiring several years.

Re-domiciling the Corporation

The state of Wyoming offers a great tool for those who are finding difficulty in capitalizing Warbucks. This concept is called re-domestication. When done offshore, it is generally referred to as re-domiciling the corporation. With this unique provision, Wyoming allows you to move an existing corporation from any state into Wyoming, as if it were a new Wyoming corporation but retaining the original date of incorporation. Here is how the process works:

Your existing corporation files Articles of Domestication in Wyoming, with a Certificate of Good Standing, not more than 30 days old from the original state of incorporation. (A certificate in good standing is a simple one-page document requested of the state to demonstrate that the corporation is then based there and its fees paid up.) When this happens, your old home state corporation becomes a Wyoming corporation with the original date of incorporation. From a tax point of view, this is a "Type F Reorganization". Next, your new, old Wyoming corporation sells your home state business to a newly formed corporation in your home state, taking back a note for the payment, and securing the note with the assets of the business. Instantly, you have put the Warbucks strategy into action! Let's go through this one more time with an example.

Red, Inc. is in California, and has a retail store. Let's say it was incorporated in 1988. Red, Inc. files Articles of Domestication in Wyoming in 2002, and becomes a Wyoming corporation, however it maintains the original incorporation date of 1988. Then, you form a new California corporation. The new corporation buys the business from the Wyoming corporation for say $100,000. Since the business was bought by a start up company, the new corporation doesn't have $100,000. The seller, now in Wyoming, agrees to finance the purchase by taking a note for $100,000. To ensure that it is paid, the new 1988 Wyoming corporation requires the assets of the business as collateral, and files a UCC-1. Then, you dissolve the old 1988 corporation in California to terminate its California connection.

The old Red, Inc. becomes Warbucks, and the new California corporation becomes the new Red, Inc. This approach may have tax consequences in certain circumstances, but it is certainly an effective way to get the strategy rolling, and it would be difficult to argue with the consideration for the debt structure of the new Red, Inc.

SECTION IV

Corporate Formalities & Forms

FORMS, MINUTES, RESOLUTIONS, NOTES
AGREEMENTS AND CONTRACTS

CHAPTER 14

FORMS, MINUTES, RESOLUTIONS, NOTES AGREEMENTS AND CONTRACTS

"The difference between death and taxes is death doesn't get worse every time Congress meets."

Will Rogers

Why Forms?

A corporation can do essentially everything you can do but think! That is the reason a corporation has a board of directors — to do it's thinking for it. If challenged, it becomes very important that the corporation be able to prove that it thought. Here's where the forms come in — as proof that the corporation thought. A corporation's thoughts are reduced to some form of writing, or record, usually in the form of a resolution or minutes. Then if the corporation ever needs to, it can prove it thought. In other words, it can prove its board of directors did its thinking. The resolutions, minutes, or other forms are all part of its corporate records.

In order to effectively keep corporate records, it is important to have a good quality corporation kit and record book. Many people tend to place little significance on these items until it's too late. That is to say, until they discover themselves a defendant in a lawsuit and plaintiff's counsel attaches their personal assets due to lax record keeping, or until a tax commission gets hold of the corporate record book and decides that since record keeping was lax, they will simply hold the stockholders responsible for any liabilities.

This is where the tightfisted "do it yourselfers" fall into the tar pit of liability and ruin. It's happened time and time again. Maybe you can picture it: A thrifty but short-sighted individual, convinced of his intelligence, decides to save a few money and files some papers at the state house, and calls it a corporation. He smugly believes he has a corporation along with all of its wonderful protection, until one day he gets to court where his corporation is being sued ... and then ... he hears a judge saying something to the effect, "This corporation just didn't act like a corporation —— it didn't keep records properly . There's no proof that its directors thought for it. There are no minutes of any meetings. There's just a form from the state! I'll order that your personal bank account, house, and any other assets you have be seized until this judgment is satisfied. Court is adjourned."

The lesson here is that it is critically important to keep good records,

206

and downright foolish not to do so. The main purpose of this section of the book is to help you perform this most important task correctly and thoroughly.

Working With Forms

The forms included in this book will be of material assistance to those organizing or managing corporations. The forms are not intended to be all-inclusive. They are intended to give you a broad enough spectrum from which, simply by using a little common sense, you or someone in your organization can word a resolution, minutes, or other form to say what you want it to so it will have the force and effect you wish.

Many of the enclosed forms may be exactly what you're looking for — for others you may want to take a part from this form and a part from another. Most of the time you can mix and match as it suits your corporation's needs. However, sometimes state laws dictate procedures or contents of forms.

The forms in this book were originated with Nevada specifically in mind. However, they should generally be acceptable in any state. Periodically you should have your forms reviewed by an attorney.

Corporate Formalities

Perhaps corporate formalities are the most important thing in the final analysis, regarding the legality of your corporation. What are corporate formalities? They are, simply stated, the responsibilities of keeping your corporate record book or records in compliance with all laws and regulations. The fewer stockholders a corporation has, the more important this becomes. Certainly in the case of a one-person corporation, it is literally everything!

You may have heard of Litigators "piercing the corporate veil." This will not happen to your corporation if corporate formalities are properly followed and there is no fraud or wrongful intent perpetrated. That is why it is all-important to observe corporate formalities. One important element courts look at to determine if the corporation has acted like a corporation is the corporate records. In good corporate records all decisions are documented to prove that it was the corporation acting and not the stockholders as functioning as individuals.

Alter Ego

This theory is applied when stockholders use their corporation in such a way that the corporation is not a separate entity from the stockholders — in other words, stockholders use the corporate entity as their "alter ego." Lack of corporate formalities is a major factor in determining if the corporation is the "alter ego" of its stockholders, and if so, the stockholders may be held liable for the corporate obligations.

The bottom line is that to be treated and recognized as a corporation, the corporation (you) must observe the corporate formalities, which are primarily as follows:

a. ARTICLES/BYLAWS: The corporation must comply with the rules and regulations set forth in these documents. Study them closely, comply with them, observe them. To do so is observing corporate formalities.

Some parts of a corporations' articles and bylaws can be changed (Some parts are required by state law and can't be changed. So — check the laws and be sure.) If you want to change a part of the articles or bylaws, it's simple. Change them.

b. DIRECTORS/OFFICERS: Be sure to appoint or elect directors and officers.

c. REQUIRED MEETINGS: Annual meetings are required of the stockholders and directors. Therefore, these must be properly recorded in the corporation record book. Under Nevada law, these meetings can be held anywhere at any time, within or out of the state. State laws differ. If you are incorporated in any other state, check the law in your state. Consult with your attorney. Know what you are doing. Do it right, and both you and the corporation will be safe.

d. MINUTES OF MEETINGS: When a meeting is held by either the stockholders or the board of directors for any purpose, it is important to observe the corporate formalities and document the meeting in the corporate record book.

e. RESOLUTIONS: Aside from required annual meetings, the easiest way to govern and observe corporate formalities in a small private corporation are by resolutions signed by a majority or quorum of its directors or stockholders, whichever is applicable. These are much simpler and faster to prepare than minutes of a meeting, and in fact they do not require a meeting; they simply require the signatures of the directors or stockholders, whichever seems most appropriate to the resolution. NRS 78.315 allows directors to take action without such a meeting, and NRS 78.320 permits stockholders to take such action if the stockholders holding at least a majority of the voting power consent in writing. Put lots of resolutions in your corporate record book concerning everything you do, and you will be protecting both the corporation and the individual stockholders.

f. CORPORATE SEAL: In many states, the corporate seal is required on official documents of the corporation. In Nevada that is not true. No seal is required. It is simply up to the whim and wish of the directors as to whether or not a corporate seal is used. Generally it is wise to have a corporate seal on hand, because some states will not recognize an official document that does not have the corporate seal affixed. You will find information regarding the corporate seal in NRS 78.065.

g. MONEY: Never commingle your personal funds or expenditures with those of the corporation. The corporation should have its own checking account, separate from your personal account. Do not pay personal expenses out of the corporate checking account. For instance, do not write a corporate check for groceries or for clothes. Do not write a corporate check for cash without a written explanation as to where the cash went. Keep your accounts clean. Do not commingle funds. Also, for tax sheltering reasons, it is vital to put adequate explanations on the corporate checks you write and to have receipts or cash tickets to back them up. For example, in the case of a company car, the corporation pays all the expenses, but the checks must be made out so that this is readily ascertainable. You as an individual may accumulate cash tickets for gasoline, oil changes, and so on. When the corporation writes you a check for those items, the check should be identified as "Reimbursement for cash tickets attached;" then they should be broken down for accounting reasons. The very separateness between you and the corporation helps to keep your accounts clean and helps you to keep better records and do a better job of bookkeeping.

h. SIGNING DOCUMENTS: Another important formality! When you sign anything on behalf of the corporation, particularly invoices, delivery receipts, contracts, or other items of indebtedness, always put the name of the corporation, by (name of individual), and then, following the individual's name, his or her title. In other words, sign everything "XYZ Corporation by John Doe, President" (or Secretary, or Treasurer, or whatever capacity you happen to acting in). That is giving public notice that you are signing as and for the corporation and not as an individual. This is one of the formalities that preclude "piercing the corporate veil." If you sign only as an individual, anyone can say that they thought you were acting as an individual, because you didn't indicate otherwise. So you may be held personally liable for the obligation that really belongs to the corporation.

To repeat: In order to be treated like a corporation, your corporation has to act like one. The corporation should have independent business activities and function independently of the stockholders.

Pre-incorporation

Before a corporation is actually created, it may be necessary to raise money for the operation of the business, although this is not always necessary.

One way of raising capital for your business venture or operation is via a stock subscription. Subscriptions can occur either before incorporation or after a corporation has been formed. The agreement included within is a pre-incorporation subscription agreement.

A pre-incorporation subscription enables promoters of a corporation to obtain commitments from investors as to money, which will be invested in the corporation upon its formation. In Nevada such a subscription is irrevocable for six months unless otherwise provided by the subscription agreement or all the subscribers consent to the revocation.

PRE-INCORPORATION STOCK SUBSCRIPTION (Part A)

OF

BLACK, INC.

A _____ Nevada _____ Corporation

The undersigned, in consideration of the mutual subscriptions hereby made, do agree among themselves, each with the others, and with the corporation to be known as _____ Black, Inc. _____, to subscribe to and purchase from the corporation, at _____ (par on book) _____ value, the class and number of shares of the corporation set forth opposite their respective signatures below. Each other undersigned hereby subscribes for the kind and number of shares set opposite his/her name, and his/her obligation hereunder shall not be dependent upon performance by any of the other signatories.

The respective subscription prices shall be due and paid in full at such time or in such installments at such times as determined by the board of directors.

In the event that such corporation is not formed on or before _____ September 1 _____, _____ 2001 _____, or such later date as may hereafter be agreed upon by all the subscribers below signed, then this agreement and the obligations of the respective subscribers shall be null and void and of no further force and effect.

In witness whereof the subscribers have executed this subscription at _____ Carson City, _____ Nevada _____, this _____ first _____ day of _____ May _____, _____ 2001 _____.

NAME OF SUBSCRIBERS	CLASS OF SHARES	NUMBER OF SHARES
I. M. Director	common	100
M. E. Rich	common	75
E. M. Bezzler	common	50

I. M. Director
SUBSCRIBER

M. E. Rich
SUBSCRIBER

E. M. Bezzler
SUBSCRIBER

PRE-INCORPORATION STOCK SUBSCRIPTION (Part B)

OF

<u>BLACK, INC.</u>

A _____Nevada_____ Corporation

We, the undersigned, in consideration of the mutual promises herein, and of the subscriptions hereby made, do hereby each for himself/herself subscribe to the capital stock of a corporation about to be organized, which corporation shall be named " _____Black, Inc._____ ", or some other name hereafter agreed on, should the _____Secretary of State_____ refuse to permit the corporation to be organized under that name, to engage in the business of _____any_____ _____lawful activity_____ , in the amounts set opposite our several names.

This subscription is to be binding only in the event that the _____Secretary of State_____ of the State of _____Nevada_____ shall issue a certificate of incorporation to the corporation and that all necessary legal steps be taken as prescribed by law to that end.

All subscriptions are to be payable in cash, immediately on the completion of all necessary legal steps and as called for by the board of directors of the corporation. Certificates are to be issued only as the subscriptions are so paid in cash.

NAME OF SUBSCRIBER	NUMBER OF SHARES	AMOUNT
I. M. Director	100	10,000.00
M. E. Rich	75	7,500.00
C. M. Bezzler	50	5,000.00

I. M. Director
SUBSCRIBER

M. E. Rich
SUBSCRIBER

C. M. Bezzler
SUBSCRIBER

Optional Subscription Provision

Payment by Transfer of Property

It is agreed among the undersigned subscribers of the corporation that the stock subscriptions of _____I.M. Director_____ and _____M.E. Rich_____ shall be fully paid by transferring and delivering to the corporation, free and clear of all liens and encumbrances, all items set forth in the attached list of _____property_____ at a value to the corporation that is hereby agreed to be the sum of _____TEN THOUSAND_____ Dollars (_____$10,000.00_____) or shall be determined by appraisal of independent appraisers selected by the Board of Directors of the corporation or as the case may be.

If the value of the property as so agreed upon or determined shall be less than the value of the shares subscribed to by the owners of the property, the balance of the subscription price shall be paid in cash by them to the corporation within _____ten_____ (_____10_____) days following the date of transfer. If the value of the property shall be greater than the value of the shares so subscribed then the excess of property value over stock value shall be paid by the corporation to said owners within _____ten_____ (_____10_____) days following the date of transfer.

I. M. Director
SUBSCRIBER

M.E. Rich
SUBSCRIBER

Subscription Receipt

Received from _____ M.E. Rich _____

the sum of _____ FIVE THOUSAND _____ Dollars ($_____ 5,000.00 _____)

being _____ ONE HUNDRED _____ percent (__100__%) of the total price of his/her

subscription.

    This receipt is to be accepted by the treasurer of the corporation, when organized, for the full amount hereof.

Dated _____ November 1 _____, ____ 2001 ____.

Paul Paypoll, Tres.

Signature

Acceptances and Resignations

When a director or an officer is appointed or elected, it's a good idea to have this person sign an acceptance of office form in order to document that the person accepted the office, and as proof that the appointment or election took place. Resignations should be formalized in writing for the same reason.

The forms included herein supplement Resolutions adopted by the stockholders or directors, which authorized these appointments, elections, or resignations. See the Resolution section that follows later in this chapter.

ACCEPTANCE OF APPOINTMENT AS DIRECTOR

I, _____ I.M. Director _____ having been appointed a Director of _____ Black, Inc. _____ a _____ Nevada _____ corporation, do hereby accept said position, effective as of the time of my appointment on ___ November 1 ___, ___ 2001 ___.

DATED this __1st__ day of ___ November ___, ___ 2001 ___.

I. M. Director
DIRECTOR

216

RESIGNATION OF DIRECTOR

I, _____Joe Worthless_____, hereby tender my resignation as a member of the
Board of Directors of _____Black, Inc._____, a _____Nevada_____
corporation, to take effect immediately.

DATED this __1st__ day of _____November_____, __2001__.

Joe Worthless

DIRECTOR

Notices of Meetings and Waivers

Whenever stockholders or directors are required to meet to take action, written notice of the meeting shall be given to every stockholder or director as required by the corporation's bylaws. The president, secretary, or authorized person must sign the notice as the bylaws indicate and must state the purpose, the time, and the place for the meeting. The notice must be given personally or by mail to each stockholder as required by the bylaws.

Notices Can Be Waived

A waiver is an intentional and voluntary giving up of a known right. For example, in the pages that follow the reference is to a stockholder or director waiving his or her right to receive written notice of an upcoming meeting. In other words, to sign a waiver means simply that you as a stockholder or a director agree that you don't require written notice of the next stockholder or director's meeting. This can be done by the stockholder or director simply signing a waiver before, during, or after a meeting.

NOTICE OF FIRST MEETING OF STOCKHOLDERS

OF

BLACK, INC.

A _____ Nevada _____ Corporation

PLEASE TAKE NOTICE that the First Meeting of the Stockholders of ___BLACK, INC.___ _____ a _____ Nevada _____ corporation, will be held on _____November 1_____, ___2001___, at _____10:00 a.m._____, at _____the corporate offic_____ for the purpose of ___electing a Board of Directors and conducting such other business as may properly come before the meeting___

Your attendance is requested, but if you are unable to attend, you may be represented by proxy.

DATED THIS _____1st_____ day of _____November_____, ___2001___.

Minnie Minutes

SECRETARY

219

NOTICE OF ANNUAL STOCKHOLDERS' MEETING

OF

BLACK, INC.

A _____Nevada_____ Corporation

NOTICE IS HEREBY GIVEN, that the annual meeting of the stockholders of _____Black, Inc._____, a _____Nevada_____ corporation, will be held on _____November 1_____, _____2001_____, at _____10:00 a.m._____, at _____the corporate office_____ for the purpose of _____electing Directors and transacting any other business as may properly come before the meeting_____

Enclosed is a proxy which you are requested to sign and return. In the event that you are present at the meeting and desire to do so, you can withdraw your proxy and vote in person.

DATED THIS _____1st_____ day of _____November_____, _____2001_____.

Minnie Minutes

SECRETARY

NOTICE OF SPECIAL MEETING OF STOCKHOLDERS

OF

BLACK, INC.

A _____ Nevada _____ Corporation

Called by Stockholders

Notice is hereby given that, pursuant to a call by stockholders holding not less than _____ 51% _____ of the voting power of _____ Black, Inc. _____, a _____ Nevada _____ corporation, a special meeting of the stockholders of _____ Black, Inc. _____ will be held on _____ November 1 _____, _____ 2001 _____, at _____ 10:00 a.m. _____, at _____ the corporate office _____ for the following purpose: to consider merging with Success, Inc. _____

The close of business on _____ October 1 _____, _____ 2001 _____ has been fixed as the record date for determining stockholders entitled to receive notice of and to vote at this meeting, or any adjournment thereof.

If you do not expect to be present in person at the meeting, you are urged to date and sign the enclosed proxy and return it promptly in the enclosed envelope which requires no postage.

DATED THIS _____ 1st _____ day of _____ November _____, _____ 2001 _____.

Minnie Minutes

SECRETARY

SAMPLE

NOTICE OF

FIRST MEETING OF BOARD OF DIRECTORS

OF

BLACK, INC.

A _____ Nevada _____ Corporation

Notice is hereby given that the first meeting of the Board of Directors of _Black, Inc._ _____, a _____ Nevada _____ corporation, will be held on _November 1_ , _2001_ , at _10:00 a.m._ , at _the corporate office_.

DATED THIS _1st_ day of _November_ _2001_ . ,

Minnie Minutes
SECRETARY

222

NOTICE OF ANNUAL

MEETING OF BOARD OF DIRECTORS

OF

BLACK, INC.

A _____ Nevada _____ Corporation

A meeting of the Board of Directors of _____ Black, Inc. _____, a _____ Nevada _____ corporation, will be held on _____ November 1 _____, 2001 _____, at _____ 10:00 a.m _____ at _____ the corporate office _____ for the following pur- pose: _____ to elect Officers and conduct such other business as may _____ properly come before the Board _____

DATED THIS _____ 1st _____ day of _____ November _____, _____ 2001 _____.

Minnie Minutes

SECRETARY

223

NOTICE OF SPECIAL MEETING

OF THE

BOARD OF DIRECTORS

OF

<u>BLACK, INC.</u>

A <u>Nevada</u> Corporation

Please take notice that a special meeting of the Board of Directors of <u>Black, Inc.</u>, a <u>Nevada</u> corporation, will be held on <u>November 1</u>, <u>2001</u>, at <u>10:00 a.m.</u> at <u>the corporate office</u> for the purpose of <u>considering a medical plan for the employees</u>.

DATED THIS <u>1st</u> day of <u>November</u>, <u>2001</u>.

<u>Minnie Minutes</u>
SECRETARY

WAIVER OF NOTICE OF FIRST MEETING OF

STOCKHOLDERS

OF

BLACK, INC.

A _____Nevada_____ Corporation

We, the undersigned, being all the stockholders, do hereby severally waive notice of the time, place, and purpose of the first meeting of stockholders of _____Black, Inc._____, a _____Nevada_____ Corporation, and consent that the meeting be held on _____November 1_____, ____2001____, at ____10:00 a.m.____ at _____the corporate office_____, and we further consent to the transaction of any business requisite to complete the organization of this Corporation and any and all such business that may properly come before the meeting.

DATED THIS ____1st____ day of _____November_____, ____2001____.

_____Jane Baker_____
STOCKHOLDER

_____Joe Baker_____
STOCKHOLDER

_____John Adams_____
STOCKHOLDER

225

Minutes of Meetings

Your corporation's bylaws will provide for an annual meeting of both stockholders and directors. For Nevada corporations these meetings may be held either within Nevada or outside the state.

The date and time as well as the place for holding annual meetings may be changed from time to time in order to suit the pleasure and convenience of stockholders or directors.

Stockholders' Meeting

All who attend the annual shareholders meeting, wherever possible, should sign stockholders minutes. This shows that all who attended agree that the minutes accurately reflect what transpired. There is a place provided for these signatures at the end of the minutes on the left under the word "ATTEST." In larger companies having all stockholders attending an annual general meeting actually sign the meeting minutes is not practical and may not be advisable in any event.

Generally, the main business at the stockholders' annual meeting is to elect a board of directors to serve for the coming year. It is also sound practice for the stockholders to adopt a resolution ratifying all the actions taken by the board of directors during the past year. Any business of the corporation that requires stockholder approval, such as amendments to the Articles of Incorporation, or a merger proposal, or what have you, may also be handled at the annual meeting.

It is important to note in the minutes that the meeting was properly called and that all stockholders received adequate notice of the meeting. It is important to show that each meeting was properly called, because actions taken at an improper meeting may be challenged and declared null and void as though they never happened.

If written notice was given, a copy of the notice should be attached to the minutes. If no written notice was given, the written consent of the stockholders to a waiver of notice should be filled out and attached to the minutes.

For any action taken by the stockholders, the minutes should state that the matter was duly proposed, seconded, and agreed to by a majority or a quorum of the stockholders. The text of any resolution adopted by the stockholders should appear in the minutes, along with any contracts, reports, or other documents relating to the resolution. Thus, the minutes provide a complete record of corporate formalities.

Actions can be taken without a meeting if authorized by the written consent of the stockholders holding a majority of the voting power.

1. Majority – Any number greater than half of the total in attendance.

2. Quorum – The number of members who must be present in a meeting before business may be transacted. This number is established in the corporate bylaws. (e.g., 75%, 2/3, 7 out of 10, or any majority established by the director in the bylaws).

Directors' Meeting

The main business at the Board of Directors' meetings is to elect officers and authorize action to run the business.

As with the stockholders' meeting, it is important to note that the meeting was properly called and all directors had proper notice. This protects the validity of the meeting. Written notice, if given, should be attached to the minutes or a waiver filled out.

As with the stockholders' meeting, minutes should state that all matters were duly proposed, seconded, and agreed to by a majority of the directors. The copies of all resolutions adopted by the directors during the past year should be attached to the minutes to provide a complete record of corporate formalities.

Since minutes can be cumbersome and difficult to draw up and meetings can be lengthy, an alternate method exists for the board of directors to run the corporation. A corporation may be run by resolutions, which are very simple to make. See the section marked RESOLUTIONS for several examples of the proper form.

MINUTES OF FIRST MEETING OF STOCKHOLDERS

OF

BLACK, INC.

A _____Nevada_____ Corporation

     The first meeting of stockholders of the above-captioned Corporation was held on the date and at the time and place set forth in the written waiver of notice signed by the stockholders, fixing such time and place, and prefixed to the minutes of this meeting.

     The meeting was called to order by the Chairman of the Board of Directors, and the following stockholders, being all of the stockholders of the Corporation, were present:

Sam Smith

Sally Smith

Tom Jones

     The Chairman noted that it was in order to consider electing a Board of Directors for the ensuing year. Upon nominations duly made, seconded and (unanimously) carried, the following person(s) was/were elected as Director(s) of the Corporation, to serve for a period of one year or until such time as his/her/their successor(s) is/are elected and qualify:

I.M. Director

There was presented to the meeting the following:

1. Copy of Certificate of Incorporation;
2. Copy of bylaws of the Corporation;
3. Resolutions adopted by the Incorporators;
4. Corporate certificate book;
5. Corporate certificate ledger.

Upon motion duly made, seconded, and (unanimously) carried, it was

RESOLVED, that the items listed above have been examined by all stockholders, and are all approved and adopted, and that all acts taken and decisions reached as set forth in such documents be, and they hereby are, ratified and approved by the stockholders of the Corporation.

There being no further business to come before the meeting, upon motion duly made, seconded, and (unanimously) carried, it was adjourned.

DATED THIS _____1st_____ day of _____November_____, _____2001_____.

Minnie Minutes
SECRETARY

ATTEST:

_____Jane Baker_____
STOCKHOLDER

_____John Adams_____
STOCKHOLDER

229

MINUTES OF ANNUAL MEETING OF STOCKHOLDERS

OF

BLACK, INC.

A _____Nevada_____ Corporation

The regular meeting of the stockholders of _____Black, Inc._____ for the year
November 1, 2000 to October 31, 2001, was held on _____November 1_____,
2001, at ____10:00 a.m_, at ___the corporate office_____.

The meeting was called to order by the Chairman, _____U.R. Important____. A
quorum being present, Chairman _____Important_____ announced that the meeting was
duly constituted and ready to proceed with business.

Prior minutes and resolutions of the stockholders and Directors to date were read. It was duly
moved, seconded, and (unanimously) carried that the minutes and resolutions be approved as read.

Reports of Directors and Officers were called for. There being none, the stockholders proceeded
to the next item of business.

_____I.M. Director_____ was/were properly nominated, seconded and
(unanimously) elected as Director of the Corporation for the coming year.

There being no unfinished business and no further business, the annual meeting of the stockholders
was adjourned until this time and date next year.

DATED THIS ___1st___ day of ____November____, ___2001___.

Minnie Minutes

SECRETARY

ATTEST:

Jane Baker

STOCKHOLDER

John Adams

STOCKHOLDER

230

MINUTES OF SPECIAL MEETING OF STOCKHOLDERS

OF

BLACK, INC.

A _____Nevada_____ Corporation

A special meeting of the stockholders was held on _____October 1_____, 2001____ at _____10:00 a.m_____, at ____the corporate office____.

The meeting was called to order by _____U.R. Important_____, the Chairman of the Board of Directors, and ____Minnie Minutes____, the Secretary of the Corporation, kept the records of the meeting.

The Secretary reported that stockholders owning _____1500_____ shares were present in person and stockholders owning _____300_____ shares were represented by proxy, the aggregate amount representing more than _____51 %_____ of the outstanding stock entitled to vote.

The Secretary reported that the following stockholders were present in person:

Names of Stockholders	Number of Shares
Sam Smith	500
Sally Smith	500
Tom Jones	500

and that the following stockholders were represented by proxy:

Names of Stockholders	Number of Shares	Name of Proxy
Red Rose	100	Sam Smith
Yellow Gladiolus	100	Sam Smith
Purple Violets	100	Sam Smith

The Chairman announced that there were present in person and represented by proxy the number of shares necessary to constitute a quorum and that the meeting was legally convened and ready to proceed.

The Secretary presented and read a waiver of notice of the meeting signed by each stockholder entitled to notice of the meeting, said waiver was ordered to be filed with the minutes of the meeting.

On motion duly made, seconded, and after due deliberation, the following resolution was voted upon:

RESOLVED, that

(Insert text of resolution here)

A vote was taken which showed:

In Favor of Motion

_____Sam Smith_____, representing _____800_____ shares

_____, representing _____ shares

_____, representing _____ shares

_____, representing _____ shares

Opposed to Motion

_____Sally Smith_____, representing _____500_____ shares

_____, representing _____ shares

232

SAMPLE

Not Voting on Motion

_____ Tom Jones _____, representing _____ 500 _____ shares

The Secretary reported that _____ 800 _____ shares had been voted in favor of the foregoing resolution and _____ 500 _____ shares had been voted against the resolution, said vote representing a quorum of the outstanding shares entitled to vote thereon.

The Chairman thereupon declared that the resolution had been adopted.

There being no further business, upon motion duly made, seconded and unanimously carried, the meeting was adjourned.

DATED THIS _____ 1st _____ day of _____ October _____, _____ 2001 _____.

Minnie Minutes
_____
SECRETARY

ATTEST:

Jane Baker
_____
STOCKHOLDER

John Adams
_____

233

MINUTES OF FIRST MEETING OF BOARD OF DIRECTORS

OF

BLACK, INC.

A _____Nevada_____ Corporation

The first meeting of the Board of Directors of _____Black, Inc._____ convened on ___November 1___, ___2001___, pursuant to waiver of notice and consent to the holding thereof executed by each Director of the Corporation. Present were all the Directors:

Sam Smith

Sally Smith

Dick Morris

_____U.R. Important_____ was elected temporary Chairman and _____Minnie Minutes_____ was elected temporary Secretary, each to serve only until permanent officers are elected.

The Chairman reported that the Articles of Incorporation of the Corporation had been filed in the Office of the Nevada Secretary of State on ___October 14___, ___2001___, that a copy thereof, certified by the Nevada Secretary of State, had been filed in the Office of the Carson City Clerk on ___October 15___, ___2001___, and that as a consequence, the Corporation is duly and validly existing and in good standing under the laws of the State of Nevada and qualified to proceed with the transactions of business. The Certificate of Incorporation of the Corporation then being exhibited, on motion duly made, seconded and carried, said Certificate of Incorporation was accepted and approved.

On motion duly made, seconded and carried, the Directors were recognized as the first Directors of the Corporation and it was further moved that they were to hold office until the first annual meeting of stockholders or until their respective successors shall be duly elected and qualified.

The temporary Chairman called for the nomination of Officers of the Corporation. Thereupon, the following persons were nominated for the Officers of the Corporation:

President:	U.R. Important
Vice President:	G.I. Gogetum
Secretary:	Minnie Minutes
Treasurer:	Paul Payroll

234

No further nominations being made, the nominations were closed and the Directors proceeded to vote on the nominees. All of the Directors present at the meeting having voted and the vote having been counted, the Chairman announced the aforesaid nominees had been duly elected to the offices set before their respective names. The permanent Officers of the Corporation then took charge of the meeting.

Upon motion duly made, seconded and carried, the following resolutions were adopted:

RESOLVED, that the Treasurer be and (s)he hereby is authorized to pay all fees and expenses incident to and necessary for the organization of this Corporation.

RESOLVED, that the proper Officers of this Corporation be and they here authorized and directed on behalf of the Corporation, to make and file such certificates, reports, or other instruments as may be required by law to be filed in any State in which Officers shall find it necessary or expedient to file the same to register or authorize the Corporation to transact business in such State.

RESOLVED, that the Treasurer be and (s)he hereby is ordered to open a bank account in the name of this Corporation with _____ Easy National Bank _____ for deposit of funds belonging to the Corporation, such funds to be withdrawn only by check of the Corporation signed by its President and/or _____ Treasurer _____.

RESOLVED, that the actions taken by Laughlin Associates, Inc. and _Brent Buscay,_ _Incorporator_ prior to the incorporation of the Corporation, on behalf of the Corporation, are hereby approved, ratified, and adopted as if done pursuant to corporate authorization.

RESOLVED, a form of Stock Certificate was presented, examined, approved, and duly adopted for use by the Corporation. Certificate No. _____ 26 _____ was directed to be inserted in the Corporate Record Book as evidence and sample thereof.

RESOLVED, that the Board of Directors of this Corporation deem it desirable and/or prudent to, from time to time, utilize an official corporate seal (optional under Nevada law) and, therefore, that the corporate seal presented to this Board, circular in form with the inscription of the corporate name, NEVADA, and the official date of incorporation, be, and the same hereby is, adopted as the official seal of the Corporation, and be it

FURTHER RESOLVED, that the impression of said seal be made upon Certificate No. _____26_____ inserted in the Corporate Record Book as evidence and sample thereof.

RESOLVED, that the fiscal year of the Corporation shall commence on __January 1__, and end on __December 31__ of each year hereafter.

FURTHER RESOLVED, that __Laughlin Associates, Inc.__ be, and hereby is, appointed Resident Agent of this Corporation, in charge of the principal office and so authorized to discharge the duties of Resident Agent, and be it

FURTHER RESOLVED, that the Secretary forthwith supply a List of Officers and Directors to the Resident Agent for filing with the Secretary of State of the State of _____Nevada_____ as required by law. (In the event the filing has not yet been accomplished), and be it

FURTHER RESOLVED, that the Secretary forthwith supply the Resident Agent with a certified copy of the Corporation Bylaws and a stock ledger statement to be kept on file at the principal office as required by _____Nevada__ law. (In the event this has not yet been done.)

There being no further business to come before the meeting, upon motion duly made, seconded, and (unanimously) carried, it was adjourned.

DATED THIS ____1st____ day of _____November_____, ____2001____.

Minnie Minutes
SECRETARY

ATTEST:

Sam Harris
DIRECTOR

Sally Harris
DIRECTOR

Dick Morris
DIRECTOR

236

MINUTES OF ANNUAL MEETING OF BOARD OF DIRECTORS

OF

BLACK, INC.

A _____ Nevada _____ Corporation

The annual meeting of the Board of Directors of _____ Black, Inc. _____ immediately followed the annual meeting of stockholders on _____ November 1 _____, _____ 2001 _____, at 10:00 a.m, at _____ the corporate office _____.

The following were present: Sam Smith

Sally Smith

Dick Morris

being all of the Directors of the Corporation.

The meeting was called to order by _____ Sam Smith _____. It was moved, seconded and (unanimously) carried that _____ Sam Smith _____ act as Chairman and _____ Sally Smith _____ act as Secretary.

The Chairman noted that it was in order to elect officers for the ensuing year. Upon nominations duly made and seconded, the following were (unanimously) elected officers of the Corporation, to serve for the ensuing year or until their successors are elected and qualify:

President:	U.R. Important
Vice President:	
Secretary:	Minnie Minutes
Treasurer:	Paul Payroll

Upon motion duly made, seconded, and (unanimously) carried all of the Resolutions adopted by the Directors in the previous year were ordered to be filed with the Secretary and attached to these minutes and are thereby made a part thereof.

237

There being no further business to come before the meeting, upon motion duly made, seconded, and (unaninously) carried, it was adjourned.

DATED THIS _____1st_____ day of _____November_____, _____2001_____.

Minnie Minutes
SECRETARY

ATTEST:

Sam Harris
DIRECTOR

Sally Harris
DIRECTOR

Dick Morris
DIRECTOR

Stock Restrictions and Resolutions

Stock is the ownership element in a corporation. Stock certificates are issued as evidence of this ownership. Space prohibits going into a lot of detail about stocks in this book, therefore, this chapter is limited to stock restrictions. The transferability of stock can be limited if the stock certificate so states. Included for your reference are several such limitations or "restrictions," as they are commonly called.

Stock that has such restrictions or limitations is frequently referred to as Lettered or restricted stock. The stock certificate is said to bear a legend. The legend on the lettered stock gives notice to everyone that the stock in question is restricted or limited as indicated by the legend. Further investigation may be warranted regarding the full extent and meaning of the legend.

On the following pages are representative examples of some wording on restrictions or limitations that may be placed upon various stock issues. This wording may go into the articles, by-laws or be the subject of an appropriate resolution. Each example also shows an appropriate accompanying Legend that goes onto the corresponding stock certificate. The legend may be printed on the stock certificate. It may, in some cases, be stamped on by a rubber stamp (usually in red ink).

Most restrictions you elect to place on stock issues can be successfully implemented. However, it can become a touchy matter with serious legal implications. The final wording and Legend should definitely be reviewed and approved by an attorney knowledgeable in securities before you go to press and/or issue stock with a legend affixed.

Anytime you are offered or encounter a stock certificate bearing a legend, you should request a full written, sworn explanation from the corporate secretary, before consummating any transaction. The stock may be placed in escrow pending an explanation subject to your approval or confirmation of stated limitation submitted with opening of escrow.

Restrictions and Options

NOTICE: This stock is not FREE trading and may have restrictions, conditions and corporate options.

SAMPLE LEGEND

No transfer of stock shall be valid, until ten (10) days after the Corporation through its Secretary shall have had written notice of the proposed sale, the number of shares proposed to be sold, the price at which the proposed sale is to be made, and the name of the prospective buyer; and during said ten (10) days, the Corporation shall have the sole option to buy the said shares at the price named. The Corporation shall also have

SAMPLE

RESOLUTION OF THE BOARD OF DIRECTORS

OF

Black, Inc.

A _____ Nevada _____ Corporation

I, the undersigned, being all of the Directors of _____ Black, Inc. _____

_____, a _____ Nevada _____ corporation, having

met and discussed the business herein set forth, have unanimously:

RESOLVED, that the President be and is hereby authorized to borrow money for the corporation and/or make loans of any size, type or kind whatsoever, at his/her discretion, on behalf of the corporation, and be it

FURTHER RESOLVED, that the President be and is hereby authorized to negotiate, consummate and/or enter into any type of financing, purchases, conditional sales contracts, leases, lease purchase agreements, co-sign for or make loans to employees or enter into and execute any documents representing debt or encumbrances or obligations of any nature, for and on behalf of the corporation, at his/her discretion and in his/her best judgment, and be it

FURTHER RESOLVED, that the President be and is hereby authorized to enter into any type of contractual agreement at his/her discretion, and be it

FURTHER RESOLVED, that the President be and is hereby authorized to handle all employment of corporate employees which in his/her discretion is in the best interest of this corporation, and be it

FURTHER RESOLVED, that the President be and is hereby authorized to make any decisions, take any actions, issue any directives, and/or consummate any business transactions whatsoever in the pursuit of the corporation's business.

DATED THIS _____1st_____ day of _____August_____ , _____2001_____ .

I M Director

DIRECTOR IN TOTO

SAMPLE

Form Committee to Manage Business

RESOLUTION OF THE BOARD OF DIRECTORS

OF

Black, Inc.

A _____ Nevada _____ Corporation

I, the undersigned, being all of the Directors of ___ Black, Inc. ___
_____, a ___ Nevada ___ corporation, having
met and discussed the business herein set forth, have unanimously:

RESOLVED, that a committee consisting of _____ one (1) _____ Directors is
hereby formed for the express and limited purpose of managing the business and affairs of this
Corporation and more specifically to make recommendations with regards to
the payment of bonuses to the various Officers of this Corporation
_____, and be it

FURTHER RESOLVED, that this committee shall be known as the _____ Bonus _____
_____ Committee, and be it

FURTHER RESOLVED, that such committee is to be in existence for a period of
_____ 30 days _____ days/months/years.

DATED THIS ___ 1st ___ day of ___ August ___, ___ 2001 ___.

I M Director

DIRECTOR IN TOTO

244

Open Bank Account

RESOLUTION OF THE BOARD OF DIRECTORS

OF

Black, Inc.
_____

A _____ Nevada _____ Corporation

I, the undersigned, being all of the Directors of _____ Black, Inc. _____
_____, a _____ Nevada _____ corporation, having
met and discussed the business herein set forth, have unanimously:

RESOLVED, that the Treasurer be and hereby is ordered to open a bank account in the name of
this Corporation with _____ Easy National Bank _____ for the deposit of
funds belonging to the Corporation, such funds to be withdrawn only by a check of the Corporation
signed by its _____ President _____ and/or
_____ Treasurer _____ .

DATED THIS ____ 1st ____ day of _____ August _____, ____ 2001 ____.

I M Director
_____
DIRECTOR IN TOTO

245

SAMPLE

RESOLUTION OF THE BOARD OF DIRECTORS

OF

Black, Inc.

A _____ Nevada _____ Corporation

I, the undersigned, being all of the Directors of _____ Black, Inc. _____

_____, a _____ Nevada _____ corporation, having met and discussed the business herein set forth, have unanimously:

RESOLVED, that _____ Paul Payroll _____ is hereby appointed

_____ Treasurer _____ of this Corporation to fill the vacancy created by the

resignation of _____ John Roe _____.

DATED THIS _____ 1st _____ day of _____ August _____, _____ 2001 _____.

I M Director

DIRECTOR IN TOTO

(Any Officerís) Salary

RESOLUTION OF THE BOARD OF DIRECTORS

OF

Black, Inc.

A _____ Nevada _____ Corporation

I, the undersigned, being all of the Directors of _____ Black, Inc. _____

_____, a _____ Nevada _____ corporation, having met and discussed the business herein set forth, have unanimously:

RESOLVED, that the salary of the _____ Any Officer _____ of this Corporation hereby is fixed at _____ Ten Thousand _____ Dollars ($_____ 10,000.00 _____) per month beginning _____ January 1 _____, _____ 2002 _____, until further action of this Board of Directors.

DATED THIS _____ 1st _____ day of _____ August _____, _____ 2001 _____.

_____

DIRECTOR IN TOTO

Acceptance of Resignation (Any Officer)

RESOLUTION OF THE BOARD OF DIRECTORS

OF

Black, Inc.

A _____ Nevada _____ Corporation

I, the undersigned, being all of the Directors of _____ Black, Inc. _____
_____, a _____ Nevada _____ corporation, having
met and discussed the business herein set forth, have unanimously:

RESOLVED, that the resignation of _____ Wylie Newcomer _____, as a
_____ Director _____ of _____ Black, Inc. _____, as
evidenced by a letter to the Corporation, dated _____ October 15 _____, _____ 2001 _____, is hereby
accepted, and the Secretary of this Corporation is hereby instructed to notify
_____ Wylie Newcomer _____ of the acceptance of his resignation.

DATED THIS _____ 1st _____ day of _____ November _____, _____ 2001 _____.

_____ ~I M Director~ _____
DIRECTOR IN TOTO

248

SAMPLE

RESOLUTION OF THE BOARD OF DIRECTORS

OF

Black, Inc.

A _____ Nevada _____ Corporation

I, the undersigned, being all of the Directors of _____ Black, Inc. _____, a _____ Nevada _____ corporation, having met and discussed the business herein set forth, have unanimously:

RESOLVED, that the Board of Directors declares it advisable to amend Article _____ Five _____ of the Articles of Incorporation of this Corporation to change the number of directors of this Corporation from three (3) to one (1) _____,

and be it

FURTHER RESOLVED, that a meeting of the stockholders of _____ Black, Inc. _____ be held on _____ November 20 _____, _____ 2001 _____, at _____ 10:00 a.m. _____, at _____ the corporate office _____ to consider said amendment.

DATED THIS _____ 1st _____ day of _____ November _____, _____ 2001 _____.

_____
DIRECTOR IN TOTO

249

SAMPLE

RESOLUTION OF THE STOCKHOLDERS

OF

<u>Black, Inc.</u>

A <u>Nevada</u> Corporation

I, the undersigned, being all of the stockholders of <u>Black, Inc.</u>

_____, a <u>Nevada</u> corporation, having

met and discussed the business herein set forth, have unanimously:

RESOLVED, that the President and Secretary are hereby authorized and instructed to amend the Articles of Incorporation of this Corporation as provided in Article <u>5</u> of the Articles of Incorporation of this Corporation to <u>Change the number of Directors of this Corporation from three (3) to one (1)</u>

and be it

FURTHER RESOLVED, that the above stated amendment to the Articles of Incorporation of this corporation shall be and is effective <u>November 1</u>, <u>2001</u> and be it

FURTHER RESOLVED, that the Secretary shall send a copy of said amendment to all stockholders of record on <u>October 1</u>, <u>2001</u>, all Directors, and all Officers of this Corporation, and be it

FURTHER RESOLVED, that the President and Secretary are hereby authorized to execute a certificate regarding said amendment as required by _____ NRS 78.390 _____ and to cause said certificate to be properly filed with the _____ Nevada _____ Secretary of State.

DATED THIS ___1st___ day of ___November___, ___2001___.

John Adams

STOCKHOLDER

Amend Bylaws (Stockholders)

RESOLUTION OF THE STOCKHOLDERS

OF

Black, Inc.

A _____ Nevada _____ Corporation

I, the undersigned, representing all or a majority of stockholders of _____ Black, Inc. _____

_____, a _____ Nevada _____ corporation, having

met and discussed the business herein set forth, have unanimously:

RESOLVED, that the President and Secretary are hereby authorized and instructed to amend the Bylaws of this Corporation as provided in Article _____ VI _____ of the Bylaws of said Corporation to indemnify any and all directors of the corpora-tion from any personal liability, as authorized by passage of S.B.6 of the 64th Session of the Nevada Legislature on March 19, 1997

and be it

FURTHER RESOLVED, that the above-stated amendment to the Bylaws of this Corporation shall be and is effective _____ (immediately/on a specific date) _____

and be it

FURTHER RESOLVED, that the Secretary shall send a copy of said amendment to all stockhold-ers of record on _____ October 1 _____, _____ 2001 _____, all Directors, and all Officers of this Corporation.

DATED THIS _____ 1st _____ day of _____ November _____, _____ 2001 _____.

John Adams

STOCKHOLDER

252

Amend Bylaws (Directors)   *SAMPLE*

RESOLUTION OF THE BOARD OF DIRECTORS

OF

Black, Inc.

A _____ Nevada _____ Corporation

I, the undersigned, being all of the Directors of _____ Black, Inc. _____ , a _____ Nevada _____ corporation, having met and discussed the business herein set forth, have unanimously:

RESOLVED, that the President and Secretary are hereby authorized and instructed to amend the Bylaws of this Corporation as provided in Article _____ VI _____ of the Bylaws of this Corporation to _____ Indemnify any and all directors or officers of the corporation from any personal liability, as authorized by passage of of S.B.6 of the 64th Session of the Nevada legislature on March 19, 1987 _____

and be it

FURTHER RESOLVED, that the above-stated amendment to the Bylaws of this Corporation shall be and is effective _____ (immediately/on a specific date) _____ , and be it

FURTHER RESOLVED, that the Secretary shall send a copy of said amendment to all stockholders of record on _____ October 1 _____ , _____ 2001 _____ all Directors, and all Officers of this Corporation.

DATED THIS _____ 1st _____ day of _____ November _____ , _____ 2001 _____ .

_____

DIRECTOR IN TOTO

253

Authorize Travel (General)

RESOLUTION OF THE BOARD OF DIRECTORS

OF

Black, Inc.

A _____ Nevada _____ Corporation

I, the undersigned, being all of the Directors of _____ Black, Inc. _____

_____ , a _____ Nevada _____ corporation, having

met and discussed the business herein set forth, have unanimously:

RESOLVED, WHEREAS, in the judgment of the Board of Directors that

_____ Hawaii, the island of Maui _____ would be an excellent location

to make some contacts with qualified individuals for the purpose of

attempting to borrow money on behalf of the Corporation

_____ , and

RESOLVED, that _____ U.R. Important _____ , _____ President _____ , and

_____ Paul Payroll _____ , _____ Treasurer _____ , be and are

hereby instructed to travel to _____ Hawaii, the island of Maui _____ , and return on the

above-indicated official company business and remain in _____ Maui _____ for a

duration of _____ two weeks _____ , and be it

FURTHER RESOLVED, that all necessary and reasonable costs and expenses are to be paid or

reimbursed by the Corporation.

DATED THIS _____ 1st _____ day of _____ November _____ , _____ 2001 _____ .

I.M. Director

DIRECTOR IN TOTO

SAMPLE

RESOLUTION OF THE BOARD OF DIRECTORS

OF

Black, Inc.

A _____ Nevada _____ Corporation

I, the undersigned, being all of the Directors of _____ Black, Inc. _____

_____ , a _____ Nevada _____ corporation, having

met and discussed the business herein set forth, have unanimously:

RESOLVED, that _____ U.R. Important _____ , _____ Minnie Minutes _____ ,

and _____ Paul Payroll _____ be and is/are hereby authorized and instructed to

travel to _____ Carson City _____ , _____ Nevada _____ and

return therefrom, to attend _____ the Board of Directorís Meeting _____ , and be it

FURTHER RESOLVED, that all necessary and reasonable costs and expenses are to be paid or
reimbursed by the Corporation.

DATED THIS _____ 1st _____ day of _____ November _____ , _____ 2001 _____ .

I M Director

DIRECTOR IN TOTO

Reimbursement for Expenditures

RESOLUTION OF THE BOARD OF DIRECTORS

OF

Black, Inc.

A _____ Nevada _____ Corporation

I, the undersigned, being all of the Directors of _____ Black, Inc. _____
_____, a _____ Nevada _____ corporation, having
met and discussed the business herein set forth, have unanimously:

RESOLVED, that the Treasurer of this Corporation or his designee is hereby authorized and
instructed to reimburse _____ Minnie Minutes _____ for moneys advanced and expenses incurred and paid for by _____ Minnie Minutes _____ in connection with the
proper business purposes of this Corporation.

DATED THIS _____ 1st _____ day of _____ November _____ , _____ 2001 _____ .

I. M. Director

DIRECTOR IN TOTO

256

RESOLUTION OF THE BOARD OF DIRECTORS

OF

Black, Inc.

A _____Nevada_____ Corporation

I, the undersigned, being all of the Directors of _____Black, Inc._____ , a _____Nevada_____ corporation, having met and discussed the business herein set forth, have unanimously:

RESOLVED, that _____U.R. Important_____ , President, is hereby authorized to establish a credit account with _____American Express_____ , and to charge to that account any travel, entertainment and other expenses related to the ordinary and necessary trade or business of this Corporation, which expenses the Treasurer is hereby directed to pay in full as they become due.

DATED THIS ___1st___ day of ___November___ , ___2001___ .

I M Director

DIRECTOR IN TOTO

257

President to Get % of Net Profits

RESOLUTION OF THE BOARD OF DIRECTORS

OF

Black, Inc.

A _____ Nevada _____ Corporation

I, the undersigned, being all of the Directors of _____ Black, Inc. _____ , a _____ Nevada _____ corporation, having met and discussed the business herein set forth, have unanimously:

RESOLVED, that in special consideration of and as special compensation for the services performed by _____ U.R. Important _____ , President of this Corporation, in effecting the consummation of numerous contracts for the sale of the products of this Corporation during the year _____ 2001 _____ , _____ President Important will receive

_____ five _____ per cent (_____ 5 %) of the net profits of this Corporation during the year _____ 2001 _____ , on the books of the Corporation, but not to exceed the sum of _____ One _____ Hundred Thousand _____ Dollars ($ _____ 100,000.00 _____), the said special compensation to be paid to _____ President Important at the end of the year _____ 2001 _____ , and be it

FURTHER RESOLVED, that for the purpose of determining said compensation, net profits shall comprise the amount available for dividends on the common stock and for surplus and reserves — that is, net income after deductions have been made for the interest on the indebtedness, expenses, all accrued taxes, and preferred dividends.

DATED THIS _____ 1st _____ day of _____ November _____ , _____ 2001 _____ .

_____ I.M. Director _____

DIRECTOR IN TOTO

258

SAMPLE

RESOLUTION OF THE BOARD OF DIRECTORS

OF

Black, Inc.

A _____ Nevada _____ Corporation

I, the undersigned, being all of the Directors of _____ Black, Inc. _____

_____, a _____ Nevada _____ corporation, having

met and discussed the business herein set forth, have unanimously:

RESOLVED, that the President and Treasurer of the Corporatin are hereby authorized to employ,

for a period not exceeding _____ six (6) _____ months, some reputable firm to

undertake the sale of the _____ printing plant _____

and other assets of the Corporation, upon such terms and conditions as the President and Treasurer

deem best for the interests of the Corporation.

DATED THIS ____ 1st ____ day of ____ November ____, ____ 2001 ____.

I M Director

DIRECTOR IN TOTO

Fire Old Auditors, Hire New Ones *SAMPLE*

RESOLUTION OF THE BOARD OF DIRECTORS

OF

Black, Inc.

A _____ Nevada _____ Corporation

I, the undersigned, being all of the Directors of _____ Black, Inc. _____

_____, a _____ Nevada _____ corporation, having

met and discussed the business herein set forth, have unanimously:

RESOLVED, that, when the employment contract expires, dated _____ December 31 _____,
_____ 2001 _____, with _____ C.P. Anderson, Inc. _____, auditors for this Corporation, the
said contract of employment shall not be renewed, and be it

FURTHER RESOLVED, that the President of this Corporation is hereby authorized to enter into a
contract with _____ Bill Closely, Ltd. _____, employing the said
_____ Bill Closely, Ltd. _____ to act as auditors for this Corporation
for a period of _____ one year _____, commencing on _____ January 1 _____,
_____ 2002 _____, at a yearly compensation of _____ Two Thousand _____ Dollars
($_____ 2,000.00 _____).

DATED THIS _____ 1st _____ day of _____ November _____, _____ 2001 _____.

I.M. Director

DIRECTOR IN TOTO

RESOLUTION OF THE BOARD OF DIRECTORS

OF

Black, Inc.

A _____ Nevada _____ Corporation

I, the undersigned, being all of the Directors of _____ Black, Inc. _____

_____, a _____ Nevada _____ corporation, having

met and discussed the business herein set forth, have unanimously:

RESOLVED, that the President of this Corporation be and hereby is authorized to enter into a

contract for _____ computer service _____ with

_____ Tapedrive, Ltd. _____, in the name and on behalf of this Corporation, upon such

terms and conditions as may be agreed upon between him and _____ Tapedrive, Ltd. _____

_____ .

DATED THIS _____ 1st _____ day of _____ November _____, _____ 2001 _____ .

I M Director

DIRECTOR IN TOTO

261

Authority to Borrow Money

RESOLUTION OF THE BOARD OF DIRECTORS

OF

Black, Inc.

A _____ Nevada _____ Corporation

I, the undersigned, being all of the Directors of _____ Black, Inc. _____

_____, a _____ Nevada _____ corporation, having

met and discussed the business herein set forth, have unanimously:

RESOLVED, WHEREAS, this Corporation desires to borrow money for its corporate purpose, it is hereby

RESOLVED, that the Board of Directors of this Corporation is hereby given authority to borrow sums of money as is needed on the notes of this Corporation, and for that purpose to pledge and assign any or all bills and accounts receivable or any other available assets of the Corporation to secure such notes.

DATED THIS _____ 1st _____ day of _____ November _____, _____ 2001 _____.

_____

DIRECTOR IN TOTO

RESOLUTION OF THE BOARD OF DIRECTORS

OF

Black, Inc.

A Nevada Corporation

I, the undersigned, being all of the Directors of Black, Inc.
, a Nevada corporation, having met and discussed the business herein set forth, have unanimously:

RESOLVED, that President U.R.Important of this Corporation be hereby designated, the name of and for the account of this Corporation, and on such terms and conditions as may be deemed proper, to borrow from the Easy National Bank of Nevada , sums of money; to sign, execute, and endorse such documents as may be necessary by the bank to prove such indebtedness, to discount or rediscount with said bank any of the bills receivable held by this Corporation; to apply and obtain from this bank letters of credit, and to endorse and execute agreements to secure said bank in connection thereof; to pledge and/or mortgage any moneys on deposit or any moneys otherwise in the possession of said bank, and/or any bonds, stocks, bills receivable, or other property of this Corporation, to secure the payment of any indebtedness, liability, or obligation of this Corporation to said bank, whether due or to become due and whether existing or hereafter incurred, however arising; to withdraw and/or substitute any property of this Corporation held at any time by said bank, and to sign and execute trust receipts for the withdrawal of same when required; and generally to do and perform all acts and sign all agreements, obligations, pledges, and/or other instruments necessary by the bank for its own protection in its dealings with this Corporation, and be it

FURTHER RESOLVED, that all transactions by any of the Officers or representatives of this Corporation in its name and for its account with said bank prior to this meeting are hereby approved and ratified, and be it

FURTHER RESOLVED, that said bank be furnished with a certified copy of these resolutions, and is hereby authorized to deal with the officers herein above named under said authority unless and until it is expressly notified in writing to the contrary by this Corporation, and shall in writing acknowledge receipt of such notifications; and said bank shall at all times be protected in recognizing as such Officers the persons named in a certificate signed by any Officer of this Corporation.

DATED THIS _____1st_____ day of _____November_____, _____2001_____.

I M Director
DIRECTOR IN TOTO

SAMPLE

RESOLUTION OF THE BOARD OF DIRECTORS

OF

<u>Black, Inc.</u>

A <u>Nevada</u> Corporation

I, the undersigned, being all of the Directors of <u>Black, Inc.</u>
<u>   </u>, a <u>Nevada</u> corporation, having
met and discussed the business herein set forth, have unanimously:

RESOLVED, WHEREAS, this Corporation wants to borrow money for corporate use, it is hereby

RESOLVED, that the designated Officers of this Corporation are hereby authorized to borrow from
the <u>Easy National</u> Bank, for and on behalf of this Corporation, a sum not
to exceed <u>One Hundred Fifty Thousan</u> Dollars ($<u>150,000.00</u>), on its promissory
note which matures <u>One Hundred Eighty</u> (<u>180</u>) days from the date
hereof, to be signed by the designated Officers of this Corporation, to bear interest at the rate of
<u>twelve</u> per cent (<u>12</u>%) per annum, with the right, however,
to renew said loan at the maturity thereof for a further period of
<u>One Hundred Eighty</u> (<u>18</u>) days, upon payment of <u>Fifteen Thousand</u>
Dollars ($<u>15,000.00</u>) on account of the principal amount thereof, and with additional
right of renewing the balance of said loan at the maturity of said further period of <u>   </u>
<u>One Hundred Eighty</u> (<u>180</u>) days, for another period of
<u>One Hundred Eight</u> (<u>180</u>) days, upon payment of
<u>Fifteen Thousand</u> Dollars ($<u>15,000.00</u>) on account of said
balance, thereby reducing said loan to <u>One Hundred Twenty Thousand</u> Dollars
($<u>120,000.00</u>), and the designated Officers of this Corporation are hereby authorized and
directed to sign any new or renewal note or notes required by said <u>   </u>
<u>Easy National</u> Bank to carry out the terms of this resolution, which new
note or notes shall bear such rate of interest as shall be agreed upon between this Corporation and
the <u>Easy National</u> Bank at the time of such renewal or renewals, and be

FURTHER RESOLVED, that President U.R. Important of this Corporation be hereby authorized, for and on behalf of this Corporation, to countersign the aforesaid promissory note of One Hundred Fifty Thousand Dollars ($ 150,000.00), or any new or renewal note or notes as stated in this resolution.

DATED THIS 1st day of November , 2001 .

I M Director

DIRECTOR IN TOTO

Buy Real Property

RESOLUTION OF THE BOARD OF DIRECTORS

OF

Black, Inc.

A _____ Nevada _____ Corporation

I, the undersigned, being all of the Directors of _____ Black, Inc. _____
_____, a _____ Nevada _____ corporation, having
met and discussed the business herein set forth, have unanimously:

RESOLVED, that _____ President U.R. Important _____ of Corporation, be and is hereby
authorized and instructed to proceed on behalf of this Corporation, using discretion and judgment to
consummate the purchase of that real property identified as:

100 Diamond Avenue

and be it

FURTHER RESOLVED, that _____ President U.R. Important _____ be and is hereby authorized
to execute any and all documents required on behalf of this Corporation pertinent to the above
authorized purchase.

DATED THIS _____ 1st _____ day of _____ November _____, _____ 2001 _____.

I.M. Director

DIRECTOR IN TOTO

267

Loan From Corporation

RESOLUTION OF THE BOARD OF DIRECTORS
OF
Black, Inc.

A _____ Nevada _____ Corporation

I, the undersigned, being all of the Directors of _____ Black, Inc. _____, a _____ Nevada _____ corporation, having met and discussed the business herein set forth, have unanimously:

RESOLVED, WHEREAS, _____ John Doe _____, a _____ stockholder _____ of this Corporation, has requested that the Corporation lend to him the sum of _____ Five Thousand _____ Dollars ($_____ 5,000.0 _____), and has offered to furnish _a Certificate of Deposit_ as security for said loan, and has agreed to pay interest on said loan at the rate of _____ twelve _____ per cent (_____ 12 _____%) per annum, it is hereby

RESOLVED, that this Corporation be and is hereby authorized to issue a check to the said _____ John Doe _____ for the sum of _____ Five Thousand _____ Dollars ($_____ 5,000.00 _____) upon receipt by it of said security.

DATED THIS _____ 1st _____ day of _____ November _____, _____ 2001 _____.

_____ I M Director _____
DIRECTOR IN TOTO

Lease Equipment   *SAMPLE*

RESOLUTION OF THE BOARD OF DIRECTORS
OF
Black, Inc.

A _____ Nevada _____ Corporation

I, the undersigned, being all of the Directors of _____ Black, Inc. _____

_____, a _____ Nevada _____ corporation, having

met and discussed the business herein set forth, have unanimously:

RESOLVED, that the President be and is hereby authorized to lease from

_____ Lotsa Info., Inc. _____, a _____ computer _____ and related

items to be used in the furtherance and pursuit of the Corporation's necessary and ordinary day to

day business.

DATED THIS _____ 1st _____ day of _____ November _____, _____ 2001 _____.

_____ I M Director _____
DIRECTOR IN TOTO

269

President Make Purchase For Corporation   *SAMPLE*

RESOLUTION OF THE BOARD OF DIRECTORS

OF

Black, Inc.
_____

A _____ Nevada _____ Corporation

I, the undersigned, being all of the Directors of _____ Black, Inc. _____

_____, a _____ Nevada _____ corporation, having

met and discussed the business herein set forth, have unanimously:

RESOLVED, that the President be and is hereby authorized and instructed to purchase now and in

the future such _____ computer software _____ as may in his/her judgment and at his/her

sole discretion be in the best interest of the business pursuits of this Corporation.

DATED THIS _____ 1st _____ day of _____ November _____ , _____ 2001 _____ .

_____
DIRECTOR IN TOTO

270

SAMPLE

RESOLUTION OF THE BOARD OF DIRECTORS

OF

Black, Inc.

A _____Nevada_____ Corporation

I, the undersigned, being all of the Directors of _____ Black, Inc. _____

_____, a _____Nevada_____ corporation, having met and discussed the business herein set forth, have unanimously:

RESOLVED, that the common stock of the Corporation be issued to the named individuals in the amount stated in exchange for cash, property, services performed, or other assets received and indicated:

NAME	NO. OF SHARES	ISSUED FOR
James Roe	100	$1,000.00
Jane Roe	100	$1,000.00

DATED THIS ___1st___ day of ___November___, ___2001___.

I M Director

DIRECTOR IN TOTO

271

SAMPLE

Subscription of Stock

RESOLUTION OF THE BOARD OF DIRECTORS
OF
Black, Inc.

A _____ Nevada _____ Corporation

I, the undersigned, being all of the Directors of _____ Black, Inc. _____ , a _____ Nevada _____ corporation, having met and discussed the business herein set forth, have unanimously:

RESOLVED, WHEREAS _____ John Doe _____ has subscribed for _____ Sixty (60) _____ shares of the stock of this Corporation for a total price of _____ Sixty Thousand _____ Dollars ($_____ 60,000.00 _____) and has proposed to pay for the same by conveying, transferring and assignment to this Corporation the following described property: _____ 100 Gold Street _____ ;

it is hereby

RESOLVED, that the proposal of _____ John Doe _____ to pay for his/her subscription to shares of this Corporation by conveying, transferring and assigning to this Corpora-tion certain assets hereinbefore described, be and the same is hereby accepted; and be it

FURTHER RESOLVED, that such property be, and hereby is, valued by this Board of Directors at the sum of _____ Sixty Thousand _____ Dollars ($_____ 60,000.00 _____).

DATED THIS ___ 1st ___ day of ___ November ___ , ___ 2001 ___ .

_____
DIRECTOR IN TOTO

272

SAMPLE

RESOLUTION OF THE BOARD OF DIRECTORS

OF

Black, Inc.

A _____ Nevada _____ Corporation

I, the undersigned, being all of the Directors of _____ Black, Inc. _____

_____, a _____ Nevada _____ corporation, having met and discussed the business herein set forth, have unanimously:

RESOLVED, that it is now the dividend policy of the Corporation to place the capital stock of the Company on a dividend basis of _____ Eighty Thousand _____ Dollars ($_____ 80,000.00 _____) per annum, payable on the first day of _____ January _____, _____ 2001 _____ , provided the earnings of the Corporation warrant the same, subject to the declaration and pleasure of said dividends from time to time by the Board of Directors.

DATED THIS _____ 1st _____ day of _____ November _____, _____ 2002 _____.

I M Director

DIRECTOR IN TOTO

Stock Dividend

RESOLUTION OF THE BOARD OF DIRECTORS

OF

Black, Inc.

A _____ Nevada _____ Corporation

I, the undersigned, being all of the Directors of _____ Black, Inc. _____
_____ , a _____ Nevada _____ corporation, having
met and discussed the business herein set forth, have unanimously:

RESOLVED, WHEREAS, this Corporation as of the _1st_ day of _November_ ,
_2001_ , has undistributed surplus funds in the sum of _Fifty Thousand_
_____ Dollars ($_50,000.00_), and

WHEREAS, a majority of the Board of Directors have decided that _Fifty Thousand_
Dollars ($_50,000.00_) should be set aside from the undistributed surplus funds for the
purpose of declaring a stock dividend to be distributed to the holders of outstanding common shares
of the Capital Stock of this Corporation; it is hereby

RESOLVED that a stock dividend be and hereby is declared in the amount of
Twenty Thousand Dollars ($_20,000.00_) per share of the
common stock of this Corporation, and that the same shall be paid by the proper Officers on
January 1 , _2002_ , to shareholders of record as of
November 1 , _2001_ , and

FURTHER RESOLVED, that the proper Officers are authorized and directed to transfer ___Fifty Thousand___ Dollars ($___50,000.00___) from earned (or other) surplus to the capital account.

DATED THIS ___1st___ day of ___November___, ___2001___.

___I M Director___
DIRECTOR IN TOTO

275

Increase/Decrease Number of Directors

RESOLUTION OF THE BOARD OF DIRECTORS
OF

Black, Inc.

A _____ Nevada _____ Corporation

I, the undersigned, being all of the Directors of _____ Black, Inc. _____
_____, a _____ Nevada _____ corporation, having
met and discussed the business herein set forth, have unanimously:

RESOLVED, that the number of Directors of this Corporation shall be increased/decreased to a total of _____ one _____ (_____1_____), and be it

FURTHER RESOLVED, that this change be and hereby is effective _____ immediately / on a
_____ specific date _____

DATED THIS _____ 1st _____ day of _____ November _____, _____ 2001 _____.

_____ I M Director _____
DIRECTOR IN TOTO

276

RESOLUTION OF THE BOARD OF DIRECTORS

OF

Black, Inc.

A _____ Nevada _____ Corporation

I, the undersigned, being all of the Directors of _____ Black, Inc. _____ , a _____ Nevada _____ corporation, having met and discussed the business herein set forth, have unanimously:

RESOLVED, that _____ Joe Worthless _____ , a member of the Board of Directors of this Corporation, be and hereby is removed as a member of the Board, and be it

FURTHER RESOLVED, that said removal be and hereby is effective immediately/on a specific date

DATED THIS _____ 1st _____ day of _____ November _____ , _____ 2001 _____ .

I. M. Director

DIRECTOR IN TOTO

277

Proxy

A proxy is an authorization given by a stockholder to someone else to exercise the voting rights attached to his/her shares. In Nevada a proxy must be written and generally is valid for six (6) months UNLESS 1.) the proxy is "coupled with an interest," or 2.) the stockholder specifies the length of time the proxy is to continue in force. However, in neither case is a proxy valid for more than seven (7) years in Nevada.

A proxy may be made irrevocable if it expressly says so AND is "coupled with an interest." The interest can be in the shares themselves. For example — a stockholder borrows money, pledges his/her shares as security for repayment, and signs an "irrevocable proxy" on the voting rights in the shares until the loan is repaid. The stockholder still owns the shares but someone else has the right to vote them. The maximum length of time an irrevocable proxy is valid is seven (7) years in Nevada. Revocation of a proxy must be in writing and be filed with the secretary of the corporation.

Proxy (limited to one meeting)   *SAMPLE*

PROXY

BLACK, INC.
_____

A _____ Nevada _____ Corporation

KNOW ALL MEN BY THESE PRESENTS, that the undersigned, _____

_____ John Adams _____, the owner of _____ 500 _____ shares of stock in

_____ Black, Inc. _____ Corporation, a _____ Nevada _____

corporation, represented by Share Certificate No. ___5___, hereby authorizes _____ Joe Baker _____

_____ to vote those shares at the meeting of stockholders of said Corporation to

be held on _____ November 1 _____, _____ 2001 _____, at _____ 10:00 a.m. _____ at

_____ the corporate office _____.

Under the authority _____ Joe Baker _____ shall have the right to vote for the

election of Directors and on any other matter as may properly be raised at the meeting.

DATED THIS _____ 1st _____ day of _____ November _____, _____ 2001 _____.

John Adams
_____
SIGNATURE OF STOCKHOLDER

(Please sign exactly as your name is printed on
this proxy. If Trustee, Guardian, Executor,
coroporation, etc., indicate official capacity.

Proxy (limited to one meeting #2)   *SAMPLE*

PROXY

BLACK, INC.
_____

A _____ Nevada _____ Corporation

KNOW ALL MEN BY THESE PRESENTS, that _____ Joe Baker _____ and

_____ Jane Baker _____, the undersigned stockholders in _____ Black, Inc. _____, a

_____ Nevada _____ corporation, hereby constitute and appoint _____ John Adams _____

our true and lawful attorney and agent for us and in our names, places and steads to vote as our proxy at the

(annual or regular or special) meeting of stockholders of the said Corporation to be held on

_____ November 1 _____, _____ 2001 _____, or at any adjournment thereof for the election of

Directors and for the transaction of any business which may legally come before the said meeting and for us

and in our names to act as fully as we could do if personally present.

DATED THIS _____ 1st _____ day of _____ November _____, _____ 2001 _____.

_____ *Joe Baker* _____
SIGNATURE OF STOCKHOLDER

_____ *Jane Baker* _____
SIGNATURE OF STOCKHOLDER

(Please sign exactly as your name is printed on
this proxy. If Trustee, Guardian, Executor,
coroporation, etc., indicate official capacity.

Certified Copy of Corporate Resolution

The certified copy of a corporate resolution is seldom properly used. When you are doing business as a corporate entity, you are repeatedly asked for a corporate resolution or a copy of the corporate resolution authorizing your corporation to do whatever it is you desire it to do. Don't give whoever is requesting the corporate resolution the actual resolution or even a copy of the resolution. The proper instrument or document to supply them with is a certified copy of corporate resolution.

It is probably worthy to note that banks, lending institutions and various others have ready-made corporate resolutions to be signed by the officers of the corporation in question for the bank's records and to keep on file before making a loan, for example. Any time you sign this type of ready-made resolution you should make a certified copy of the corporation resolution as illustrated in this section and place it in your corporate record book for your records. The resolution is just as important for you to have on record as it is for the bank. If in a hurry, you may simply photocopy the bank's resolution and put it in your book. That's a lot better than having nothing. If you take the time, you will find it very enlightening to carefully read one of those prepared resolutions that the bank or lending institution has you sign. You might find it very revealing and eye-opening. Usually people don't read this already-prepared resolution and are shocked at some time in the future to find out what they signed and agreed to.

Certified Copy of Corporate Resolution (Stockholders)

CERTIFIED COPY OF CORPORATE RESOLUTION

OF

BLACK, INC.

A _____ Nevada _____ Corporation

I, _____ Minnie Minutes _____, Secretary of _____ Black, Inc. _____, a

_____ Nevada _____ corporation, hereby certify that the following is a true and correct

copy of a resolution duly adopted by all/a majority of the stockholders of said Corporation, and that said

resolution has not been modified or rescinded and is still in full force and effect:

RESOLVED,

(insert text of resolution here)

I further certify that said Corporation is duly organized and existing and has the power to take the

action called for by the aforesaid resolution.

IN WITNESS WHEREOF, I have hereunto affixed by hand this _____ 1st _____ day of

_____ November _____, _____ 2001 _____.

Minnie Minutes

SECRETARY

(acknowledgement)

282

SAMPLE

CERTIFIED COPY OF CORPORATE RESOLUTION

OF

BLACK, INC.

A _____Nevada_____ Corporation

I, ____Minnie Minutes____, Secretary of ____Black, Inc.____, a
____Nevada____ corporation, hereby certify that the following is a true and correct copy of a resolution duly adopted by the Board of Directors of said Corporation, and that said resolution has not been modified or rescinded and is still in full force and effect:

RESOLVED,

(insert text of resolution here)

I further certify that said Corporation is duly organized and existing and has power to take the action called for by the aforesaid resolution.

IN WITNESS WHEREOF, I have hereunto affixed my hand this ____1st____
day of ____November____, ___2001___.

Minnie Minutes
SECRETARY

(acknowledgement)

283

SAMPLE

CERTIFICATE AMENDING ARTICLES OF INCORPORATION

OF

BLACK, INC.

A _____ Nevada _____ Corporation

The undersigned, being the President and Secretary of _____ Black, Inc. _____, a _____ Nevada _____ corporation, hereby certify that by majority vote of the Board of Directors and majority vote of the stockholders at a meeting held on _____ November 1 _____, _____ 2001 _____, it was agreed by unanimous vote that this CERTIFICATE AMENDING ARTICLES OF INCORPORATION be filed.

The undersigned further certify that the original Articles of Incorporation of _____ _____ Black, Inc. _____ were filed with the Secretary of State of _____ Nevada _____ on the _____ 1st _____ day of _____ September _____, _____ 2001 _____, and a Certified copy of said Articles were filed with the _____ Carson City _____ Clerk on the _____ 15th _____ day of _____ September _____, _____ 2001 _____. The under-signed further certify that _____ Section V _____ of the Articles of Incorporation filed on the _____ 1st. _____ day of _____ September _____, _____ 2001 _____ herein is amended to read as follows:

(insert new text of Articles here)

The undersigned hereby further certify that they have executed this Certificate Amending the Articles of Incorporation heretofore filed with the Secretary of State of _____ Nevada _____.

DATED THIS _____1st_____ day of _____November_____, _____2001_____.

U. R. Important
PRESIDENT

Minnie Minutes
SECRETARY

(acknowledgement)

Promissory Notes

A promissory note is a written promise to pay a specified sum of money at a certain time or on demand. The person promising to pay signs the note and is the "maker." Enclosed are several examples plus a list of "optional provisions" that you can insert as needed.

Promissory Note (on demand with interest)   *SAMPLE*

PROMISSORY NOTE

On demand for value received I, the undersigned, promise to pay to _____ Black, Inc.
_____, at _____ 100 Easy Street _____,
_____ Anytown, U.S.A. _____, the sum of _____ Five Thousand ___ Dollars
($_____ 5,000.00 _____), with interest thereon at the rate of _____ thirteen ___ per cent
(___1___%) per _(day or month or year____, payable(monthly or quarterly or
semiannually or on specified dates as the case may be)_____ thereafter.

If default is made in the payment when due of any part or installment of interest, then the whole sum of principal and interest shall become immediately due and payable at the option of the payee without notice.

In the event of commencement of suit to enforce payment of this note, I agree to pay such additional sum as attorneys' fees as the court may adjudge reasonable.

(insert other provisions if needed)

DATED THIS ___1st.___ day of _____ November _____, ___2001___.

Pauline Payroll

(NAME OF MAKER)

(acknowledgement)

Promissory Note (installments with interest)

PROMISSORY NOTE

$ __5,000.00__   Carson City, NV   November 1 , 2001

For value received, _____ Black, Inc. _____, a _____ Nevada _____

corporation, promises to pay to _____ Blue, Inc. _____, a _____ Any State _____

corporation, at _____ 100 Sapphire Street _____, _____ Any Town _____,

__USA__ , _____ Five Thousand _____ Dollars ($__5,000.00__)

with interest from _____ November 1 _____, __2001__, at the rate of _____ Thirteen _____

per cent (__1__ %) per __(day, month or year__ until paid, payable __(monthly or__

quarterly or semiannually or annually or on specified dates as the case may be) _____ thereafter.

If default is made in the payment when due of any part or installment of interest, then the entire amount of principal and interest shall become immediately due and payable at the option of the holder of this note, without notice.

IN WITNESS WHEREOF, __(insert other provisions if needed)__ , a

_____ Nevada _____ corporation, has caused this note to be executed by its duly

authorized Officers.

_____ Black, Inc. _____
(NAME OF CORPORATION) MAKER

U. R. Important
PRESIDENT

Minnie Minutes
SECRETARY

(SEAL - Optional in Nevada)

(acknowledgement)

288

SAMPLE

PROMISSORY NOTE

FOR A GOOD AND VALUABLE CONSIDERATION, the receipt and sufficiency of which is hereby acknowledged, _____MY CORPORATION, INC._____, a _____Any State_____ corporation, promises to pay to _____BLACK, INC._____, a _____Nevada_____ corporation, the sum of _____Twenty Thousand_____ Dollars ($_____20,000.00_____) _____twenty_____ (_____20_____) years from the date of this document with interest thereon at the rate of _____fifteen_____ per cent (_____15_____%) per year payable _____yearly_____ thereafter.

Upon the death of _____John Cleveland_____ any remaining obligation of _____My Corporation Inc._____ to _____Black, Inc._____ due and owing under this note is automatically forgiven.

IN WITNESS WHEREOF, _____My Corporation Inc._____, a _____Any State_____ corporation, has caused this note to be executed by its duly authorized Officer.

_____MY CORPORATION, INC._____
(NAME OF CORPORATION) MAKER

Martha Washington
PRESIDENT

(SEAL - Optional in Nevada)

(acknowledgement)

Promissory Note (installments with interest)

SAMPLE

PROMISSORY NOTE

Carson City, Nevada

_____November 1_____, __2001__

For value received, the undersigned promises to pay to _____John Adams_____, the
sum of _____Five Thousand_____ Dollars ($_____5,000.00_____), payable only in
lawful money of the United States and payable as is hereafter set forth. No interest will be charged against
the above amount as long as the payments as set forth below are made on schedule. Should the maker
deviate from the payment schedule, interest will be charged at the rate of
_____thirteen_____ per cent (___13___%) per (day, month or year)
and added to the payments accordingly.

The maker hereto agrees to pay to the holder of this note the sum of Two Hundred Fifty
_____ Dollars ($___250.00___) per month on the first day of
each month commencing on _____December 1_____, __2001__, and a like amount on the
first day of each and every month for a period of ___one___ years and ___seven___
months, with a final payment of __Two Hundred Fifty__ Dollars ($___250.00___) on
_____July 1_____, __2002__.

If default is made in the payment of any installment under this note and if default is not vacated within
ten (10) days after the due date thereof, the holder of this note shall have the option to declare the entire
principal sum and accrued interest, if any, immediately due and payable without notice.

Failure to exercise this option shall not constitute a waiver of the right to exercise the same in the
event of any subsequent default.

The maker waives demand, notice, protest and diligence and further promises that if this note is not
fully paid as above provided, the maker will pay all costs and expenses, including a reasonable attorneys'
fee, that may be incurred in connecting this note or any part thereof.

290

The maker shall have the right to prepay the principal amount or any part thereof without penalty at any time.

(Insert other provisions if needed)

DATED THIS _____1st_____ day of _____November_____, ___2001___,

at _____Carson City_____, _____Nevada_____.

_____BLACK, INC._____
(NAME OF CORPORATION)

U. R. Important
_____
(TITLE)

(acknowledgement)

Security Agreements and Deeds of Trust

A security agreement is a written agreement granting a creditor a security interest in the debtor's personal property (everything but real property). Once this agreement is signed, the named creditor can attach (take over) the debtor's personal property if the debtor defaults in payment to the creditor.

A security interest must be "perfected" to be made effective against most of the rest of the world. That is —— so the creditor will be first in line to get the debtor's personal property if the debtor defaults. "Perfection" is accomplished by filing a UCC-1 Financing Statement in the proper place (either in the secretary of state's office or in the county recorder's office where the personal property is located).

UCC-1 FINANCING STATEMENT - These forms can be obtained from the secretary of state's office and most office supply stores.

Some states refer to a deed of trust as a mortgage or a trust deed. A deed of trust is a security instrument by which the legal title to real property is placed in a trust until the repayment of a sum of money or the debtor performs on some pre-determined condition.

Included below is a sample Deed of Trust for Nevada together with optional covenants which can be incorporated.

SECURITY AGREEMENT

Agreement made _____ November 1 _____, _____ 2001 _____, between
_____ Blue, Inc. _____, _____ 100 Sapphire Street _____,
_____ Any Town, Any Stat ___, herein referred to as Debtor, and _ Black, Inc. _____,
_____ 100 Easy Street _____, _____ Any Town, Any State
herein referred to as Secured Party.

In consideration of the mutual covenants and promises set forth herein, Debtor and Secured Party
agree:

I

The collateral subject of this security agreement, herein referred to as Collateral, is the personal
property of the following description: All cash, moneys, inventory, equipment, real estate
estate, supplies receivables, or furnishings of the Debtor Corporation
now or in the future.

all of which shall be a component part of Collateral.

II

Debtor hereby grants to Secured Party a security interest in said Collateral, hereinbefore described to
secure the performance and payment of Debtor's note dated _____ November 1 _____,
_____ 2001 _____, in the amount of _____ Five Thousand _____, (_ 5,000.00 _),
given to Secured Party as principal and interest as therein provided; in all expenditures by Secured Party for taxes,
insurance, repairs to and maintenance of the Collateral and all costs and expenses incurred by Secured Party in
the collection and enforcement of the note and other indebtedness of Debtor; in future advances to be evidenced
by like notes to be made by Debtor to Secured Party at Secured Party's option; and in all liabilities of Debtor to
Secured Party now existing or hereafter incurred, matured or unmatured, direct or contingent, and any renewals
and extensions thereof and substitutions therefore.

III

Secured Party shall make the loan to Debtor as agreed and as evidenced by the above-mentioned note.

IV

Debtor shall pay to Secured Party the sum evidenced by the above-mentioned note or by any renewals or extensions thereof executed pursuant to this security agreement in accordance with the terms of such note and any other obligations that now exist or may hereafter accrue from Debtor or Secured Party as provided herein.

V

Debtor hereby grants to Secured Party a security interest in and to all proceeds of Collateral, as defined in Section I. The provisions shall not be constructed to mean that Debtor is authorized to sell, lease, or dispose of Collateral without the consent of Secured Party.

VI

At the request of Secured Party, Debtor will join in executing, or will execute as appropriate, all necessary financing statements in a form satisfactory to Secured Party, and will pay the cost of filing such statements. Debtor will execute all other instruments deemed necessary by Secured Party and pay the cost of filing such documents. Debtor warrants that no financing statement covering Collateral or any part thereof or any proceeds thereof is presently on file in any public offfice.

VII

Debtor will not, without the written consent of Secured Party, sell, contract to sell, lease, encumber, or otherwise dispose of Collateral or any interest therein until this security agreement and all debts secured thereby have been fully satisfied.

VIII

If in the judgment of Secured Party, Collateral has materially decreased in value, or if Secured Party shall at any time deem itself insecure, Debtor shall either provide additional Collateral sufficient to satisfy Secured Party or reduce the total indebtedness by an amount sufficient to satisfy Secured Party.

IX

Debtor shall insure Collateral with companies acceptable to Secured Party against such casualties and in such amounts as Secured Party shall require. The insurance shall be for the benefit of Debtor and Secured Party as their interests may appear. Secured Party is hereby authorized to collect from the insurance company any amount that may become due under any of such insurance, and the Secured Party may apply the same to the obligations hereby secured.

X

Debtor will keep Collateral separate and identifiable and at the address of Debtor shown herein, and Debtor will not remove Collateral from such address without the written consent of Secured Party.

XI

Debtor shall keep Collateral in good order and repair; Debtor shall not waste or destroy Collateral or any part thereof; and Debtor shall not use Collateral in violation of any statute or ordinance. Secured Party shall have the right to examine and inspect Collateral at any reasonable time.

XII

Secured Party may at its option and at any time discharge taxes, liens, or interest on Collateral; perform or cause to be performed for and on behalf of Debtor any action or conditions, obligations, or covenants that Debtor has failed or refused to perform; or pay for the repair, maintenance, and preservation of Collateral. All sums so expended shall bear interest from the date of payment at the rate of

<u>   thirteen   </u> per cent (<u>   13   </u>%) per year, shall be payable at the place designated in the above-mentioned note, and shall be secured by this security agreement.

XIII

Debtor shall pay promptly when due all taxes and assessments levied on Collateral or on its use and operation.

XIV

When performing any act under this security agreement and the note secured hereby, time shall be of the essence.

XV

If Debtor fails to pay when due any amount payable on the above-mentioned note or on any other indebtedness of Debtor secured hereby, or shall fail to observe or perform any or the provisions of this agreement, Debtor shall be in default.

XVI

Failure of Secured Party to exercise any right or remedy, including but not limited to the acceptance of partial or delinquent payments, shall not be a waiver of any obligation of Debtor or right of Secured Party or constitute a waiver of any other similar default subsequently occurring.

XVII

On any default, and any time thereafter:

(1) Secured Party may declare all obligations secured hereby immediately due and payable

and may proceed to enforce payment of the same, and exercise any and all of the rights and remedies provided in this Security Agreement as well as any and all other rights and remedies possessed by Secured Party.

(2) Secured Party shall have the right to remove Collateral from Debtor's premises. Secured Party may require Debtor to assemble Collateral and make it available to Secured Party at any place to be designated by Secured Party that is reasonably convenient to both parties. For purposes of removal and possession of Collateral, Secured Party or its representatives may enter any premises of Debtor without legal process, and Debtor hereby waives and releases Secured Party of and from any and all claims in connection therewith or arising therefrom.

(3) Unless Collateral is perishable or threatens to decline speedily in value or is of type customarily sold on a recognized market, Secured Party shall give Debtor reasonable notice of the time and place of any public sale thereof or of the time after which any private sale or other intended disposition thereof is to be made. The requirements of reasonable notice shall be met if such notice is mail, postage prepaid, to the address of Debtor shown herein at least _____ twenty _____ (___ 20 ___) days before the time of the sale or disposition. Expenses of retaking, holding, preparing for sale, selling, or the like shall include reasonable attorneys' fees and legal expenses incurred by Secured Party.

XVIII

This Security Agreement shall be constructed according to ___ the Nevada Revised ___, ___ Statutes ___ and other applicable laws of the State of ___ Nevada ___, and all obligations of the parties created hereunder are to be performed in the State of ___ Nevada ___.

IN WITNESS WHEREOF, the parties have executed this agreement at ____Carson City____

_____, _____Nevada_____ the day and year first above written.

_____BLUE, INC._____   _____BLACK, INC._____

(NAME OF CORPORATION) - DEBTOR   (NAME OF CORPORATION) - SECURED PARTY

By: _____   By: _____

    (TITLE)   (TITLE)

DEED OF TRUST

(Direct)

THIS DEED OF TRUST, made this ____1st____ day of ____November____,
____2001____, by and between ____Blue, Inc.____, a Nevada Corporation, hereinafter
referred to as "Grantor," ____Black, Inc.____, whose address is
2533 N. Carson St., Carson City, Nevada 89701
hereinafter referred to as "Trustee," and ____Red. Inc.____, hereinafter
referred to as "Beneficiary," who maintains an office and place of business at ____Penn Street,
Anytown, Anystate____.

WITNESSETH, that for and in consideration of $1.00 and other good and valuable consideration, receipt of which is hereby acknowledged, the Grantor does hereby bargain, sell, grant, assign, and convey unto the Trustee, his successors and assigns, all of the following described property situated and being in the County of ____any coaunty____, State of Nevada:

Together with and including all buildings, all fixtures, including but not limited to all plumbing, heating, lighting, ventilating, refrigerating, incinerating, air conditioning apparatus, and elevators (the Trustor hereby declaring that it is intended that the items herein enumerated shall be deemed to have been permanently installed as part of the realty), and all improvements now or hereafter existing hereon; the hereditaments and appurtenances and all other rights thereunto belonging, or in anywise appertaining, and the reversion and reversions, remainder and remainders, and rents, issues, and profits of the above-described property. To have and to hold the same unto the Trustee, and the successors is interest of the Trustee, forever, in fee simple or such other estate, if any as is stated herein in trust, to secure the payment of a promissory note dated July 14, 2001 and maturing ____July 14, 2001____, in the principal sum of $____42,500.00____, signed by ____Real Money, President____ in behalf of ____Blue, Inc.____, a Nevada Corporation. The beneficial owner and holder of said note and of the indebtedness evidenced thereby is the Beneficiary.

1. This conveyance is made upon and subject to the further trust that the said Grantor shall remain in quiet and peaceable possession of the above granted and described premises and take the profits thereof to his own use until default be made in any payment of an installment due on said

299

note or in the performance of any of the covenants or conditions contained therein or in this Deed of Trust; and, also to secure the reimbursement of the Beneficiary or any other holder of said note, the Trustee or any substitute trustee of any and all costs and expenses incurred including reasonable attorneys' fees on account of any litigation which may arise with respect to this Trust or with respect to the indebtedness evidenced by said note, the protection and maintenance of the property, herein-above described or in obtaining possession of said property after any sale which may be made as hereinafter provided.

2. Upon the full payment of the indebtedness evidenced by said note and in the interest thereon, the payment of all other sums herein provided for, the repayment of all monies advanced or expended pursuant to said note or this instrument, and upon the payment of all other proper costs, charges, commissions, and expenses, the above described property shall be released and reconveyed to and at the cost of the Grantor.

3. Upon default in any of the covenants and conditions of this instrument or of the note or loan agreement secured hereby, the Beneficiary or his assigns may without notice and without regard to the adequacy of security for the indebtedness secured, either personally or by attorney or agent without bringing any action or proceeding, or by a receiver to be appointed by the court, enter upon and take possession of said property, collect and receive the rents, royalties, issues, and profits thereof, including rents accrued and unpaid, and apply the same, less costs of operation and collec-tion, upon the indebtedness secured by this Deed of Trust, said rents, royalties, issues, and profits, being hereby assigned to Beneficiary as further security for the payment of such indebtedness. Exercise of rights under this paragraph shall not cure or waive any default or notice of default hereunder or invalidate any act done pursuant to such notice but shall be cumulative to any right and remedy to declare a default and to cause notice of default to be recorded as hereinafter provided, and cumulative to any other right and/or remedy hereunder, or provided by law, and may be exercised concurrently or independently. Expenses incurred by Beneficiary hereunder including reasonable attorneys' fees, shall be secured hereby.

4. The Grantor covenants and agrees that if he shall fail to pay said indebtedness, or any part thereof, when due, or shall fail to perform any covenant or agreement of this instrument or of the promis-sory note secured hereby, the entire indebtedness hereby secured shall immediately become due, payable, and collectible without notice, at the option of the Beneficiary or assigns, regardless of maturity, and the

Beneficiary or assigns may enter upon said property and collect the rents and profits thereof. Upon such default in payment or performance, and before or after such entry, the Trustee, acting in the execution of this Trust, shall have the power to sell said property, and it shall be the Trustee's duty to sell said property (and in the case of any default of any purchaser, to resell) at public auction, to the highest bidder, first giving four weeks' notice of the time, terms, and place of such sale, by advertisement not less than once during each of said four weeks in a newspaper published or distributed in the county or political subdivision in which said property is situated, all other notice being hereby waived by the Grantor (and the Beneficiary or any person on behalf of the Beneficiary or any person on behalf of the Beneficiary may bid and purchase at such sale). Such sale will be held at a suitable place to be selected by the Beneficiary within said county or political subdivision. The Trustee is hereby authorized to execute and deliver to the purchaser at such sale a sufficient conveyance of said property, which conveyance shall contain recitals as to the happening of a default upon whcih the execution of the power of sale herein granted depends; and the said Grantor hereby constitutes and appoints the Trustee as his agent and attorney in fact to make such recitals and to execute said conveyance and hereby covenants and agrees that the recitals so made shall be binding and conclusive upon the Grantor, and said conveyance shall be effectual to bar all equity or right of redemption, homestead, dower, right of appraisement, and all other rights and exemptions of the Grantor, all of which are hereby expressly waived and conveyed to the Trustee. In the event of a sale as hereinabove provided, the Grantor, or any person in possession under the Grantor, shall then become and be tenants holding over and shall forthwith deliver possession to the purchaser at such sale or be summarily dispossessed, in accordance with the provisions of law applicable to tenants holding over. The power and agency hereby granted are coupled with an interest and are irrevocable by death or otherwise, and are granted as cumulative to all other

remedies for the collection of said indebtedness. The Beneficiary or Assigns may take any other appropriate action pursuant to state or Federal statute either in state or Federal court or othewise for the disposition of the property.

5. In the event of a sale as provided in paragraph 4, the Trustee shall be paid a fee by the Beneficiary in an amount not in excess of _____ per cent of the gross amount of said sale or sales, provided, however, that the amount of such fee shall be reasonable and shall be approved by the Beneficiary as to reasonableness. Said fee shall be in addition to the costs and expenses incurred by the Trustee in conducting such sale. The amount of such costs and expenses shall be deducted and paid from the sale's proceeds. It is further agreed that if said property shall be advertised for sale as herein provided and not sold, the Trustee shall be entitled to a reasonable fee, in an amount acceptable to the Beneficiary for

the services so rendered. The Trustee shall also be reimbursed by the Beneficiary for all costs and expenses incurred in connection with the advertising of said property for sale if the sale is not consummated.

6. The proceeds of any sale of said property in accordance with paragraph 4 shall be applied first to payment of fees, costs, and expenses of said sale, the expenses incurred by the Beneficiary for the purpose of protecting or maintaining said property and reasonable attorneys' fees; secondly, to payment of the indebtedness secured hereby; and thirdly, to pay any surplus or excess to the person or persons legally entitled thereto.

7. In the event said property is sold pursuant to the authorization contained in this instrument or at a judicial foreclosure sale and the proceeds are not sufficient to pay the total indebtedness secured by this instrument and evidenced by said promissory note, the Beneficiary will be entitled to a deficiency judgment for the amount of the deficiency without regard to appraisement, the Grantor having waived and assigned all rights of appraisement to the Trustee.

8. The Grantor covenants and agrees as follows:

a. He will promptly pay the indebtedness evidenced by said promissory note at the times and in the manner therein provided.

b. He will pay all taxes, assessments, water rates, and other governmental or municipal charges, fines, or impositions, for which provisions have not been made hereinbefore, and will promptly deliver the official receipts therefor to the Beneficiary.

c. He will pay such expenses and fees as may be incurred in the protection and maintenance of said property, including the fees of any attorney employed by the Beneficiary for the collection of any or all of the indebtedness hereby secured, or such expenses and fees as may be incurred in any foreclosure sale by the Trustee, or court proceedings or in any other litigation or proceeding affecting said property, and attorneys' fees reasonably incurred in any other way.

d. The rights created by this conveyance shall remain in full force and effect during any postponement or extension of the time of the payment of the indebtedness evidenced by said note or any part thereof secured hereby.

302

e. He will continuously maintain hazard insurance of such type or types and in such amounts as the Beneficiary may from time to time require, on the improvements now or hereafter on said property, and will pay promptly when due any premiums therefor. All insurance shall be carried in companies acceptable to Beneficiary and the policies and renewals thereof shall be held by Beneficiary and the policies and renewals thereof shall be held by Beneficiary and have attached thereto loss payable clauses in favor of and in form acceptable to the Beneficiary. In the event of loss, Grantor will give immediate notice in writing to Beneficiary and Beneficiary may make proof of loss if not made promptly by Grantor, and each insurance company concerned is hereby authorized and directed to make payment for such part thereof, may be applied by Beneficiary at its option either to the reduction of the indebtedness hereby secured or to the restoration or repair of the property damaged. In the event of a Trustee's sale or other transfer of title to said property in extinguishment of the indebtedness secured hereby, all right, title, and interest of the Grantor in and to any insurance policies then in force shall pass at the option of the Beneficiary to the purchaser or Beneficiary.

f. He will keep the said premises in as good order and condition as they are now and will not commit or permit any waste thereof, reasonable wear and tear excepted, and in the event of the failure of the Grantor to keep the buildings on said premises and those to be erected on said premises, or improvements thereon, in good repair, the Beneficiary may make such repairs as in the Beneficiary's discretion it may deem necessary for the proper preservation thereof, and any sums paid for such repairs shall bear interest from the date of payment at the rate specified in the note, shall be due and payable on demand and shall be fully secured by this Deed of Trust.

g. He will not without the prior written consent of the Beneficiary voluntarily create or permit to be created against the property subject to this Deed of Trust any lien or liens inferior or superior to the lien of this Deed of Trust and further that he will keep and maintain the same free from the claim of all persons supplying labor or materials which will enter into the construction of any and all buildings now being erected or to be erected on said premises.

h. He will not rent or assign any part of the rent of said property or demolish, remove, or substantially alter any building without the written consent of the Beneficiary.

9. In the event the Grantor fails to pay any Federal, state, or local tax assessment, income tax or other tax lien, charge, fee, or other expense charged to the property hereinabove described, the Beneficiary is hereby authorized to pay the same and any sum so paid by the Beneficiary shall be added to and become a part of the principal amount of the indebtedness evidenced by said promissory note. If the Grantor shall pay and discharge the indebtedness evidenced by said promissory note, and shall pay such sums and shall discharge all taxes and liens and the costs, fees, and expenses of making, enforcing, and executing this Deed of Trust, then this Deed of Trust shall be canceled and surrendered.

10. The Grantor covenants that he is lawfully seized and possessed of and has the right to sell and convey said property; that the same is free from all encumbrances except as hereinabove recited; and that he hereby binds himself and his successors in interest to warrant and defend the title aforesaid thereto and every part thereof against the lawful claims of all persons whomsoever.

11. For better security of the indebtedness hereby secured, the Grantor, upon the request of the Beneficiary, its successors or assigns, shall execute and deliver a supplemental mortgage or mortgages covering any additions, improvements, or betterments made to the property hereinabove described and all property acquired after the date hereof (all in form satisfactory to Grantee). Furthermore, should Grantor fail to cure any default in the payment of a prior or inferior encumbrance on the property described by this instrument, Grantor hereby agrees to permit Beneficiary to cure such default, but Beneficiary is not obligated to do so; and such advances shall become part of the indebtedness secured by this instrument, subject to the same terms and conditions.

12. That all awards of damages in connection with any condemnation for public use of or injury to any of said property are hereby assigned and shall be paid to Beneficiary, who may apply the same to payment of the installments last due under said note, and the Beneficiary is hereby authorized, in the name of the Grantor, to execute and deliver valid acquittances thereof and to appeal from any such award.

13. The irrevocable right to appoint a substitute trustee or trustees is hereby expressly granted to the Beneficiary, his successors or assigns, to be exercised at any time hereafter without notice and without specifying any reason therefor, by filing for record in the office where this instrument is recorded an instrument of appointment. The Grantor and the Trustee herein named or that may hereinafter be substituted hereunder expressly waive notice of the exercise of this right as well as any requirement or application to any court for the removal, appointment or substitution of any trustee hereunder.

14. Notice of the exercise of any option granted herein to the Beneficiary or to the holder of the note secured hereby is not required to be given the Grantor, the Grantor having hereby waived such notice.

15. If more than one person joins in the execution of this instrument as Grantor or if anyone so joined be of the feminine sex, the pronouns and relative words herein shall be read as if written in the plural or feminine, respectively, and the term "Beneficiary" shall include any payee of the indebtedness hereby secured or any assignee or transferee thereof whether by operation of law or otherwise. The covenants herein contained shall bind and the rights herein granted or conveyed shall inure to the respective heirs, executors, administrators, successors, and assigns of the parties hereto.

16. In compliance with section 101.1(d) of the Rules and Regulations of the Small Business Administration [13 C.F.R. 101.1(d)], this instrument is to be construed and enforced in accordance with applicable Federal law.

17. A judicial decree, order, or judgment holding any provision or portion of this instrument invalid or unenforceable shall not in any way impair or preclude the enforcement of the remaining provisions or portions of this instrument.

IN WITNESS WHEREOF, the Grantor has executed this instrument and the Trustee and Beneficiary have accepted the delivery of this instrument as of the day and year aforesaid.

Blue, Inc.
_____

A NEVADA CORPORATION

Real Money
_____

PRESIDENT

Minnie Minutes
_____

SECRETARY

STATE OF NEVADA   )
) SS.

COUNTY OF _____Carson_____   )

On this _____13th_____ day of _____August_____, _____2001_____, personally appeared before me, a Notary Public in and for said County and State, _____Real Money/Minutes_____, known to me to be the persons described in and who executed the within instrument on behalf of _____Blue, Inc._____ Corporation, in their capacity as _____President_____ and _____Secretary_____ respectively, and who acknowledged to me that they executed the same freely and voluntarily and for the uses and purposes therein mentioned.

Beasely Sean
_____

Notary Public, State of Nevada

Contract With Independent Contractor

A contract with an independent contractor is a written agreement between parties to do some form of work. One of the parties is an independent contractor, which means that he/she retains control of the means, method, and manner of accomplishing the work contracted. The other party pays for the work done by the independent contractor.

CONTRACT WITH INDEPENDENT CONTRACTOR

Contract made _____ November 1 _____, _____ 2001 _____, between
_____ BLACK, INC. _____, _____ 100 Easy Street, Anytown, U.S.A. _____
herein referred to as Corporation, and _____ I.A. Doer _____,
_____ 100 Work Street, Anytown, U.S.A. _____ herein referred to as Contractor.

Corporation owns and operates a _____ (type of business) business at the
address set forth above, and desires to have the following services performed _____.
_____ (type of services to be contracted for) _____

Contractor agrees to perform these services for Corporation under the terms and conditions
set forth in this contract.

In consideration of the mutual promises set forth herein, it is agreed by and between
Corporation and Contractor:

I

The work to be performed by the Contractor includes all services generally performed by
Contractor in his usual line of business, including, but not limited to, the following:
_____ (description of work to be performed) _____
_____.

II

Corporation will pay contractor the total sum of _____ (total amount of contract) _____
Dollars ($_____) for the work to be performed under this contract, according to the
following schedule: _____ (insert the work schedule here) _____.

308

III

The work to be performed under this contract will be performed entirely at Contractor's risk, and Contractor assumes all responsibility for the condition of tools and equipment used in the performance of this contract. Contractor will carry, for the duration of this contract, public liability insurance in an amount acceptable to Corporation. Contractor agrees to indemnify Corporation for any and all liability or loss arising in any way out of the performance of this contract.

IV

The parties intend that an independent contractor-employer relationship will be created by this contract. Corporation is interested only in the results to be achieved, and the conduct and control of the work will lie solely with Contractor. Contractor is not to be considered an agent or employee of Corporation for any purpose, and the employees of Contractor are not entitled to any of the benefits that Corporation provides for Corporation employees. It is understood that Corporation does not agree to Contractor exclusively. It is further understood that Contractor is free to contract for similar services to be performed for other corporations while under contract with Corporation.

V

Either party may cancel this contract on _____ thirty _____ (____ 30 ____) day's written notice; otherwise, the contract shall remain in force for a term of _____ one year _____ from date.

IN WITNESS WHEREOF, the parties have executed this agreement at ____ Carson City ____ _____, _____ Nevada _____ the day and year first above written.

_____ BLACK, INC. _____   _J.A Doer_

(NAME OF CORPORATION)   (INDEPENDENT CONTRACTOR)

By:_A. R. Important_

(TITLE)

309

Corporate Changes of the Guard

The forms included below relate to major changes your corporation may undergo. Many of these changes, such as merger, dissolution, and bankruptcy are governed by state laws. Be sure to check the laws in the state your corporation resides when faced with a major corporate change of affairs.

MERGER – A merger occurs when one corporation is absorbed into another corporation. The corporations that participate in a merger are called "constituent" corporations. After a merger is completed, the remaining corporation is known as the "surviving" corporation.

CONSOLIDATION – A consolidation occurs when two or more existing corporations combine to form a wholly new corporation. The corporations that participate in a consolidation are called "constituent" corporations. After a consolidation is completed, the new corporation is known as the "consolidated" corporation.

S CORPORATION – This is a regular corporation, but instead of the corporation paying income tax, the profit or loss of the corporation flows through to the individual stockholders' personal tax return.

BANKRUPTCY – This happens when a debtor is unable to pay his debts as they become due. The process is governed by the Federal Bankruptcy Act or in some cases by state bankruptcy laws.

REORGANIZATION – This occurs under the Federal Bankruptcy Act when most of the assets of the old corporation are transferred to a newly formed corporation.

DISSOLUTION – This is ending your corporation's status as a legal entity. State laws regulate this process and the forms included here follow Nevada law.

LIQUIDATION – This is a process of winding up the affairs of a corporation after dissolution, such as paying debts and distributing assets.

Merger

SAMPLE

RESOLUTION OF THE BOARD OF DIRECTORS

OF

Black, Inc.
_____

A _____ Nevada _____ Corporation

I, the undersigned, being all of the Directors of _____ Black, Inc. _____, a

_____ Nevada _____ corporation, having met and discussed the business herein set

forth, have unanimously:

RESOLVED, that in the opinion of the Board of Directors of this Corporation, it is deemed advis-

able to adopt the Articles of Merger, set forth below, for the purpose of merging

_____ India Inc. _____ into this Corporation; and be it

FURTHER RESOLVED, that a special meeting of the stockholders of this Corporation is hereby

called, to be held on _____ December 1 _____, _____ 2001 _____, at _____ 10:00 a.m. _____, at

_____ the corporate office _____, to take action upon this recommendation and that the

Secretary is hereby instructed to give notice of such meeting to the stockholders in accordance with

the Articles and Bylaws of this Corporation.

DATED THIS _____ 1st _____ day of _____ November _____, _____ 2001 _____.

I. M. Director
_____
DIRECTOR IN TOTO

311

Merger

RESOLUTION OF THE STOCKHOLDERS

OF

BLACK, INC.
_____

A _____ Nevada _____ Corporation

I, the undersigned, being all of stockholders of _____ Black, Inc. _____, a
_____ Nevada _____ corporation, having met and discussed the business herein set
forth, have unanimously:

RESOLVED, WHEREAS, this Corporation now owns all the stock of _____ India, Inc. _____
_____, a corporation organized and engaged in business similar and
incidental to that of this Corporation, and

WHEREAS, it is deemed advisable that this Corporation merge with said _____ India, Inc. _____
_____, in order that all the estate, property, rights, privileges, and
franchises of said Corporation shall vest in and be possessed by this Corporation, it is hereby

RESOLVED, that the stockholders of _____ Black, Inc. _____ hereby approve the
adoption of a certain Agreement of Merger, approved on _____ November 1 _____,
_____ 2001 _____, by the respective Boards of Directors of _____ Black, Inc. _____,
and _____ India, Inc. _____, and entered into by a majority of the directors of each of
such corporations, respectively, on such date, in which Agreement of Merger are prescribed the terms
and conditions of the proposed merger of _____ India, Inc. into
_____ Black, Inc. _____, and the mode of carrying the same into effect, and be it

FURTHER RESOLVED, that the said Agreement of Merger and the terms and conditions therein
set forth and provided are hereby in all respects approved, adopted, authorized, and agreed to, and
be it

FURTHER RESOLVED, that a copy of said Agreement of Merger submitted to this meeting is hereby ordered to be filed with the minutes of this meeting.

DATED THIS ____1st____ day of ____November____, ____2001____.

M.E. Rich

STOCKHOLDER

SAMPLE

PLAN AND AGREEMENT OF MERGER BETWEEN

BLACK, INC.

A ___Nevada___ Corporation

AND

INDIA, INC.

A ___Anystate___ Corporation

Plan and Agreement of Merger made and entered into on the ___1st___ day of ___November___, ___1998___ by and between ___Black, Inc.___ ___, a ___Nevada___ Corporation, and ___India, Inc.___, a ___Anystate___ Corporation, said Corporations hereinafter sometimes referred to jointly as the Constituent Corporations.

WITNESSETH:

WHEREAS, ___Black, Inc.___ is a Corporation organized and existing under the laws of the State of ___Nevada___, its Certificates of Incorporation having been filed in the Office of the Secretary of State of the State of ___Nevada___ on ___May 30___, ___2001___ and recorded in the office of the Recorder for ___Carson City___ in the said State, on ___June 5___, ___2001___, and the registered office of ___Black, Inc.___ being located at ___2533 N. Carson St.___, in the City of ___Carson City___, and its registered agent being ___Laughlin Associates, Inc.___.

WHEREAS the total number of shares of stock which ___Black, Inc.___ has authority to issue is ___2,500___ shares, of which ___2,000___ ___Nevada___ shares are now issued and outstanding, and

WHEREAS, ___India, Inc.___ is a corporation organized and existing under the laws of the State of ___Anystate___, its Articles of Incorporation having been

314

filed in the office of the Secretary of State of the State of _____ Anystate _____ on the
_____ 12th _____ day of _____ July _____, _____ 2001 _____, and a
Certificate of Incorporation having been issued by said Secretary of State on that date, said Certificate of
Incorporation having been recorded in the office of the Recorder of _____ Any _____ County,
_____ Anytown _____, on the _____ 15th _____ day of
_____ July _____ 2001 _____, and the registered office of _____ India, Inc. _____
_____ being located at _____ 100 Anystreet _____,
in the City of _____ Anytown _____, and its registered agent being _Pigment, Inc_.
_____, and

     WHEREAS, the aggregate number of shares which _____ India, Inc. _____ has
authority to issue is _____ 2,500 _____ of which _____ 2,000 _____ shares are issued and outstanding; and

     WHEREAS, the Board of Directors of each of the Constituent Corporations deems it
advisable that _____ India, Inc. _____ be merged into _____ Black, Inc. _____ on
the terms and conditions hereinafter set forth in accordance with the applicable provisions of the statutes of
the State of _____ Anystate _____ and _____ Nevada _____ respectively,
which permit such merger

     NOW, THEREFORE, in consideration of the promises and of the agreements, covenants and provisions
hereinafter contained, _____ Black, Inc. _____, and _____ India, Inc. _____ by their respective Board of Directors, have agreed and do hereby agree, each with the other as follows:

ARTICLE I

_____ Black, Inc. _____ and _____ India, Inc. _____ shall be merged into a single
corporation, in accordance with applicable provisions of the laws of the State of _____ Nevada _____ and of the
State of _____ Anystate _____, by _____ India, Inc. _____ merging into
_____ Black, Inc. _____, which shall be the surviving corporation.

SAMPLE

ARTICLE II

Upon the merger becoming effective, as provided in the applicable laws of the State of
_____ Nevada _____, and of the State of _____ Anystate _____

1. The two Constituent Corporations shall be a single corporation, which shall be
_____ Black, Inc. _____ as the Surviving Corporation, and the separate
existence of _____ India, Inc. _____ shall cease except to the extent provided by
the laws of the State of _____ Anystate _____ in the case of a corporation after
its merger into another corporation.

2. _____ Black, Inc. _____ shall thereupon and thereafter possess all the
rights, privileges, immunities and franchises, as well as the public and private nature of each of the
Constituent Corporations; all property, real, personal and mixed, all debts due on whatever account,
including subscriptions to shares, all other cases in action, and all and every other interest of or
belonging to or due to each of the Constituent Corporations which shall be taken and deemed to be
vested in the Surviving Corporations which shall not revert or be in any way impaired by reason of
this merger.

3. _____ Black, Inc. _____ shall thenceforth be responsible and liable for all
of the liabilities and obligations of each of the Constituent Corporations; and any claim
existing or action or proceeding pending by or against either of the Constituent Corporations may be
prosecuted to judgment as if the merger had not taken place, or the Surviving Corporation may be
substituted in its place and neither of the rights of creditors nor any liens upon the property of either of the
Constituent Corporations shall be impaired by the merger.

4. The Surviving Corporation hereby agrees that it may be served with process in the State
of _____ Anystate _____ in any proceeding for the enforcement of any obligations of _____ India, Inc. _____, arising from the merger, including the rights of any
dissenting stockholders thereof, and hereby irrevocably appoints the Secretary of State of
_____ Anystate _____ as its agent to accept service of process in any such suit or
other proceedings and agrees that service of any such process may be made by personally delivering to and leaving with such Secretary of State of the State of

316

_____ Anystate _____ duplicate copies of such process; and hereby authorizes the Secretary of State of the State of _____ Anystate _____ to send forthwith by registered mail one of the such duplicate copies of such process addressed to the Surviving Corporation, unless said Surviving Corporation shall hereafter designate in writing to such Secretary of State of _____ Anystate _____ a different address for such process, in which case the duplicate copy of such process shall be mailed to the last address so designated.

5. The aggregate amount of the net assets of the Constituent Corporation which was available for the payment of dividends immediately prior to the merger to the extent that the value thereof is not transferred to stated capital by the issuance of shares or otherwise shall continue to be available for the payment of dividends by the Surviving Corporation.

6. The Bylaws of _____ Black, Inc. _____ as existing and constituted immediately prior to the effective date of merger shall be and constitute the bylaws of the Surviving corporation.

7. The Board of Directors, the members thereof, and the Officers of _____ Black, Inc. _____ immediately prior to the effective date of this merger shall be and constitute the Board of Directors, the members thereof, and the Officers of the Surviving Corporation.

ARTICLE III

The Certificate of Incorporation of _____ Black, Inc. _____ shall not be amended in any respect by reason of this Agreement of Merger, and said Certificate of Incorporation, as filed in the office of the Secretary of State of the State of _____ Nevada _____ on the _____ 30th _____ day of _____ May _____, _____ 2001 _____, shall constitute the Certificate of Incorporation of the Surviving Corporation until amended in the manner provided by law and is set forth in Exhibit A attached hereto and made a part of this Plan and Agreement of Merger with the same force and effect as if set forth in full herein. The Certificate of Incorporation as set forth in said Exhibit A and separate and apart from this Plan and Agreement of Merger may be certified separately as the Certificate of Incorporation of the Surviving Corporation.

ARTICLE IV

The manner and basis of converting the shares of each of the Constituent Corporations into shares of the Surviving Corporation is as follows:

1. The ___2,000___ shares of stock of ___India, Inc.___ now owned and held by ___Stockholders___ shall be cancelled and no shares of stock of ___India, Inc.___ shall be issued in respect thereof, and the capital of ___India, Inc.___ shall be deemed to be reduced by the amount represented by said ___2,000___ shares of stock.

2. Each of the ___2,000___ shares of ___India, Inc.___ shall be converted into one fully paid and nonassessable share of capital stock of ___Black, Inc.___. After the effective date of the merger, each owner of an outstanding certificate or certificates theretofore representing shares of ___India, Inc.___ ___ shall be entitled, upon surrendering such certificate or certificates to the Surviving Corporation, to receive in exchange therefore a certificate or certificates representing the number of shares of stock of the Surviving Corporation into which the shares of ___India, Inc.___ theretofore represented by the surrendered certificate or certificates shall have been converted as hereinbefore provided. Until so surrendered, each outstanding certificate which, prior to the efffective date of the merger, represented shares shall be deemed, for all corporate purposes, to represent the ownership of the stock of the Surviving Corporation on the basis hereinbefore provided.

ARTICLE V

___India, Inc.___, as the Surviving Corporation, shall pay all expenses of carrying this Agreement of Merger into effect and accomplishing the merger herein provided for.

ARTICLE VI

If at any time the Surviving Corporation shall consider or be advised that any further assignment of assurance in law are necessary or desirable to vest in the Surviving Corporation the title to any property or rights of _____India, Inc._____, the proper Officers and Directors of _____India, Inc._____ shall and will execute and make all such proper assignments and assurances in law and do all things necessary or proper to thus vest such property or rights in the Surviving Corporation, and otherwise to carry out the purposes of this Plan and Agreement of Merger.

ARTICLE VII

This Plan and Agreement of Merger shall be submitted to the stockholders of each of the Constituent Corporations as provided by law and shall take effect, be deemed and be taken to be the Plan and Agreement of Merger of said Corporations upon the approval or adoption thereof by the stockholders of each of the Constituent Corporations in accordance with the requirements of the laws of the State of _____Nevada_____ and the State of _____Anystate_____ and upon the execution, filing and recording of such documents and the doing of such acts and things as shall be required for accomplishing the merger under the provisions of the applicable statutes of the State of _____Nevada_____ and of the State of _____Anystate_____ as heretofore amended and supplemented.

ARTICLE VIII

Anything herein or elsewhere to the contrary notwithstanding this Plan and Agreement of Merger may be abandoned by either of the Constituent Corporations by an appropriate resolution of its Board of Directors at any time prior to its approval or adoption by the stockholders thereof or by the mutual consent of the Constituent Corporations evidenced by appropriate resolution of their respective Board of Directors at any time prior to the effective date of the Merger.

IN WITNESS WHEREOF, <u>President U.R. Important</u> and <u>Secretary</u> <u>Minnie Minutes</u>, pursuant to the approval and authority duly given by resolutions adopted by their respective Board of Directors have caused this Plan and Agreement of Merger to be executed by the President and Attested by the Secretary of each party hereto, and the corporate seal affixed.

ATTEST:

George Washington

PRESIDENT

ATTEST:

Martha Washington

SECRETARY

ATTEST:

U. R. Important

PRESIDENT

ATTEST:

Minnie Minutes

SECRETARY

I, _____ Minnie Minutes _____ , Secretary of _____ Black, Inc. _____ ,
under the laws of the State of _____ Nevada _____ , hereby certify, as Secretary and
under the seal of the said corporation, that the Plan and Agreement of Merger to which this certificate is
attached, after having been first duly signed on behalf of said corporation by the President and Secretary of
_____ Black, Inc. _____ , a corporation of the State of
_____ Nevada _____ , was duly submitted to the stockholders of said
_____ Black, Inc. _____ , at a special meeting of said stockholders called and held separately from the stockholders of any other corporation, upon waiver of notice, signed by all the stockholders
for the purpose of considering and taking upon said Agreement of Merger, that
_____ 4,000 _____ shares of stock of said corporation were on said date issued and
outstanding and that the holders of _____ 3,500 _____ shares voted by ballot in favor
of said Agreement of Merger and the holders of _____ 500 _____ shares voted
by ballot against same, the said affirmative vote representing at least a majority of the total number of shares
of the outstanding capital stock of said corporation, and that thereby the Agreement of Merger was at said
meeting duly adopted as the act of the stockholders of said _____ Black, Inc. _____ , and
the duly adopted agreement of the said corporation.

WITNESS my hand and seal of said _____ Black, Inc. _____ on this
_____ 1st _____ day of _____ November _____ , _____ 2001 _____ .

Minnie Minutes
SECRETARY

321

THE ABOVE PLAN AND AGREEMENT OF MERGER, having been executed by the President and Secretary of each corporate party thereto, and having been adopted separately by the stockholders of each corporate party thereto, in accordance with the provisions of the _____

<u>Nevada Revised Statutes</u>

of the State of _____Nevada_____, and the fact having been certified on said Plan and Agreement of Merger by the Secretary of each corporate party thereto, the President and Secretary of each corporate party thereto do now hereby execute the said Plan and Agreement of Merger under the

corporate seals of their respective corporations, by the authority of the directors and stockhodlers thereof, as the respective act, deed and agreement of each of said corporation, on the _____1st_____ day of

_____November_____, __2001___.

ATTEST: ATTEST:

George Washington   *A. R. Important*

PRESIDENT   PRESIDENT

ATTEST: ATTEST:

Martha Washington   *Minnie Minutes*

SECRETARY   SECRETARY

Dissolve Corporation

RESOLUTION OF THE BOARD OF DIRECTORS

OF

BLACK, INC.

A _____ Nevada _____ Corporation

I, the undersigned, being all of the Directors of _____ Black, Inc. _____, a

_____ Nevada _____ corporation, having met and discussed the business herein set

forth, have unanimously:

RESOLVED, that in the judgment of this Board of Directors, it is deemed advisable and for the benefit of

_____ Black, Inc. _____ that said Corporation should be

dissolved; and to that end as required by law it is ordered that a meeting of those stockholders of said

Corporation having voting power to take action upon this resolution is hereby called to be held on

_____ December 1 _____, _____ 2001 _____, at _____ 10:00 a.m. _____, at

_____ Nevada _____, and be it

FURTHER RESOLVED, that the Secretary of this Corporation is hereby authorized and directed

within _____ ten _____, (_____ 10 _____) days after the adoption of this resolution

to cause notice of the adoption of this resolution to be mailed to each

stockholder of this Corporation.

DATED THIS _____ 1st _____ day of _____ November _____, _____ 2001 _____.

I. M. Director

DIRECTOR IN TOTO

323

Dissolve Corporation

RESOLUTION OF THE STOCKHOLDERS

OF

BLACK, INC.

A _____Nevada_____ Corporation

I, the undersigned, being all of stockholders of _____Black, Inc._____, a
_____Nevada_____ corporation, having met and discussed the business herein set
forth, have unanimously:

RESOLVED, that _____Black, Inc._____ surrender its charter to the State of
_____Nevada_____ and that it cease to be and exist as a corporation; and be it

FURTHER RESOLVED, that _____U. R. Important_____, the President, and
_____Minnie Minutes_____, the Secretary, of _____Black, Inc._____,
are hereby authorized and directed to file the necessary certificate of dissolution of this Corporation
with the Secretary of State of the State of _____Nevada_____ and with the
_____Carson City_____ Clerk; and be it

FURTHER RESOLVED, that the Board of Directors of this Corporation is hereby
authorized, empowered, and directed to do all things necessary and requisite to settle the affairs of
the Corporation, to collect the outstanding debts, to provide for the payment
of the liabilities and obligations of the Corporation, to distribute its assets, and to do all other things
necessary to carry into effect the foregoing resolution.

DATED THIS ___1st___ day of ___November___, ___2001___.

_____M. E. Rich_____
STOCKHOLDER

324

Officers

CERTIFICATE OF DISSOLUTION

OF

BLACK, INC.

A _____Nevada_____ Corporation

The undersigned Officers of _____Black, Inc._____, a _____Nevada_____
Corporation, as designated after our respective signatures below in compliance with the provisions of Section
____78.580____ of the _____Nevada Revised Statutes_____,
and being authorized and directed by the Board of Directors of said Corporation, do hereby certify:

That at a meeting of the Board of Directors of said Corporation regularly convened on
____November 1____, ____2001____, at ____10:00 a.m____, at ____the corporate____
____office____, a resolution was duly adopted declaring that in the judgment of
said Board it is desirable and for the benefit of the Corporation that it be dissolved; and called a meeting of
the stockholders having voting power to take action upon such resolution, to-wit:

RESOLVED, that it is deemed desirable in the judgment of this Board of Directors, and for the benefit of
the Corporation that it should be dissolved, and a meeting of the stockholders of this Corporation having
voting power to take action upon this resolution is hereby called to be held on
____December 1____, ____2001____, at ____10:00 a.m.____, at
____the corporate office____ of which meeting written notice is hereby directed to be given
to all stockholders having voting power in the manner and for the period of time prescribed by
____NRS 78.730____ and the bylaws of the Corporation; and be it

FURTHER RESOLVED that if, at such meeting of stockholders, or any adjournment thereof, the
holders of stock entitled to exercise a majority of the voting power shall by resolution consent that
the dissolution shall take place, then the President, the Secretary, and the
Treasurer shall, and they are hereby authorized and directed to make, execute and file in the office
of the Secretary of State of the State of ____Nevada____, the certificate
required by law to be filed therein, and to do any and all other things necessary or desirable to effect
the dissolution of this Corporation.

That, pursuant to said resolution, and as required by _____NRS 78.730_____,
due notice of the meeting thus called was given to all stockholders of record of the Corporation having
voting power, and that such meeting of stockholders was regularly convened and held on
____November 1____, ____2001__, at _____10:00 a.m.____, at
____the corporate office__.

That at the date of said meeting there were issued and outstanding the following of the authorized
capital stock of the Corporation having voting power:

CLASS OF SHARES   NUMBER OUTSTANDING

(This is to be filled out from the stock ledger in the Corporate Record Book and
includes only the class or classes of stock entitled to vote.)

and that there were present at said meeting, in person or by written proxies duly filed with the Secretary of
the Corporation, stockholders holding the number of shares having voting power, listed below:

| | | VOTING |
| CLASS OF SHARES | NUMBER OUTSTANDING | IN PERSON/BY PROXY |

(This is to be filled out from the Corporate or Secretary's records
and includes only the class or classes of stock entitled to vote)

That the resolution of the Board of Directors above referred to was duly considered at said meeting,
and upon motion duly made and seconded, the following resolution, to-wit:

RESOLVED, that the resolution of the Board of Directors regularly adopted by them on the
_____1st_____ day of ____November____, ____2001____,
proposed the dissolution of this Corporation, be, and the same is hereby adopted as the resolution
of the stockholder of this Corporation.

was adopted by the following vote of the holders of stock of all classes having voting power, present in
person or by proxy at said meeting, viz.:

326

_____1,500_____ shares of all classes were voted for the adoption of said resolution;

_____500_____ shares of all classes were voted against the adoption of said resolution;

and that the shares voting for the adoption of said resolution constituted at least a majority of all the voting power of stockholders of the Corporation.

That the names and residence addresses of the present Officers and Directors of the Corporation are as follows:

NAME AND TITLE	RESIDENCE ADDRESS
U.R. Important, President	1001 Fortune Dr., Carson City, NV 89701
Minnie Minutes, Secretary	292 Merit Dr., Carson City, NV 89703
Paul Payroll, Treasurer	244 Ledger Way, Carson City, NV 89703

DATED THIS _____1st_____ day of _____November_____, _____2001_____.

U.R. Important
_____
PRESIDENT

Minnie Minutes
_____
SECRETARY

Paul Payroll, Tres.
_____
TREASURER

(acknowledgement)

327

President and Secretary

CERTIFICATE OF DISSOLUTION

OF

BLACK, INC.

A _____ Nevada _____ Corporation

We, the President and Secretary of _____ Black, Inc. _____, in accordance with
the requirements of the _____ Nevada Revised Statutes _____
of the State of _____ Nevada _____, and in order to obtain the dissolution of said Corporation, as
provided by said Law,

DO HEREBY CERTIFY AS FOLLOWS:

The registered office of _____ Black, Inc. _____ in the State of _____ Nevada _____ is
at 2533 N.Carson St.,Carson City and the Resident Agent thereof, upon whom process
against this corporation may be served, is Laughlin Associates, Inc.

The dissolution of said _____ Black, Inc. _____ has been duly authorized in accordance with the provisions of Section _____ 78.58 _____ of the Nevada Revised Statutes.

The following is a list of the names and residence addresses of the Directors and of the Officers of
said Corporation:

NAME	TITLE	ADDRESS
	(provide appropriate information from corporate records)	

On _____ November 1 _____, _____ 2001 _____, the stockholders having voting power of
_____ Black, Inc. _____ met upon due notice and a majority of the stockholders having voting
power consented by resolution to the dissolution. A certified copy of said resolution is attached hereto.

DATED THIS _____1st_____ day of _____November_____, _____2001_____.

_____*U. R. Important*_____
PRESIDENT

_____*Minnie Minutes*_____
SECRETARY

_____*Paul Payroll, Tres.*_____
TREASURER

(acknowledgement)

Distribution of Assets to Stockholders after Liquidation   *SAMPLE*

RESOLUTION OF THE BOARD OF DIRECTORS

OF

BLACK, INC.

A _____ Nevada _____ Corporation

I, the undersigned, being all of the Directors of _____ Black, Inc. _____,
a _____ Nevada _____ corporation, having met and discussed the business herein
set forth, have unanimously:

RESOLVED, that the sum of _____ Fifty Thousand _____ Dollars
($ 50,000.00) per share be distributed to the stockholders of this Corporation upon production
to _____ C.D. Light _____ Trustee, of the certificate therefor, in order that the amount
of said distribution may be endorsed thereon; and be it

FURTHER RESOLVED, that _____ Trustee aC.D. Light _____ be requested upon
presentation of the certificate for that purpose to stamp upon each certificate an endorsement
showing the amount paid per share and the date of such payment; and be it

FURTHER RESOLVED, that the President and the Treasurer of this Corporation be
authorized upon receipt of the remaining payment specified in the agreement with _____
_____ Trustee C.D. Light _____ and of the other amount due this Corporation to make from time
to time further distribution to the stockholders of this Corporation in liquidation of its assets in the
same manner as provided in the foregoing resolutions; and be it

FURTHER RESOLVED, that the Board of Directors does hereby approve of the plan to send
to the stockholders of this Corporation the following letter prepared by the President, announcing the
liquidation, together with a letter to _____ Trustee C.D. Light _____, and that it does hereby
approve the form of receipt for the certificate.

DATED THIS _____ 1st _____ day of _____ November _____, _____ 2001 _____.

_____ I. M. Director _____
DIRECTOR IN TOTO

330

SECTION V

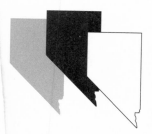

Appendices

Introduction to the Appendices

This book was prepared to aid you in understanding the basic concepts of how to use legal structures to protect yourself, your assets, your business affairs, your family possessions, reduce your taxes, increase profit and income and build a better and more secure future in these tumultuou times. This book has also provided me with an opportunity to expand somewhat on what I view as the "sea change" going on before us.

If you are an American it should be clear to you that if you HAV anything, or you have more than one income source, you should have least one Nevada corporation and perhaps several. If you are from any where else and you want to do business in the U.S. you will need one more Nevada companies. If you're from Canada you may be want reread the state-to-state strategy described in Chapter 7 and consider ho it might be used as a country-to-country strategy.

As a reminder, when you activate your Nevada Corporation wi the IRS by securing a tax identification number, be certain to declare fiscal year date ending different from that of the calendar year. This acti will allow you future flexibility in shifting income between your corpo tion and yourself for any given year. A good date you may want to co sider is having your fiscal year end January 31st.

Why is the fiscal year date important? A U.S. person filing a jo return can earn up to $45,200 and still only be subject to 15% fed income tax. And, your "C" corporation is only assessed 15% up to the f $50,000 of net income annually. Which means that with some car planning you and your corporation can earn up to $95,200 collectiv and only be subject to a maximum of 15% federal income tax. And keeping your company qualified in Nevada you eliminate state inc tax altogether!

Your circumstances may well warrant participation with an offsh corporation or limited liability company, and you may find it adva: geous to invoke a domestic or offshore asset protection trust in con with a Nevada, Wyoming, or offshore corporation. However, it is opinion that regardless of whether or not you intend to enter the offsh world, in most cases you are still well advised to have at least one Ne Corporation

A comment about a related matter not addressed in this book - you are an American and have not set up a Living Trust, then do s living trust should be established to prevent your heirs from suffering the complicated and very expensive issues related to probate after death. A living trust does not provide YOU with improved privac though it can keep particulars about your estate out of the newspap required by probate. A living trust does not provide YOU with asset tection although it can provide your heirs with critical protection regarding your estate. And, a living trust does not provide YOU with any real tax advantages, but again it can do so for your heirs.

As to how to invoke a Living Trust domestically I suggest that you contact a professional to prepare the necessary documents for you. It is really a rather simple process and one you can do with standard forms purchased from an office products store but for the few dollars extra you should review the concept with a lawyer skilled in this arena.

As you take the steps to implement strategies to take back your privacy, invoke real world asset protection mechanisms, reduce your taxes where possible, and simply MAKE and KEEP a great deal more money, do not forget your heirs. This means you need to address some basic estate planning issues. One little understood value in having a properly structured corporation as part of your legacy, may be summed up in the statement: a corporation never dies, it just elects a new president!

Having two classes of stock in your corporations allows your future heirs to own the vast majority of the stock immediately, thus eliminating problems with probate and punitive estate taxes. Perhaps 98% of the shares could be non-voting stock held by your children or grandchildren, and the controlling, or voting shares held by you. Even better, have all the shares in your family business held by a Family Limited Partnership, with only about 2% of the shares issued to the General Partner — that's you. You will recall that the General Partner calls all the shots. Either way you maintain 100% control of your business assets and stay in control until you wish to make a change or they are passed on in your will.

WHY NEVADA CORPORATIONS?

SUPERIOR NEVADA CORPORATION ADVANTAGES AND BENEFITS TO YOU:
SELECTED TAXES IMPOSED BY WESTERN STATES

State	Franchise	Corporate Income (Percent)	Personal Income (Percent)	Sales (Percent)	Property Per $100
NEVADA	NO	NO	NO	6.5	1.03
ARIZONA	YES*	1.0-6.5	3.0-5.6	5	1.56
CALIFORNIA	YES	9.3	1.0-9.3	6	.66
OREGON	YES	6.6	5-9	NO	2.07
UTAH	YES*	5	2.55-7.0	4.875	1.43
COLORADO	YES	5	5	3	1.04
IDAHO	YES	8	2-8.2	5	1.94
MONTANA	YES*	6.75	2-11	NO	1.46
WYOMING	NO**	NO	NO	4	.76
WASHINGTON	NO	NO	NO	6.5	1.01
NEW MEXICO	YES	4.8-7.6	1.7-8.5	5	1.27

* Corporate income tax
** Filing fee based on corporate property and assets located and employed in Wyoming.

COMPARE THE ADVANTAGES OF THE LIMITED LIABILITY COMPANY

Attribute	LLC	Sole Proprietor	General Partnership	Limited Partnership	Regular Corporation	S-Corporation
Asset Protection	Yes	-	-	Some[1]	Yes	Yes
Protection from lawsuit within Co.	Yes	-	-	Some[1]	Yes	Yes
Pass-Through Profit and Loss	Yes	Yes	Yes	Yes	-	Yes
Escapes Double Taxation	Yes	Yes	Yes	Yes	-	Yes
Stands as a Separate Entity	Yes	-	-	Yes	Yes	Yes
Affords Anonymity	Yes	-	-	-	Yes	Yes
Allows Foreign Owners/ Shareholders	Yes	Yes	Yes	Yes	Yes	-
Protection from Seizure of Ownership Interest	Yes	-	-	Yes	Yes	Yes
Employees Benefits paid w/pre-tax $'s	Some[2]	-	Some[2]	Some[2]	Yes	Some[2]

[1] Limited Partnerships offer protection for the limited partner so his liability is limited to the amount of his investment. The general partner is liable for whatever encumbrance the partnership is held liable to pay. Also, there is no liability protection when an investor or partner sues the other owners as may be provided by an LLC or a corporation.

[2] LLCs share similar treatment with partnerships and S-Corporations. Pre-tax benefits are available to only those owning less than 2% of the business. IRS Code 1372 defines this. The intent is to justify the taxing of the pass-through profit and loss. Fringe benefits can be provided for employees with little or no monetary interest in the business.

State	LLC Act Exists	State Income Tax Classification of LLCs	Entity-Level Tax on Partnerships LLCs[3]	LLP Act Exists
Alabama**	Yes	State classification follows federal classification of LLC[1]	No	Yes[2]
Alaska	Yes	State classification follows federal classification of LLC	$100/year - domestic $200/year - foreign	Yes
Arizona**	Yes	State classification follows federal classification of LLC[1]	No	Yes[2]
Arkansas	Yes	State taxes domestic LLCs as partnerships; follows federal classification of foreign LLC	Annual $103 franchise tax	Yes
California	Yes	State classification follows federal classification of LLC[1]	Annual $800 minimun franchise tax and maximum gross receipts tax of $4,500	Yes[2]
Colorado*	Yes	State classification follows federal classification of LLC	No	Yes[2]
Connecticut**	Yes	State classification follows federal classification of LLC	No	Yes[2]
Delaware**	Yes	State classification follows federal classification of LLC	$100 annual tax on domestic & foreign LLCs (LLPs subject to $100/partner/year fee w/$120,000 cap)	Yes[2]
Distrist of Columbia	Yes	State classification follows federal classification of LLC	14.5% tax on D.C. source income earned by unincorporated business	Yes[2]
Florida**	Yes	State taxes LLCs as corporations (no state personal income tax)	LLCs subject to 5.5% artificial entity tax (LLPs subject to $100/ FL partner/year fee w/$10,000 cap)	Yes

State	LLC Act Exists	State Income Tax Classification of LLCs	Entity-Level Tax on Partnerships LLCs[3]	LLP Act Exists
Georgia	Yes	State classification follows federal classification of LLC	LLC/LLP pays 4% withholding tax on distributions to nonresident members/ partners, with exemptions	Yes[2]
Hawaii	Yes	State classification follows federal classification of LLC[1]	(LLPs subject to $100/ partner/year fee w/$10,000 cap)	Yes
Idaho	Yes	State classification follows federal classification of LLC	No	Yes[2]
Illinois**	Yes	State classification follows federal classification of LLC	1.5% income tax on partnerships and LLCs (LLPs subject to $100/ partner/year fee with $5,000 cap)	Yes
Indiana	Yes	State classification follows federal classification of LLC[1]	LLC/LLP pays witholding tax on nonresident member's/ partner's distributive share on IN income at highest state rate	Yes[2]
Iowa**	Yes	State classification follows federal classification of LLC[1]	LLC/LLP pays witholding tax on nonresident member's/ partner's distributive share on IA income at highest state rate	Yes
Kansas**	Yes	State classification follows federal classification of LLC	LLCs subject to franchise tax on net capital accounts (LLPs subject to $75/Kansas partner/year fee with $2,500 cap)	Yes
Kentucky	Yes	State classification follows federal classification of LLC (but statute unclear whether SMLLC can be disregarded)	No	Yes

State	LLC Act Exists	State Income Tax Classification of LLCs	Entity-Level Tax on Partnerships LLCs[3]	LLP Act Exists
Louisiana**	Yes	State classification follows federal classification of LLC[1]	No	Yes
Maine	Yes	State classification follows federal classification of LLC[1]	No	Yes
Maryland	Yes	State classification follows federal classification of LLC[1]	LLC/LLP pays 5% withholding tax on nonresident member's/ partner's distributive share of MD income	Yes[2]
Massachusetts	Yes	State classification follows federal classification of LLC[1]	No	Yes[2] (Mass. Gen. L. ch. 108A, §§ 45-49
Michigan	Yes	LLCs subject to single business tax; members subject to tax on LLC income	2.3% of specified LLC tax base	Yes
Minnesota	Yes	State classification follows federal classification of LLC[1]	LLC/LLP pays 8.5% withholding tax on nonresident member's/ partner's distributive share of MN income (annual flat fee for non-farming partnerships)	Yes[2]
Mississippi	Yes	State classification follows federal classification of LLC	No	Yes
Missouri	Yes	State classification follows federal classification of LLC[1]	No (LLCs) (LLPs subject to $25/ partner/year fee w/$100 cap)	Yes[2]
Montana	Yes	State classification follows federal classification of LLC	No	Yes[2]
Nebraska	Yes	State classification follows federal classification of LLC[1]	No	Yes[2]

State	LLC Act Exists	State Income Tax Classification of LLCs	Entity-Level Tax on Partnerships LLCs[3]	LLP Act Exists
Nevada*	Yes	No state income tax	No	Yes
New Hampshire	Yes	State classification follows federal classification of LLC (but entity-level tax on dividends, interest and business profits)	5% dividends and interest; 7% on business profits	Yes
New Jersey**	Yes	State classification follows federal classification of LLC[1]	No	Yes
New Mexico	Yes	State classification follows federal classification of LLC	No	Yes[2]
New York	Yes	State classification follows federal classification of LLC[1]	$50/member/partner annual fee; w/$10,000 cap	Yes[2]
North Carolina	Yes	State classification follows federal classification of LLC[1]	No	Yes
North Dakota	Yes	State classification follows federal classification of LLC[1]	No (LLCs) ($25/LLP partner/ year with $250 cap)	Yes[2]
Ohio	Yes	State classification follows federal classification of LLC[1]	LLC/LLP pays 5% withholding tax on distributions to nonresident members/ partners after certain adjustments	Yes
Oklahoma**	Yes	State classification follows federal classification of LLC[1]	No	Yes[2]
Oregon	Yes	State classification follows federal classification of LLC	No	Yes[2]

State	LLC Act Exists	State Income Tax Classification of LLCs	Entity-Level Tax on Partnerships LLCs[3]	LLP Act Exists
Pennsylvania	Yes	Act 97-7 conforms state tax treatment to federal tax treatment for CNI tax purposes	No-LLCs RPC pays withholding tax on member's distributive share of PA income at highest state rate ($300/Pa. member or $200/Pa. partner annual fee)	Yes
Rhode Island**	Yes	State classification follows federal classification of LLC	No	Yes
South Carolina	Yes	State classification follows federal classification of LLC[1]	LLC/LLP pays 5% withholding tax on nonresident member's/ partner's distributive share of S.C. income	Yes
South Dakota	Yes	No state income tax	No	Yes[2]
Tennessee	Yes	State classification follows federal classification of LLC[1]	$50/member or partner annual fee with $3,000 cap; 6% tax on dividends & interest on bonds attributed to TN; disregarded foreign SMLLCs with corporate member subject to TN franchise/exise tax	Yes
Texas*	Yes	LLCs subject to corporate franchise tax (no state personal income tax)	.25% of capital; 4.5 of earned surplus of LLCs (LLPs subject to $100/partner/year fee; legislation to extend corporate franchise tax to RLLPs and LPs died)	Yes[2]
Utah**	Yes	State classification follows federal classification of LLC[1]	No	Yes

342

State	LLC Act Exists	State Income Tax Classification of LLCs	Entity-Level Tax on Partnerships LLCs[3]	LLP Act Exists
Vermont	Yes	State classification follows federal classification of LLC[1]	Annual $150 entity tax; LLC/LLP must make estimated tax payments on nonresident member/partner's distributive share	No
Virginia*	Yes	State classification follows federal classification of LLC[1]	No	Yes[2]
Washington	Yes	State taxes LLC as partnership (no state personal income tax)	B&O Tax of .012% to 2.5% of gross income	Yes
West Virginia*	Yes	State classification follows federal classification of LLC	Greater of $50 or .75% of "capital" (generally, balance of partners' capital accounts per Form 1065) LLC/LLP pays 4% withholding tax on nonresident member's/partner's distributive share of W. VA income	Yes
Wisconsin	Yes	State classification follows federal classification of LLC[1]	If treated as partnership, subject to temporary surcharge tax of up to $9,800	Yes[2]
Wyoming*	Yes	No state income tax	No	No

1   Indicates that state taxing authority has publicly announced that it will follow I.R.S. "check-the-box" regulations for state income tax purposes or state LLC act adopts the regulations either explicitly or implicitly.

2   Indicates "bulletproof" (broad form liability shield) RLLP statute.

3   Assuming the entity is classified as a partnership and has filed any required nonresident member jurisdictional consents.

*   State has received an IRS ruling holding that an LLC organized under this state's statute will be classified as a partnership for federal income tax purposes under pre-"check-the-box" ruling guidelines.

**   State has received an IRS ruling holding that an LLC organized under this state's statute may be classified either as a partnership or an association taxable as a corporation, depending upon the articles or organization and operating agreement, under pre-"check-the-box" ruling guidelines.

This chart is necessarily only a summary of the applicable laws and rulings and should not be relied on as a definitive source of information. Readers should consult their tax advisors and, perhaps, local counsel, regarding the application of state law to their particular circumstances.

STATE CORPORATE INCOME OR FRANCHISE TAXES AND THEIR AMOUNT

Alabama .... Income: 5% of taxable net income Franchise: $10 per 1,000 of capital stock, minimum $50

Alaska 1% 1st $10,000   2% $10-20,000   3% $20-30,000   4% $30-40,000   5% $40-50,000
                     6% $50-60,000   7% $60-70,000   8% $70-80,000   9% $80-90,000   9.4% over $90,000

Arizona .... Income: 7.968%, minimum tax $50

Arkansas .... Franchise: 27% of proporation of subscribe capital stock employed in the state. No par stock: valued at $25 per share.
                    Minimum $50. Maximum $1,075,000 Income: 1% of first 3,000 net income; 2% of next $3,000; 3% of next $5,000; 5% of
                    next $14,000; 6% of next $75,000. If net corp income exceeds $100,000, entire net income taxed at 6.5%

California.......... Franchise: 8.84 of net income. S-Corporations 1.5% Minimum Tax: $800 (waived for corporations formed in 2000 & 2001.)
                    Income: Direct tax on net income on corps not taxable under franchise tax. Rates are identical

Colorado .... Income: 4.75% of Colorado net income.

Connecticut .... Franchise/Income: 10.75% of net corporate income. Minimum $250. Maximum $1,000,000. 8.5%

Delaware.......... Franchise: Graduated rate depending on capitalization. Minimum $30, Maximum: $130,000
                   Income: 8.7% of taxable Delaware income

D.C. .... 9.975%, minimum $100

Florida .... 5.5% of Federal taxable income attributable to Florida. $5,000 of net income is exempt

Georgia .... Franchise: Graduated rates determined by net worth. Minimum $10, Maximum $5,000
                    Income: 6% of adjusted federal taxable income

Hawaii .... 4.4% 1st $25,000; 5.4% of next $75,000, 6.4% over $100,000

Idaho .... 8%, minimum $20

Illinois .... Franchise: 1/10% of paid in capital, minimum $25, maximum $1 million
                     Income: 4.8% of federal taxable income. Additional personal property replacement tax of 2.5% on net income of corporations;
                     1.5% of net income of S-Corps and partnerships.

Indiana .... Income: 3.4% of taxable income, plus supplemental net income tax of 4.5%

Iowa .... 6% 1st $25,000; 8% next $75,000; 10% next $150,000; 12% over $250,000

Kansas .... Income: 4% of federal taxable income less Kansas sources deductions. 3.35% surtax on income over $50,000
                    Franchise: $1 per $1,000 of Kansas shareholders equity attributable to Kansas.

Kentucky .... Franchise: $2.10 per $1,000 total capital employed in business, minimum $30
                    Income: 4% of first $25,000 taxable Kentucky income; 5% on next $25,000; 6% on next $50,000; 7% on next $150,000;
                    8.25% on income over $250,000

Louisiana .... Franchise: $1.50 per $1,000 in first $300,000 of capital and surplus. $3 per $1,000 of the remainder
                    Income: 4% of first $25,000; 5% of next $25,000; 6% of next $50,000; 7% of next $100,000; 8% of excess over $200,000.

Maine .... 3.5% 1st $25,000; 7.93% of next $50,000; 8.33% of next $175,000; 8.93% over $250,000

Maryland.......... 7%; 5% tax on share of non-resident shareholder's interest in S-Corps.

Massachusetts ... 9.5% of net income; excise tax of $2.60 per $1,000 of tangible values or net worth in Massachusetts; $456 minimum

Michigan .... 2.2%; the first $45,000 of federal taxable adjusted income is exempt

Minnesota .... Income: 9.8% of taxable income. Additional tax (5.8%) on difference between basic tax and alternative minimum tax

Mississippi .... Franchise: $2.50 per $1,000 of book capital, Minimum $25
                    Income: 3% of first $5,000; 4% of next $5,000' 5% of excess over $10,000

Missouri .... Franchise: .05% value of outstanding shares and surplus over $200,000 in Missouri
                    Income: 6.25% of adjusted federal taxable income

Montana .... Income: 6.75% . 7% for waters edge filers, minimum $50

344

Nebraska .... Franchise: Graduated rates applied to paid up capital stock and foreign capital employed in Nebraska. Minimum $13, Maximum $15,000 Income: 5.58% of first $50,000 at taxable income. 7.81% of taxable income over $50,000.

NEVADA .... NO CORPORATE TAX

New Hampshire Income: 8% of federal net income. Also, .25% of taxable enterprise tax base, if gross profits exceed $100,000 or if tax base exceeds $50,000

New Jersey .... C-Corporations 7.5% 1st $100,000; 9% over $100,000. S-Corporations .5% 1st $100,000; 2% of income over $100,000.

New Mexico ..... 4.8% 1st $500,000; 6.4% of 2nd $500,000; 7.6% over $1 million. $50 franchise tax

New York .... Large business ($290,000) at 8%. Small businesses (up to $200,000) have income taxed at 7.5%. If income is between $200,000 and $290,000, tax is $15,000 plus 8% of income between $200,000 and $250,000 and 2.5% of income over $250,000. S-Corporations are also taxed at special rates. Additionally, surcharge of 5% or 10%, depending on applicable
.... tax year; and 17% surcharge on business activity in Metropolitan Commuter Transportation District.

North Carolina .. Franchise: $1.50 per $1,000 of issued stock, surplus and undivided profits, minimum $35
Income: 7% of federal taxable income

North Dakota ... Income: 3% 1st $3,000; 4.5% next $5,000; 6% of next $12,000, 7.5% next $10,000; 9% next $20,000; 10.5% over $50,000

Ohio .... 5.1% of first $50,000; plus 8.5% over $50,000, or 5.82 mills multiplied by net worth plus a litter tax of .11% on first $50,000 and .22% over $50,000 or .00014 of net worth — whichever is greater

Oklahoma .... Franchise: $1.25 per $1,000 used, invested or employed in state. Minimum $10, maximum $20,000
Income: 6% of adjusted federal taxable income

Oregon .... Excise/Income; 6.6% of taxable income attributable to Oregon activities. Minimum $10

Pennsylvania ..... Franchise: 12.75 mills per dollar of capital stock value Income: 9.99% of federal taxable income

Rhode Island ..... Franchise: $2.50 per $10,000 authorized capital stock. Minimum $250
Income: 9% of net income, surtax for non-operating companies. $250 minimum

South Carolina .. 5% of net income. Franchise: $15 plus 1 mill per $1 capitalized stock and surplus, $25 minimum

South Dakota .... From $40 for $25,000 or less authorized capital stock to $500 for more than $450,000 and less than $500,000. Plus $40 per $500,000 over $5,000,000 up to maximum of $16,000

Tennessee .... Franchise: $.25 per $100 of issued and outstanding stock, minimum $10.
Income; 6% of state net earnings

Texas .... No corporate income tax Franchise Tax: .25% of net taxable capital and 4.5% net taxable earned surplus

Utah: .... Income: 5% minimum $100

Vermont .... Income: 7% of first $10,000 net income; 8.1% of next $15,000; 9.2% of next $225,000; 9.75% of excess over $250,000, minimum $150

Virginia .... Franchise: $50 on first 5,000 authorized shares; $15 for each additional $5,000 shares. Maximum $850.
Income: 6% of the net income attributable to Virginia

Washington .... No corporate income tax. However, 6.5% of value of tangible personal property used in business, and/or additional business and occupation tax may apply (.011% to 7.8%)

West Virginia .... Franchise: Graduated from $20 on $5,000 or less authorized stock to $2,500 on authorized stock of $15,000,000 or more (75% higher for non-domestic corporation.) Additionally, business franchise tax of $50 or .75% (.70% beginning July 1997) of the value of business capital, whichever is greater Income: 9% of taxable income.

Wisconsin .... Income: 7.9% of net income, plus recycling surcharge of $25 or 2.75% of gross tax liability, whichever is greater. Maximum surcharge $9,800.

Wyoming .... Franchise: Based on value of property and assets located and used in Wyoming. Graduated from $25 on $50,000 or less; to $200 on value of property between $500,000 and $1 million; plus $200 for each $1 million in property value. Maximum: $50,000 per year.

Revised 3/2000

Birth of A Nation

Great men like George Washington, Thomas Jefferson and Benjamin Franklin could not naturally see beyond their own limited vision of the future, none could really know what role they might play in creating a new world perspective based upon truth and freedom. Each of these Founding Fathers initially believed that the way forward was through the reform of existing government and the securing of favors from a benevolent monarch. Over time this understanding changed.

George Washington's Discovery

During the French and Indian war, George Washington was a Colonel for Great Britain. It was during his military career for England and specifically in this campaign that he discovered his purpose of life and developed an unshakeable dependence upon God.

The British General in command (during the war with the French and Indians) was determined to lead his army in a march toward what Washington believed would be an ambush. Obedient to his senior officer, Washington supported his commanding officer. The ambush was well planned and the British army soon found themselves in the middle of withering gunfire. The General was hit and killed, leaving Washington in command. Seeing the futile circumstances, a retreat was called. In the process of trying to collect his men in an organized retreat, two horses were shot out from under Washington and four balls passed through his coat. Today this may not seem important, but in those days with the fine tailoring, this was as close to hitting someone without touching him as possible.

When the French realized that a retreat was called, they wanted the Indians to pursue and help kill every "Red Coat." The Chief refused. Later in Washington's life, he learned the rest of the story from the Chief himself.

> "I am a chief and ruler of my tribes. My influence extends to the waters of the great lakes, and to the far Blue mountains. I have traveled a long and weary path, that I might see the young warrior of the great battle. It was on the day when the white man's blood mixed with the streams of our forest, that I first beheld the chief. I called to my young men and said, "Mark yon tall and daring warrior? He is not of the red coat tribe–he hath an Indian's wisdom, and his warriors fight as we do–he himself, is alone exposed. Quick, let your aim be certain, and he dies. " Our rifles were leveled, rifles which, but for him, knew not how to miss. Twas all in vain, a power mightier far than we, shielded him from harm. He cannot die in battle.
>
> I am old, and soon shall be gathered to the great council fire of my fathers in the land of shades, but ere I go, there is something bids me speak in the voice of prophecy. Listen!
> The Great Spirit protects that man, and guides his destinies — he will become the chief of nations, and a people yet unborn will hail him as the founder of a mighty empire."[1]

(All footnotes are at the end of this section, on page 359)

Washington wrote to his son John on July 18, 1755 "by the miraculous care of Providence, that protected me beyond all human expectation; I had 4 Bullets through my coat, and two horses shot under me, and yet escaped unhurt."[2]

Washington knew his life had been spared for a purpose, yet to be revealed. He entrusted his life into God's hands. One year prior to our Independence Day he wrote,

> "The General most earnestly requires, and expects, a due observance of those articles of war, established for the Government of the army, which forbid profane cursing, swearing and drunkenness; and in like manner requires and expects, of all Officers, and Soldiers, not engaged on actual duty, a punctual attendance on divine Service, to implore the blessings of heaven upon the means used for our safety and defense."[3]

There was no question about the allegiance Washington held to his creator. There was no question that he knew his life had been spared for some wise purpose, but what was that purpose?

American Prophesy – December 1775

As the Colonies had struggled through eighteen months of strife with Great Britain, a plan to devise a new relationship with England was put into place. A group of colonists were chosen to design a flag that would represent the thirteen colonies as separate but loyal citizens of England. Empowered with the equal rights extended to English citizens. This however overlooked the need England faced of increasing income from this bountiful land; and taxes would be levied to earn that money regardless of fairness.

Among those chosen to this committee were George Washington, Ben Franklin and a mysterious gentleman referred to as the Professor. It is the visit of this Professor that shed the light on the future and destiny of this great country. The time is December 1775. The following is taken from a book written by Robert Allen Campbell, entitled *Our Flag*. "Little seems to have been known concerning this old gentleman; and in the materials from which this account is compiled his name is not even once mentioned, for he is uniformly spoken of or referred to as "the Professor." He was evidently far beyond his three score and ten years; and he often referred to historical events of more than a century previous just as if he had been a living witness of their occurrence; still he was erect, vigorous and active–hale, hearty, and clear-minded—as strong and energetic every way as in the mature prime of his life. He was tall, of fine figure, perfectly easy, and very dignified in his manners; being at once courteous, gracious and commanding. He was, for those times and considering the customs of the Colonists, very peculiar in his method of living; for he ate no flesh, fowl or fish; he never used as food any "green thing," any roots or anything unripe; and he drank no liquor, wine or ale; but confined his diet to cereals and their products, fruits that were ripened on the stem in the sun, nuts, mild tea and the sweets of honey, sugar or molasses.

The Professor was well educated, highly cultivated, of extensive as well as varied information, and very studious. He spent considerable of his time in the patient and persistent conning of a number of very rare old books and ancient manuscripts, which he seemed to be deciphering, translating or rewriting. These books and manuscripts, together with his own writings, he never showed to any one; and he did not even mention them in his conversations with the family, except in the most casual way; and he always locked them up carefully in a large, old fashioned, cubically shaped, iron bound, heavy, oaken chest, whenever he left his room, even for his meals. He took long and frequent walks alone, sat on the brows of the neighboring hills, or mused in the midst of the green and flower-gemmed meadows. He was fairly liberal –but in no way lavish– in spending his money, with which he was well supplied. He was a quiet, though a very genial and very interesting, member of the family; and he was seemingly at home upon any and every topic coming up in conversation. He was, in short, one whom everyone would notice and respect, whom few would feel well acquainted with, and whom no one would presume to question concerning himself — as to whence he came, why he tarried, or whither he journeyed.

He was firmly, and in a dignified and assured way, one who was in favor of demanding and of securing justice on the part of the Mother Country toward the Colonies. One of his favorite forms of stating the matter was: "We demand no more than our just due; we will accept and be satisfied with nothing less than we demand."

Franklin suggested that time be allotted to the Professor to speak. His suggestion was accepted, and the Professor was invited to present his design and the reasons for its adoption. There is no full report of what he said, but the following was recorded:

> "Comrade Americans: We are assembled here to devise and suggest the design for a new flag, which will represent, at once, the principles and determination of the Colonies to unite in demanding and securing justice from the Government to which they still owe recognized allegiance. We are not, therefore, expected to design or recommend a flag, which will represent a new government or an independent nation, but one, which simply represents the principle that even kings owe something of justice to their loyal subjects. This, I say, is what we are expected to do, because this is the publicly announced, as well as the honestly entertained intent of the great majority of the people of these Colonies, as well as their representatives in Congress, and of their soldiers in the field. This is unquestionably true *now;* for the sun of our political aim, like the sun in the heavens, is very low in the horizon– just now approaching the winter solstice, which it will reach very soon. But as the sun rises from his grave in Capricorn, mounts toward his resurrection in Aries and passes onward and upward to his glorious culmination in Cancer, so will our political sun rise and continue to increase in power, in light and in glory; and the exalted sun of summer will not have gained his full strength of heat and power in the starry Lion until our Colonial Sun will be, in its glorious exaltation, demanding a place in the governmental firmament alongside of, coordinate with, and in no wise subordinate to, any other sun of any other nation upon the earth.
>
> "We are now self-acknowledged Colonies–dependencies of Great Britain, which government we, as loyal subjects, humbly sue for justice. We will, ere long, be a self-declared, independent nation, bestowing upon ourselves the justice for which we now vainly sue.

We must, therefore, design and recommend a flag, which will now recognize our loyalty to Great Britain, and at the same time, announce our earnest and united suit and demand for our rights as British Subjects.

"These demands will, of course, in the future as in the past, be neglected or denied. Our justice-demanding and our freedom-loving companions will soon learn that there is no hope for us as British Colonists; and that we can secure the rights we now contend for—as well as many more, and more to be prized rights—only as the loyal and united citizens of a free and independent American nation.

"*General Washington, here, is a British Subject; aye, he is a British soldier; and he is in command of British troops; and they are only attempting to enforce their rights as loyal subjects of the British Crown. But General Washington will soon forswear all allegiance to everything foreign; and he will ere many months appear before his own people, the people of these Colonies, and before the world, as the general commanding the armies of a free and united people, organized into a new and independent nation.*

"The flag which we now recommend must be one designed and adapted to meet the inevitable—and soon to be accomplished—change of allegiance. The flag now adopted must be one that will testify our present loyalty as English Subjects; and it must be one easily modified—but needing no radical change—to make it announce and represent the new nation which is already gestating in the womb of time; and which will come to birth—and that not prematurely, but fully developed and ready for the change into independent life—before the sun in its next summer's strength ripens our next harvest.

"The field of our flag must, therefore, be an entirely new one. For this there are two reasons, either one of which is amply sufficient why it should be so. First, the field must be new, because it will soon represent a new nation. Second, the field must be one hitherto unused as a national flag; because it will represent an entirely new principle in government — *the equal rights of man as man.*

"While the field of our flag must be new in the details of its design, it need not be entirely new in its elements. It is fortunate for us that there is already in use a flag with which the English Government is familiar, and which it has not only recognized, but also protected for more than half a century, the design of which can be readily modified, or rather extended so as to most admirably suit our purpose. I refer to the flag of the English East India Company, which is one with a field of alternate longitudinal red and white stripes, and having the cross of St. George for a union. I, therefore, suggest for your consideration a flag with a field composed of thirteen equally wide, longitudinal, alternate, red and white stripes, and with the Union Flag of England for a union.

Such a flag can readily be explained to the masses to mean as follows: The Union Flag of the Mother Country is retained as the union of our new flag to announce that the Colonies are loyal to the just and legitimate sovereignty of the British Government. The thirteen stripes will at once be understood to represent the thirteen Colonies; their equal width will type the equal rank, rights and responsibilities of the Colonies. The union of the stripes in the field of our flag will announce the unity of the interests and the cooperative union of the efforts, which the Colonies recognize and put forth in their common cause. The white stripes will signify that we consider our demands just and reasonable; and that we will seek to secure our rights through peaceable, intelligent and statesmanlike means–if they prove at all possible; and the red stripes at the top and bottom of our flag will declare that first and last–and always–we have the determination, the enthusiasm, and the power to use force, whenever we deem force necessary. The alternation of the red and white stripes will suggest that our reasons for all demands will be intelligent and forcible, and that our force in securing our rights will be just and reasonable.

All this is in strict accordance with the present public sentiment in the Colonies; for, as I have already said, the masses of the people, and a large majority of the leaders of public opinion, desire a removal of grievances, and a rectification of wrongs, through a fuller recognition of their rights as British Subjects; and few of them desire, and very few of them expect–at this time–any complete severance of their present political and dependent relations with the English Government.

There are other weightier and eternal reasons for a flag having the field I suggest; but it will be time enough to consider them when, in the near future, we, or our successors, are considering — not a temporary associated and dependent Colonies but —— a permanent standard for a united and an independent nation.

Thanking you, one and all, for your complimentary courtesy and for your patient attention, I submit this miniature drawing of the suggested flag for your intelligent consideration."[4]

The remarks of the Professor made a most profound impression; and the design, which he submitted, was, in every particular, satisfactory to every one present. It was enthusiastically endorsed, General Washington and Doctor Franklin giving it especial approval and unstinted praises.

It was formally and unanimously adopted; and shortly before midnight the Committee adjourned. The 13th of December, 1775, therefore, witnessed the presentation, consideration and approval of the only official flag of the Cooperating American Colonies; and the extreme probability is that until that time a flag with a field of alternate red and white stripes, much less a field of thirteen stripes, had never been made or seen in the American Colonies."

Following this prophecy, there must have been renewed evaluations of what lay in store for the Colonies and their relationship with England. Washington and Franklin must have discussed how they had felt the truth of the Professors message, pondered on the meaning and impact of a Declaration of Independence, and then shared with those around them the inevitable fate that awaited this country.

That evening a rock had been set in motion down the mountain of fate, and no power could withstand the avalanche that was beginning to gain strength and momentum. One rock moving another and then two moving four, etc; at first the movement seems slow and insignificant, then more and more until the whole mountainside appears to give way. Those caught in the excitement and cause could only see the dust and hear the thunder of the rolling boulders, others remaining firm on the surrounding mountains could not understand what the commotion was all about.

July 1776

As predicted, the relationship with Mother England had only decreased. Thomas Jefferson led an inspired work in drafting the Declaration of Independence stating the position of the Colonies. When praise for the work rendered his reply was "A far mightier hand than mine, hath penned this document."

This country seemed poised to face the destiny stated six months earlier, with a bold proclamation declaring beliefs, rights and principles of a government ordained by God, to which they were entitled. The only step that now awaited the Colonies was the ratification of this Declaration of Independence.

On July 2, 1776, representatives met in Philadelphia to decide the course for their future. The speakers however were not in tune with the vision shared by the Professor in December. One after another rose from their seats and presented why signing such a document would invoke the wrath of one of the most powerful nations on the earth. Changes were proposed to the document to soften or hide the meanings that were clearly stated in the original document. By the latter part of July 3, 1776 every line in the document had one or more proposed changes.

As Franklin looked upon his friend Jefferson, he could not help but notice the total despair and agony written on his face. This inspired instrument had been turned into an edited disaster. Franklin leaned over and shared with Jefferson a story of a friend in the hat making business who wanted to put a sign in front of his shop. He drafted the sign which read "Thomas the Hatter, maker of fine quality, fashionable and affordable hats" with a picture of a top hat at the end. Each time Thomas presented his idea for the sign, each friend would recommend one change after another. Of course you make fine quality hats, if not you would not be in business; there is no need to state that. No one would make hats that are not fashionable. If your hats were not affordable, no one would ever purchase them, to state such insults their intelligence. Why would you state that you are a Hatter when the picture speaks plainly to that fact. One after another went on, commenting and critiquing until finally Thomas ended up with a sign that simply said "Thomas" with a picture of a hat. Franklin then commented to Jefferson, "such is the outcome when one's thoughts are shared with another."

It was the first time Jefferson had smiled all day. For a moment the pain and stress had been averted by the wisdom of an accomplished statesman. This wisdom was still insufficient to change the mood of the congregation as the debates continued into the 4th of July. Manly P. Hall sheds the following light on the events that turned these men from a position of opposition to support.

"It was during the evening of July 4, 1776, that the second of these mysterious episodes occurred. (*The first was the appearance of the Professor in December*) In the old State House in Philadelphia, a group of men were gathered for the momentous task of severing the tie between the old country and the new. It was a grave moment, and not a few of those present feared that their lives would be forfeit for their audacity. In the midst of the debate a fierce voice rang out. The debaters stopped and turned to look upon the stranger. Who was this man who had suddenly appeared in their midst and transfixed them with oratory? They had never seen him before, none knew when he had entered; but his tall form and pale face filled them with awe. His voice ringing with a holy zeal, the stranger stirred them to their very souls. His closing words rang through the building, *"God has given America to be free"*. As the stranger sank into a chair exhausted: the Declaration of Independence was signed. But where was the man who had precipitated the accomplishment of this immortal task–who lifted for a moment the veil from the eyes of the assemblage and revealed to them a part at least of the great purpose for which the new nation was conceived? He had disappeared, nor was he ever seen or his identity established."[5]

Thomas Jefferson tells that on the day of our nations birth in the little hall in Philadelphia, debate had raged for hours. The men gathered there were honorable men hard-pressed by a King who had flouted the very laws they were willing to obey. Even so, to sign a Declaration of Independence was such an irretrievable act that the walls re-sounded with the words "TREASON, THE GALLOWS, THE HEADMAN'S AXE," and the issue remained in doubt. Then a man rose and spoke.

Jefferson described him as not a young man, but one who had to summon all his energy for an impassioned plea. He cited the grievances that had brought them to this moment and finally, his voice failing, he said,

> "They may turn every tree into a gallows, every home into a
> grave, and yet the words of that parchment can never die. To the
> mechanic in the workshop, they will speak hope, to the slave in the
> mines, freedom. Sign that parchment. Sign if the next moment the
> noose is around your neck, for the parchment will be the textbook
> of freedom. The Bible of the rights of man forever."

He fell back exhausted. The 56 delegates swept up by his eloquence, rushed forward and signed a document to be as immortal as a work of man can be. When they turned to thank him for his timely oratory, he was not be found, nor could any be found who knew who he was or how he had come in or gone out through the locked and guarded doors. Fifty-six men, a little band so unique, we have never seen their like since, had pledged their lives, their fortunes and their Sacred Honor.[6]

Not all 56 delegates were present for this original signing of the Declaration of Independence on July 4, 1776. The document itself had every line marked and edited. It was decided to prepare a polished document that all could sign. Then word was sent to all those not present of the miraculous event of this day and requesting that they join with them a few days later to sign the document as originally inspired and penned by Jefferson, with only a few changes. This is the document that we now revere and respect as the official Declaration of Independence.

No longer was there hesitation for this bold act. The fear of the hangman's noose or the headman's axe was gone. For the veil had been lifted from their eyes. They now could clearly see the eternal destiny of this country and the new light and freedom it would bring to the world. Most importantly each of these men knew their purpose as ordained of God; to carry the torch of freedom to the world. Without God there was no other way of explaining the events that had transpired.

Daniel Webster not only recorded John Adams sentiments, but the sentiments at large from the signers of the Declaration of Independence.

> "Sink or swim, live or die, survive or perish, I give my hand and

my heart to this vote. It is true, indeed, that in the beginning we aimed not at independence. But there's a divinity, which shapes our ends…why, then, should we defer the Declaration? You and I, indeed, may rue it. We may not live to the time when the Declaration shall be made good…but whatever may be our fate, be assured…. that this Declaration will stand. It may cost treasure, and it may cost blood: but it will stand, and it will richly compensate for both… My judgment approves this measure, and my whole heart is in it. All that I have, and all that I am, and all that I hope, in this life, I am now ready here to stake upon it; and I leave off as I began, that live or die, survive or perish, I am for the Declaration. It is my living sentiment, and by the blessing of God it shall be my dying sentiment, independence, now, and independence forever."[7]

For most of these men it meant losing their earthly wealth, health or loved ones. It will be an honor one day on the other side of the veil, to seek these men out and thank them for their personal sacrifices offered so willingly in our behalf.

Vision of Valley Forge

As with each personal step of progression in life, that step forward is followed by trials and temptations to see if we will remain true and faithful to the light and knowledge given. So must it also be with these men and with our nation. These men were tested and tried to see if they would remain true and faithful to the light and knowledge God had shared with them. The early battles did not fare well for the country. England had a powerful army and navy, well equipped and trained. Washington was gathering farmers, woodsmen, tradesmen, etc. and trying to make an army. Defeat after defeat depleted precious supplies and hope for victory. Valley Forge became the test of tests. The forging of this nations metal would determine if it would withstand the pressure of breaking away from a world steeped in oppressive traditions. This nation must first rise above these traditions, and then carry the whole world to a new understanding of freedom and human rights, as ordained by God.

Nine months of difficulties had left men penniless and without supplies. The weather had turned bitter cold. Shoes and gloves had long since worn out. Bleak was an optimistic outlook for this worn and tattered army. What hope did Washington have of victory with an army so destitute? Deserters were leaving daily diminishing what ever hope remained. During these dark hours there was only one place Washington had to turn for light and hope. In the quotes that follow we see the concept evolve of "One Nation, under God."

General Orders, May 15, 1776, "The Continental Congress having ordered, Friday the 17th. Instant to be observed as a day of "fasting, humiliation and prayer, humbly to supplicate the mercy of Almighty God, that it would please him to pardon all our manifold sins and transgressions, and to prosper the Arms of the United Colonies, and finally, establish the peace and freedom of America, upon a solid and lasting foundation"

The General commands all officers and soldiers, to pay strict obedience to the Orders of the Continental Congress, and by their unfeigned, and pious observance of their religious duties, incline the Lord, and Giver of Victory, to prosper our arms."

General Orders, December 17, 1777, "Tomorrow being the day set apart by the Honorable Congress for public Thanksgiving and Praise; and duty calling us devoutly to express our grateful acknowledgments to God for the manifold blessings he has granted us.

The General directs that the army remain in its present quarters, and that the Chaplains perform divine service with their several Corps and brigades. And earnestly exhorts, all officers and soldiers, whose absence is not indispensably necessary, to attend with reverence the solemnities of the day."[8]

As these quotations reveal it was on many occasions that Washington, his army and Congress sought help from a loving, caring Eternal Father. The benefit from this life of devotion to God was finally granted at Valley Forge when all hope from worldly sources had fled and God was the only power sufficiently strong to ensure victory. This prayer at Valley Forge should be embedded in the hearts and minds of every true American.

"The last time I ever saw Anthony Sherman was on the fourth of July, 1859, in Independence Square. He was then ninety-nine years old, and becoming very feeble. But though so old, his dimming eyes rekindled as he gazed upon Independence hall, which he had come to look upon once before he was gathered home.

"Let us go into the hall," he said. "I want to tell you an incident of Washington's life-- one which no one alone knows of except myself; and, if you live, you will before long see it verified. Mark the prediction; you will see it verified.

"From the opening of the Revolution we experienced all phases of fortune, now good and now ill, on time victorious, an another conquered. The darkest period we had, I think, was when Washington, after several reverses, retreated to Valley Forge, where he resolved to pass the winter of '77. Ah! I have often seen the tears coursing down our dear old commander's careworn cheeks, as he would be conversing with a confidential officer about the condition of his poor soldiers. You have doubtless heard the story of Washington going to the thicket to pray. Well, it was not only true, but he used often to pray in secret for aid and comfort from God, the interposition of whose Divine Providence brought us safely through those dark days of tribulation.

One day, I remember it well, the chilly winds whistled through the leafless trees, though the sky was cloudless and the sun shone brightly, he remained in his quarters nearly all the afternoon alone. When he came out I noticed that his face was a shade paler than usual, and there seemed to be something on his mind of more than ordinary importance. Returning just after dusk, he dispatched an orderly to the quarters of the officer I mention who was presently in attendance. After a preliminary conversation of about a half hour, Washington, gazing upon his companion with that strange look of dignity that he alone could command, said to the later:

"I do not know whether it is owing to the anxiety of my mind or what, but this afternoon as I was sitting at this very large table engaged in preparing a dispatch, something in the apartment seemed to disturb me. Looking up, I beheld standing opposite to me a singularly beautiful female. So Astonished was I, for I had given strict orders not to be disturbed, that it was some moments before I found language to inquire the cause of her presence. A second, a third, and even a fourth time, did I repeat my question, but received no answer from my mysterious visitor except a slight raising of the eyes.

By this time I felt strange sensations spreading through me. I would have risen, but the riveted gaze of the being before me rendered volition impossible. I essayed once more to address her, but my tongue had become powerless. Even thought itself suddenly became paralyzed. A new influence, mysterious, potent, irresistible, took possession of me. All I could do was to gaze steadily, vacantly, at my unknown visitant. Gradually the surrounding atmosphere seemed as though becoming filled with sensations, and grew luminous. Everything about me seemed to rarefy, the mysterious visitor herself becoming more airy, and yet more distinct to my sight than before. I now began to feel as one dying, or rather to experience the sensations which I have sometimes imagined accompany dissolution. I did not think, I did not reason, I did not move, all were alike impossible. I was only conscious of gazing fixedly, vacantly, at my companion.

"Presently I heard a voice saying, "Son of the Republic, look and learn." While at the same time my visitor extended her arm eastwardly. I now beheld a heavy vapor at some distance rising fold upon fold. This gradually dissipated, and I looked upon a strange scene. Before me lay spread out in one vast plain all the countries of the world, Europe, Asia, Africa and America. I saw rolling and tossing between Europe and America the billows of the Atlantic, and between Asia and America lay the Pacific. "Son of the Republic," said the same mysterious voice as before, "look and learn." At that moment I beheld a dark shadowy being like an angel standing or rather floating in mid-air between Europe and America. Dipping water out of the ocean in the hollow of each hand, he sprinkled some upon America with his right hand, while with his left hand he cast some on Europe.

Immediately a dark cloud rose from these countries and joined in mid-ocean. For a while it remained stationary and then moved slowly westward, until it enveloped America in its murky folds. Sharp flashes of lightning gleamed through it at intervals, and I heard the smothered groans and cries of the American people. A second time the angel dipped water from the ocean, and sprinkled it as before. The dark cloud was drawn back to the ocean, in whose heaving billows it sank from view. A third time I heard the mysterious voice saying, "Son of the Republic, look and learn." I cast my eyes upon America and beheld villages and towns and cities springing up, one after another until the whole land from the Atlantic to the Pacific was dotted with them. Again I heard the mysterious voice say, "Son of the Republic, the end of the century cometh, look and learn."

"At this the dark, shadowy angel turned his face southward and from Africa I saw an ill-omened spectre approach our land. It flitted slowly and heavily over every town and city of the latter. The inhabitants presently set themselves in battle array against each other. As I continued looking, I saw a bright angel, on whose brow rested a crown of light on which was traced the word "union," bearing the American flag, which he placed between the divided nation and said "Remember ye are brethren." Instantly the inhabitants, casting from them their weapons, became friends once more, and united around the National Standard.

"And again I heard the mysterious voice say, "Son of the

Republic, look and learn." At this the dark, shadowy angel placed a trumpet to his mouth and blew three distinct blasts; and taking water from the ocean, he sprinkled it upon Europe, Asia and Africa. Then my eyes beheld a fearful scene: From each of these countries arose thick, black clouds that were soon joined into one. And throughout this mass there gleamed a dark <u>red</u> light by which I saw hordes of armed men, who moved with the cloud, marching by land and sailing by sea to America, which country was enveloped in the volume of the cloud. And I dimly saw these vast armies devastate the whole country and burn the villages, towns and cities that I had beheld springing up. As my ears listened to the thundering of the cannon, clashing of swords and shouts and cries of millions in mortal combat, I again heard the mysterious voice saying, "Son of the Republic, look and learn: When the voice had ceased the dark shadowy angel placed his trumpet once more to his mouth and blew a long and fearful blast.

"Instantly a light as of a thousand suns shone down from above me, and pierced and broke into fragments the dark cloud which enveloped America. At the same moment the angel upon whose head still shone the word "Union," and who bore our national flag in one hand and a sword in the other, descended from heaven attended by legions of bright spirits. These immediately joined the inhabitants of America, who, I perceived, were well-nigh overcome, but who, immediately taking courage again, closed up their broken ranks and renewed the battle. Again, amid the fearful noise of the conflict, I heard the mysterious voice saying, "Son of the Republic, look and learn." As the voice ceased, the shadowy angel for the last time dipped water from the ocean and sprinkled it upon America. Instantly the dark cloud rolled back, together with the armies it had brought, leaving the inhabitants of the land victorious.

"Then once more I beheld villages, towns and cities springing up where they had been before, while the bright angel, planting the azure standard he had brought into the midst of them cried with a loud voice: "While the stars remain and the heavens send down dew upon the earth, so long shall the Republic last." And taking from his brow the crown on which was blazoned the word "Union," he placed it upon the standard while the people, kneeling down, said "Amen."

"The scene instantly began to fade and dissolve and I at last saw nothing but the rising, curling vapor I at first beheld. This also disappearing, I found myself once more gazing upon my mysterious visitor, who, in the same voice I had heard before said, "Son of the Republic, what you have seen is thus interpreted: Three great perils will come upon the Republic. The most fearful is the third, passing which the whole world united shall not prevail against her. Let every child of the Republic learn to live for his God, his land and union. With these words the vision vanished, and I started from my seat and felt that I had seen a vision wherein had been shown me the birth, progress and destiny of the United States.'"

"Such, my friends," concluded the venerable narrator, "were the words I heard from Washington's own lips, and America will do well to profit by them."[9]

Living the Dream

Consistent with revelations of the past and future, the Lord did not reveal what should be done at Valley Forge to win the war. The way to find funding and supplies was not revealed. The Lord revealed to Washington the future, so that he would know that there was a way to win. In this manner Washington's free agency was still in place to learn on his own, how he might realize the success witnessed in this vision. Trials and defeat still lay ahead, but the knowledge of the outcome from this war was no longer a question. Equipped with this knowledge, Washington knew that the divine hand of Providence would assist them in the future as the Lord had done in the past.

Some attempt to pin point the turning point of the war. For the most part the battles they point to are unknown by the general public. The battle of Yorktown was one of the final nails in the coffin, removing all doubt about the Americans ability to be protected by God in their fight for their country and rights. This battle also demonstrated by miraculous events, sparing French ships and American soldiers, while at the same time destroying British ships and troops, that God was fighting the war. When the large and slow French ships engaged in battle with the swift metal bottom British ships, they should have been outmaneuvered and destroyed. Instead, each time the British fired their cannons, the ship would pitch from the weather and they could not hit the French vessels. On the other hand the French ships with their larger and more powerful cannons, could not miss the British when they fired. The British were forced to flee rather than be totally destroyed.

The second wall around Yorktown was a critical barrier to holding Yorktown. While more than 100 Frenchmen lost their lives in this orchestrated attack, less than 40 Americans were killed, and these small numbers were credited to a miracle. Once the second wall was captured, the French could mount their larger cannons and begin bombing the English. Certain destruction was assured if the English did not retreat. The first 1,000 men were safely transported across the river to the Fort on the other side. But, when the second wave of soldiers was attempting to cross, a storm came out of nowhere, sinking the ships and killing almost all of the men. Without transportation and only three thousand men left to defend their position, surrender was the only option left for the British.

With all of this known, the last moment of darkness was left behind at Valley Forge. Washington had passed the test, and he had remained true to the Lord and worthy of the further light and knowledge necessary to lead this country in the fight for freedom.

Was this then the purpose for which Washington's life had been spared? Was his mission in life complete with the freeing and establishment of this nation? Washington himself remained uncertain as to the purpose and the mission for which his life was spared. It was not until after the war when the people desired to make him King that Washington realized his mission. For a nation to experience a new Republic, someone must lead them away from the oppressive monarchies and forms of government previously known. Washington must lead them in understanding that government should operate under the eternal laws of free agency. Wisely he fought for a leadership that would donate their time and talents for their country. The only compensation required should be for expenses incurred and nothing more. Washington's position was to become clear, term limitation were essential; otherwise powerful leaders could attain the same control as Kings.

Had Washington been successful in teaching all men these truths, we would not have the corruption present in our government today. Valiantly Washington served for two terms, his health suffered and his spirit longed for time at home with family and friends.

After his first two years in office, Washington called for the following commitment from his countrymen:

> "Do not let anyone claim to be a true American — don't let them claim the tribute of American Patriotism, if they ever attempt to remove religion from politics, if they do that they cannot be called true Americans."

In his farewell address Washington warned the nation against the pitfalls of putting party or other countries above the welfare of the nation. Included were warnings against the evil designs of conspiring men. His most poignant concerns were relative to the removal of morality and religion from government.

> "Of all the dispositions and habits which lead to political prosperity, religion and morality are indispensable supports. In vain would that man claim the tribute of patriotism who should labor to subvert these great pillars of human happiness—these firmest props of the duties of men and citizens. The mere politician, equally with the pious man, ought to respect and cherish them. A volume could not trace all their connections with private and public felicity. Let it simply be asked, "where is the security for property, for reputation, for life, if the sense of religious obligation desert the oaths which are the instruments of investigation in courts of justice?" And let us with caution indulge the supposition that morality can be maintained without religion. Whatever may be conceded to the influence of refined education on minds of peculiar structure, reason and experience both forbid us to expect that national morality can prevail in exclusion of religious principle."
>
> It is substantially true that virtue and morality is a necessary spring of popular government. Who that is a sincere friend to it can look with indifference upon attempts to shake the foundation of the fabric?
>
> Promote, then, as an object of primary importance, institutions for the general diffusion of knowledge. In proportion as the structure of government gives force to public opinion, it is essential that public opinion should be enlightened....
>
> Observe good faith and justice toward all nations. Cultivate peace and harmony with all. Religion and morality enjoin this conduct. And can it be that good policy does not equally enjoin it? It will be worthy of a free, enlightened, and at no distant period a great nation to give to mankind the magnanimous and too novel example of a people always guided by an exalted justice and benevolence.
>
> Who can doubt that in the course of time and things the fruits of such a plan would richly repay any temporary advantages, which might be lost by a steady adherence to it? Can it be that Providence has not connected the permanent felicity of a nation with its virtue?"[10]

What a shame it is that this nation has forgotten the wise words of the father of America. A greater shame is cast upon those who have forgotten the divine hand of Providence that brought this nation forth as a light unto the world.

Washington's Proclamation for a Day of Prayer – October 3, 1789

"WHEREAS it is the duty of all nations to acknowledge the providence of Almighty God, to obey His will, to be grateful for His benefits, and humbly to implore His protection and favor; and Whereas both Houses of Congress have, by their joint committee, requested me "to recommend to the people of the United States a DAY OF PUBLIC THANSGIVING and PRAYER, to be observed by acknowledging with grateful hearts the many and signal favors of Almighty God, especially by affording them an opportunity peaceably to establish a form of government for their safety and happiness:"

NOW THEREFORE, I do recommend and assign THURSDAY, the TWENTY-SIXTH DAY of NOVEMBER next, to be devoted by the people of these States to the service of that great and glorious Being who is the beneficent author of all the good that was, that is, or that will be; that we may then all unite in rendering unto Him our sincere and humble thanks for His kind care and protection of the people of this country previous to their becoming a nation; for the signal and manifold mercies and the favorable interpositions of His providence in the course and conclusion of the late war; for the great degree of tranquility, union, and plenty which we have since enjoyed; for the peaceable and rational manner in which we have been enabled to establish Constitutions of government for our safety and happiness, and particularly the national one now lately instituted;— for the civil and religious liberty with which we are blessed, and the means we have of acquiring and diffusing useful knowledge;— and, in general, for all the great and various favors which He has been pleased to confer upon us.

And also, that we may then unite in most humbly offering our prayers and supplications to the great Lord and Ruler of Nations and beseech Him to pardon our national and other transgressions;— to enable us all, whether in public or private stations, to perform our several and relative duties properly and punctually; to render our National Government a blessing to all the people by constantly being a Government of wise, just, and constitutional laws, discreetly and faithfully executed and obeyed; to protect and guide all sovereigns and nations (especially such as have shown kindness unto us); and to bless them with good governments, peace, and concord; to promote the knowledge and practice of true religion and virtue, and the increase of science among them and us; and, generally to grant unto all mankind such a degree of temporal prosperity as he alone knows to be best.

GIVEN under my hand, at the city of New York, the third day of October, in the year of our Lord, one thousand seven hundred and eighty-nine.

(signed) G. Washington

This document is an edited excerpt from a paper entitled *From Birth to Birth* prepared by James Biorge addressed to his children and reprinted with permission.

[1] Recollection and Private Memoirs of Washington, by George Washington Park Custis, 1860, p. 303

[2] MAXIMS of George Washington, John Frederick Schroeder, D.D. pg. 167

[3] MAXIMS of George Washington, John Frederick Schroeder, D.D. pg. 183

[4] Our Flag, Robert Allen Campbell, pg 36–48

[5] The Secret Teachings of All Ages, Manly P. Hall pg. CC

[6] Author Unknown

[7] The Works of Daniel Webster, 4th ed., 1851, 1:133–36

[8] Maxims of George Washington; pg. 183

Facts About Nevada

The Territory of Nevada was created by an Act of Congress, signed by President James Buchanan and became effective March 2, 1861. President Abraham Lincoln appointed James W. Nye of New York as Nevada's first Territorial Governor.

On October 31, 1864, President Lincoln proclaimed Nevada's admission to the Union as the 36th state. The creation of the Nevada Territory, and its admission to the Union, were related to both the Civil War and the mineral wealth of the Comstock Lode. During the next 75 years, many mining towns flourished, if only briefly, all over the state. Since 1931, tourism, particularly entertainment and legalized gaming, have become increasingly important to Nevada's economy. Mining also has rebounded in recent years, and Nevada now produces more gold than any other state. Federal legislation enacted in 1986 created the Great Basin National Park, the only national park in the state, which includes the area around Wheeler Peak and Lehman Caves in eastern Nevada.

Nevada Nicknames: Sagebrush State, Silver State, Battle-Born State
The origin of the state's name is Spanish, meaning "snow-capped."

Preliminary population estimate as of November, 1998: 1,852,650
Rank: 39th (1990)

Area: 110,540 square miles, 86 percent federally controlled Rank: 7th largest

Capital: Carson City, population - 51,860 (November, 1998)

Most populous city: Las Vegas - 441,230 (November, 1998)

Most populous county: Clark - 1,255,200 (November, 1998)

Highest elevation: Boundary Peak in Esmeralda County - 13,140 feet

Lowest elevation: On the Colorado River in Clark County - 470 feet

NEVADA
Name officially adopted in 1861 when territory was established by Congress; from Spanish meaning snow-capped.

1851 — First settlement — Genoa, near Carson City, permanently
        settled by Mormons, then called Mormon Station in Utah

Territory. Dayton, also near Carson City, permanently settled by miners and traders, then called Gold Canyon in Utah Territory.

1854—Carson County created as part of Utah Territory.

1861—Created as Territory of Nevada on March 2

1864—Admitted as State of Nevada October 31; a state holiday since 1939.

STATE FLAG

The new Nevada state flag; cobalt blue background; in upper left quarter is a five-pointed silver star between two sprays of sagebrush crossed to form a half wreath; across the top of wreath is a golden scroll with the words, in black letters "Battle Born." The name "Nevada" is below the star and above the sprays in golden letters. Design modified June 8, 1991, original design approved on March 21, 1929.

STATE SEAL

Designed in July 1864 and adopted February 24, 1866. A gold seal is embossed with the words "The Great Seal of the State of Nevada" around the outer edge. Within this is a composite picture showing the mining, agriculture, industry and scenery of Nevada, under which is a scroll with the State motto, "All for our Country".

STATE MOTTO - "ALL FOR OUR COUNTRY"

How did it originate?

The motto has always been part of the state seal but there is no documented source of its originality.

Nevada entered the Union as a state during the Civil War and just before the presidential election of 1864. The Constitutional Convention met in Carson City on July 4, 1864, just one year after the terrible battle at Gettysburg. The Union needed another state, another supporter of President Lincoln, to prove to the Confederacy that the Union was strong. Patriotism was running high here and those assembled for the Convention felt very loyal to the Union and quite willing to do what they could to support it.